Organizations and Activism series

Series Editors: **Daniel King**, Nottingham Trent University and **Martin Parker**, University of Bristol

Organizations and Activism publishes books that explore how politics happens within and because of organizations, how activism is organized, and how activists change organizations.

Forthcoming in the series:

Reimagining Academic Activism:
Learning From Feminist Anti-Violence Activists
Ruth Weatherall

Sociocracy at Work:
Possibilities and Limitations of an Alternative Democratic Model of Organization
Martyn Griffin, Daniel King,
Ted Jennifer Rau and **Jerry Koch Gonzalez**

Organizing Food, Faith and Freedom:
Imagining Alternatives
Ozan Alakavuklar

Out now in the series:

Anarchist Cybernetics:
Control and Communication in Radical Politics
Thomas Swann

Find out more at
bristoluniversitypress.co.uk/organizations-and-activism

Organizations and Activism series

Series Editors: **Daniel King**, Nottingham Trent University and **Martin Parker**, University of Bristol

International advisory board:

Find out more at
bristoluniversitypress.co.uk/organizations-and-activism

GUERRILLA DEMOCRACY

Mobile Power and Revolution in the 21st Century

Peter Bloom,
Owain Smolović Jones
and Jamie Woodcock

BRISTOL
UNIVERSITY
PRESS

First published in Great Britain in 2021 by

Bristol University Press
University of Bristol
1-9 Old Park Hill
Bristol
BS2 8BB
UK
t: +44 (0)117 954 5940
e: bup-info@bristol.ac.uk

Details of international sales and distribution partners are available at
bristoluniversitypress.co.uk

British Library Cataloguing in Publication Data
A catalogue record for this book is available from the British Library

ISBN 978-1-5292-0561-9 hardcover
ISBN 978-1-5292-0564-0 paperback
ISBN 978-1-5292-0567-1 ePub
ISBN 978-1-5292-0566-4 ePdf

Cover design: blu inc, Bristol
Front cover image: Alamy/EyeEm/Jonathan Diaz
Bristol University Press uses environmentally responsible print partners.
Printed and bound by CMP, Poole

Contents

Series Editors' Preface

Organizations and Activism

Series editors: Professor Daniel King, Nottingham Trent University, and Professor Martin Parker, University of Bristol

Organizing is politics made durable. From co-operatives to corporations, Occupy to Facebook, states and NGOs, organizations shape our lives. They shape the possible futures of governance, policy making and social change, and hence are central to understanding how human beings can deal with the challenges that face us, whether that be pandemics, populism or climate change. This book series publishes works that explore how politics happens within and because of organizations and organizing. We want to explore how activism is organized and how activists change organizations. We are also interested in the forms of resistance to activism, in the ways that powerful interests contest and reframe demands for change. These are questions of huge relevance to scholars in sociology, politics, geography, management and beyond, and are becoming ever more important as demands for impact and engagement change the way that academics imagine their work. They are also important to anyone who wants to understand more about the theory and practice of organizing, not just the abstracted ideologies of capitalism taught in business schools.

Our books will offer critical examinations of organizations as sites of or targets for activism, and we will also assume that our authors, and hopefully our readers, are themselves agents of change. Titles may focus on specific industries or fields, or they may be arranged around particular themes or challenges. Our topics might include the alternative economy; surveillance, whistleblowing and human rights; digital politics; religious groups; social movements; NGOs; feminism and anarchist organization; action research and co-production; activism and the neoliberal university, and any other subjects that are relevant and topical.

'Organizations and Activism' will also be a multidisciplinary series. Contributions from all and any relevant academic fields will be welcomed. The series will be international in outlook, and proposals from outside the English-speaking global north are particularly welcome.

This book, the second in our series, explores the potential of the digital to alter the possibilities of the social, producing new sociodigital arrangements which can and are reshaping what we mean by organizing. Historically, we have tended to assume that organizations were entities that were bounded in time and space, requiring a certain kind of proximity to centres of power in order to achieve co-ordination. The extension of organizing was often troublesome, involving delays and confusions which were attendant on action and information at a distance, or over time, or at scale and so on. At the present moment, it seems that we are moving into an era when power has become mobile in ways that it never has been, and hence that hegemony can be viral in the sense that it reaches 'across' and 'down' into areas of life that were previously rather hard to reach. *Guerrilla Democracy* explores both the 'negative' and 'positive' aspects of these changes, though deciding which of those is which does very much depend on who is judging.

On the one hand, sociodigital capitalism underpins a new form of domination which is predicated on innovation, flexibility, agility and so on, a particular sort of subject who is attentive to the demands placed on them and responds in creative ways to assist in capital accumulation. On the other hand, and as the previous book in this series by Thomas Swann also suggested, the affordances of communication and information technologies can also produce new forms of sociality, new ways to organize. This is what Bloom, Smolović Jones and Woodcock theorize as a radical democratic politics which infects and disrupts the present order in order to remake it in different formations, with new connections and new ways of imagining what organizing might look like. Such novelty also raises the question of how we might recognize organizing when we see it, an epistemological politics in itself. Variously metaphorized as an opening up of matters which were generally closed to all but a few, or the creation of a commons, or an insurrection from below, or mobility against and around centres of power, the point is that new forms of politics appear to become possible, simply because new forms of organizing have become possible. Creative resistance to platform capitalism, to ubiquitous surveillance and algorithmic discrimination is now not hard to find, whether in workers' campaigns, new networks of sharing and making, or distributed knowledge production. The space for digital activism is clear, and well-described in this book, but can it produce more enduring alternatives, or is it a moment which must be followed by a period of institution building, by 'constitutionalizing' the sorts of distributed, grassroots and lateral organization that it is often predicated on? We might well be sceptical as to whether such ephemeral flows of information and desire can congeal into something more enduring, but the authors of this book give us reasons for optimism. In viral times, if neoliberalism is the disease, perhaps digital technologies can provide a vaccination, even if they are often the vector for infection.

We hope you enjoy this book, and if you want to discuss a proposal yourself, then email the series editors. We look forward to hearing from you.

Preface

Democratic guerrillas in the midst of global crisis

This manuscript was completed in the middle of a global pandemic and international uprising. As we wrote our final words, the COVID-19 virus and Black Lives Matters movement were sweeping the world. It would thus seem a strangely appropriate time to theoretically and practically explore the possibilities of mobile resistance and viral revolutions. After decades of being convinced we were at the neoliberal end of history, the prospect of creating a different, freer society is suddenly not only probable but urgently necessary. This book is a work of revolutionary optimism based on our ability to reboot political resistance and radically reinvent our democracy.

For this purpose, this book seeks to fundamentally reconsider power and the basis of social order in light of recent and rapid technological changes. Established views associating strength with stability and hegemony with uniformity are being quickly dismantled by the sheer speed of events and how rapidly they spread across physical and digital borders. Instead, today, perhaps more than at any other time in history, power is strongest when it is mobile and hegemony when it is viral. Above all, it is adaptable, flexible and malleable to diverse cultural contexts and populations, allowing domination to be user-friendly and fully 'customizable'.

We too need to learn to craft our struggle and promote our own radical alternatives in a way that similarly speaks across different networks and forges new ones. This demands that we embrace experimentation as much as we do opposition, that our movements are local in their focus and global in their ambitions, that we bring together the excitement and urgency of creative disruptions with the inventiveness of actual disruptive concretions. Doing so means that we embrace a new political ethos that is mobile, viral and totally transformative.

'Smart' technologies are rapidly expanding the capabilities of state and corporate authority, increasingly disciplining us to be 'innovative' problem-solvers, continually updating and discovering fresh opportunities for preserving and spreading their capitalist status quo. At stake, then, is how to stop the ongoing mutation and infection of this racist, patriarchal, free market social 'virus'. Most immediately, this entails that we cultivate local inoculations against this international neoliberal epidemic. Looking further ahead, it requires us to produce our own contagious 'commons-based' global alternatives.

This proposed 21st-century revolutionary theory and praxis must combine the inventiveness of guerrillas and the inclusiveness of democracy. It means being able to do more than 'hack' the system, but politically repurposing and completely reconfiguring its entire social programming and structural architecture. 'Guerrilla', here, then denotes the ability to creatively use existing materials and institutions in radically fresh ways as well as to form localized spaces of emancipation and experimentation. Yet it is democratic in that it is ultimately global in scope, asking collectively who matters and in what way, cultivating international networks of contagious revolutionary knowledge exchange, skills-building and solidarity.

The possibility of revolution in viral times

This book was inspired and written, perhaps above all else, to illuminate the dynamic character of power and, therefore, to better understand how existing social orderings can be radically reimagined and concretely transformed. Traditionally, domination is conceived as a force for creating social paralysis – the attempt to impose a perceived, unchanging status quo on a subjugated population. It conjures up images of an entrenched elite or a violent state that can impose their will and achieve their interests with little to no serious resistance. However, the reality is much messier and rich in political possibilities – though no less exploitative or repressive. Instead we find regimes and elites who are constantly 'on the move' in terms of their policies and tactics. Indeed, they may have a bedrock faith in a specific ideology or a given status quo but remain utterly agnostic in how they institute, protect and expand these principles and power relations in practice. The question, then, is whether movements for revolutionary change can similarly mix a principled commitment to emancipatory values with fluid and responsive strategies for achieving these radical goals.

A key insight of our work is that power is paradoxically strongest when it is at its most diverse and adaptive to different contexts. We present power as fundamentally a viral phenomenon – one that spreads and morphs rapidly. Hegemony, then, is ultimately infectious, a highly transmittable set of ideas, relations and practices that can infect a wide range of 'host contexts' with profound short- and long-term consequences. The point of resistance is, at the very minimum, to politically build up immunities to these hegemonic epidemics; more radically still, it is to incubate 'contagious' alternatives that can positively challenge such viral domination across numerous and culturally different infected places and populations. It is an incessant battle between 'infectious hegemony' and 'contagious revolution'.

The spread of COVID-19 has been a world-changing event. It has shown how a communicable virus can completely upend social relations once thought unchangeable. It has also revealed the limits of the ability of some present systems to respond to this crisis, as well as the effectiveness of others. At the most basic level, the pandemic has focused attention on the 'life-and-death' quality of politics – in which the choice of government and the belief systems underpinning this choice are literally a matter of collective survival. It is a reflection of how infectious our increasingly globalized culture has become and how dangerous the spread of ideas in this international context can be. Yet it also represents something much more hopeful and profound: the capacity of activists to create local change and watch it go potentially global. It also showed how new forms of mutuality can perhaps become vibrant political communities, serving as a progressive contagion and an antidote to diseased status quos.

The danger, of course, is not only the understandable desire to 'return to normal' but also the struggle that lies ahead as to what this new 'normal' will end up being. To a certain extent this will be, as is true with all political struggles, a battle of ideology and organizing. Yet it must also be a matter of who can best reimagine and rematerialize the social in new and exciting ways. The aftermath of COVID-19 will undoubtedly see the forces of the free market, militarism and corporatism come back with a vengeance. Nevertheless, if history is any indication, they will do so not by simply imposing their homogenous vision on the world. Rather, it will be through their exploiting this changed situation across a wide range of host contexts with marked differences in culture, institutions, politics, and history. Domination is, as always, culturally opportunistic and creative in its application. Its reaction, in this regard, will mirror its ascent – one defined by a constant mobility and adjustability to ever-changing circumstances. So too, then, must its alternatives be culturally opportunistic and creative, as 21st-century revolution must be every bit as mobile and viral as the domination it opposes and seeks to replace.

Viral threats and guerrilla possibilities

An immediate question, though, may be why the focus is on the word 'guerrilla'? Why not just concentrate on how viral power fundamentally is and is presently becoming? The answer is that while the viral aspect of power is interesting and absolutely essential for comprehending social order (across time and in our contemporary era), it tells us very little about the potential for small- and large-scale political transformation. Put differently, all domination and change are 'viral' to a certain extent, yet further attention and greater conceptual development is needed to grasp how mobile power can be practically disrupted and supplanted. A guerrilla politics – and more precisely a 'guerrilla democracy'– hopes to provide a modern revolutionary theory and praxis for radically reimagining and rematerializing this fluid hegemony.

The threat of infection is, right now, at the foremost of our political consciousness. COVID-19 has invaded entire continents and shut down whole nations. While this has been an almost unprecedented event in our present times, it symbolizes the viral spread of capitalist ideologies that increasingly define our existence. Beginning in the 1980s, the free market invaded country after country, upending the economic and political fates of entire regions the world over. Marx rightly noted that capitalism is at its heart insatiable, and the end of the 20th century and the start of the new millennium witnessed its insatiable hunger for introducing a global corporate takeover. The infectious discourse of the market became a full-on hegemonic epidemic with debilitating symptoms of privatization, marketization and financialization.

Capitalism has, hence, 'gone viral'– spreading rapidly, like a virus, across the world. Nevertheless, like all outbreaks, it is far from uniform in its appearance. It has constantly adjusted to the on-the-ground reality of host contexts and, to a degree, learned from them. It was a dynamic colonization – continuously updating, culturally sensitive and drawing its power from the sheer diversity of its possible applications. The free market of East Asia differed from that of Latin America, which differed from what was found in Africa. While their symptoms were the same, the intensity and timing of those symptoms contrasted markedly.

Driving this dynamism in no small measure were the ongoing and constant resistances to this viral capitalist threat. Each host context sought to produce its own antibodies to fight off this free market infection. These could range from sustained mass strikes to progressive political movements, or more recently the rise of right-wing populism. At times these cures can feel relatively powerless to stem the tide of this epidemic, or (as is the case with populism, which fuses racism and virulent nationalism with discourses of protectionism) can feel worse than the disease.

Despite their vast differences in ideology and approach, these movements put on full display how, in order to be successful, resistances must also 'go viral'. They must be able to spread and adapt. Going one step further, they must also form vibrant networks for sharing knowledge and, when necessary, material support. The 'red state' teachers' strike in the US began as a spark of outrage on Facebook and became a viral national movement with concrete demands for greater public investment in education. Black Lives Matter similarly grew into a global network of activists and protests to challenge systemic racism and police brutality throughout the world. Less positively, but every bit as illuminating, right-wing populism has ironically turned resurgent nationalism into a global struggle with deep transnational connections. In response, supposed 'moderates' have recast themselves as 'nasty' and as 'radicals' to directly confront, on the street, in the ballot box and on social media, the rise of fascism.

Emerging from the right, left and centre, thus, is a nascent but effective guerrilla politics. These are movements and activists who are willing to work from the 'bottom up' to organize and find ways to creatively subvert contemporary political boundaries to achieve their goals. Significantly, theirs is a politics that combines direct resistance with innovative 'sideways' oppositions. It involves both in-person and digital community building of groups that can span vast geographic boundaries. They are learning how to share ideas, forge alliances, moderate internal discussions and make democratic decisions. They are both decentralized and connected, global in their scale and local in their focus.

Hence, the point is not merely that information is viral, but rather that it is giving rise to a new generation of guerrillas who are diverse in their beliefs and innovative in their methods. At stake is a more flexible form of political engagement. It is at one and the same time broad and international in the scale of its possibilities and context specific in its concrete manifestations. This is the era when elections are fought, increasingly, between digital organizations who can quickly allocate funds where needed across entire nations and help frame broader shared principles and platforms in accordance with local cultures, or when activists connected primarily through mobile phones can share with each other advice and knowledge about effective protest techniques.

The ultimate question, though, is how such guerrilla resistance can be transformed into sustainable types of guerrilla revolution? How can we move from building viral antibodies to building contagious concrete alternatives for remaking the world from the bottom up? In a sense, it is a matter of understanding the theory and praxis of making places and people into host contexts for emancipation rather than oppression. And that is what is at the heart of this book. It is an attempt to make sense of and provide insight into the reimagining and rematerializing of the social through these new hi-tech methods of what we term 'guerrilla democracy'. In the face of mobile power, what are the opportunities for mobile revolutions?

Introducing Mobile Power and Guerrilla Politics

Che Guevera, opening his famous book *Guerrilla Warfare*, proclaimed that the Cuban revolution 'showed plainly the capacity of the people to free themselves by means of guerrilla warfare from a government that oppresses them'. These words were written over half a century ago. Since then, the world and politics have changed dramatically. The Soviet Union has fallen, neoliberalism reigns supreme, and Cuba and China have almost completely abandoned 'really existing socialism' for the promises of capitalist progress. And yet the more things change, the more they seem to stay the same. The 21st century has been marked by disastrous US imperialist adventures, a global financial crisis, a pandemic wherein the poor and precarious have suffered disproportionately to the wealthy, and the resurgence of socialist ideas the world over. New movements are arising, challenging the ideology of the free market and the rule of corporations. And just as importantly, new populist reactions have emerged embracing the rebirth of ethno-nationalism and political authoritarianism.

It is precisely in this contemporary context of revolution and reaction, radical change and an evolving status quo that guerrilla politics becomes once more so socially inspiring and strategically significant. Yet the terrain and composition of these insurrectionary movements have necessarily changed with the times. Now it is not professional armies that are the primary combatants but predictive algorithms which shape our behaviour and guide our exploitation. It is not only armed insurrections that will bring about revolutionary conditions but international mobile movements aided by digital platforms. And it is not the countryside that will be the main field of battle but a digital commons through which outdated capitalist structures and divisions between city, town and countryside can be subverted and new collaborative social relations can arise and thrive.

These rebooted guerrilla revolutionaries, admittedly, are more incipient than fully formed at this point in history. Yet their presence is being felt as insurgent groups are emerging, ushering in technologically sophisticated forms of 'insurrectionary' actions. Perhaps the best known of these is the hacktivist group tellingly named Anonymous, which has 'incited online vigilantism from Tunisia to Ferguson' (Kushner, 2014). This has included campaigns targeting the alleged abuses of Scientology, the leaking of the names of hundreds of KKK members, and 'Operation Egypt', which sought to evade the media blackout imposed by the Egyptian government during the Arab Spring by sending thousands of faxes updating people about what was happening there.

These actions are part of a now (at least) decade-long movement to exploit information and communication technologies (ICTs) and big data in order to foster a more open and democratic world order. 'This insider's drive to expose institutional secrets – to conscientiously blow the whistle or vindictively dump their superior's dirty laundry – has always existed', Andy Greenberg observes in his book *This Machine Kills Secrets: How WikiLeakers, Cyberpunks, and Hacktivists Aim to Free the World's Information*, 'but the technology that enables spillers of secrets has been accelerating its evolution since the invention of computing' (Greenberg, 2012, p 11). Such famous whistle-blowers as Chelsea Manning, who exposed secret actions undertaken by the US in its 'war on terror', Edward Snowden, who revealed the full extent of the NSA mass digital-surveillance strategy, and the still anonymous leaker of the Panama papers which brought to light the massive tax evasion of the economic elite, reflect for many a new type of political hero. Recently, these efforts have been technologically aided by the rise of 'digital whistleblowing platforms' (Di Salvo, 2020) – encrypted platforms allowing for the confidential and secure transferring of documents and communication between whistle-blowers and journalists and activities.

It is tempting, perhaps, to minimize the impact of such politics – to dismiss them as innovative but ultimately peripheral movements, mere disruptions as opposed to representatives of a fundamental shift in the politics of the new millennium. Nevertheless, they do reflect a novel and increasingly ubiquitous ethos for political action. While, for instance, Anonymous has been described as 'cyberlibertarian' (Golumbia, 2013), in fact the group reflects a complex ethos mixing nihilism and idealism as well as dystopianism and utopianism that both limits and enhances its potential political impact (Goode, 2015, p 84). Moreover, it shows the power of an innovative form of digital activism, or, as it is often referred to, hacktivism (George & Leidner, 2019). The power of hacktivism is more than simply the merging of technology with protest but is also its capacity to push forward radical social alternatives often marginalized by the political establishment and conventional politics. Nevertheless, it reveals a now three-decade-old historical trajectory that has witnessed it evolve from an outsider form of 'firebrand activism' into one that is increasingly mainstream and to an extent tamed (Karatzogianni, 2015), as anyone who has let loose a deep sigh of dejection at the futility of completing yet another digital petition can attest.

Yet it is our argument that mobile technologies still contain the promise to completely reconfigure the possibility of social movements and activism. Over the last decade alone, there have been insurrections both small and large scale all over the world prominently featuring smart technologies (Eagle, 2010). The so-called Arab Spring was aided, in part, by the prevalence of mobile phones which allowed activists and citizens to quickly communicate, coordinate and share information. The act that is widely credited with sparking the movement, the self-immolation of a fruit vendor in Tunisia in protest of unjust economic and social conditions, was publicized in an online post by his cousin the following day that went viral, showing the growing protest at City Hall against the treatment of street vendors (see Saroshisar, 2016). Mobile phones were used to similar effect by Black Lives Matters protestors, who drew on them to rapidly coordinate their actions and share the truth about what was happening with a wider audience on social media.

Mobile phones are, furthermore, reinvigorating 'everyday democracy' in these places. Indeed, 'mobile phones do not only transmit political information needed for rational deliberation in the public sphere, but also transgress cultural and social borders and hierarchies in ways they refashion identities and create informal economies and communicative networks' (Wasserman, 2011, p 146). These are not simply tools for reproducing conventional power relations and political struggles. Rather, they can allow for novel social orderings to emerge – ones that are decentralized, autonomous and indicative of a complete reconfiguration of traditional liberal democracies (De Filippi & Loveluck, 2016). Emerging are 'decentralized autonomous organisations' which require different modes of governance than are conventionally proposed and implemented. Significantly, they experiment with the repurposing of capitalist technologies for progressive and collaborative economic orderings and systems (Dupont, 2017). These are witnessed in participatory budgeting initiatives and platform-aided direct democracy efforts wherein citizens can directly discuss and vote how to best address problems and allocate funds. Citizens in Paris had the opportunity recently, to give but one example, to digitally vote on the use of up to a half a billion euros for projects aimed at fostering urban regeneration and sustainability. These initiatives offer the possibility of establishing 'a deeper, more supple democracy' (Feguet et al, 2015, p 60). However, they also present an alternative social and political reality that brings with it 'real-world' opportunities and challenges (Garrod, 2016).

These mobile radical interventions can lead, in turn, to exciting revolutionary possibilities. They hold out the prospect of combining digital media and communication with desires for broad-based and far-reaching social and economic change (Fenton, 2016). 'The mass protests that have broken out during the past year in Asia, Europe, Africa, Latin America and the Middle East share other important characteristics', according to a recent article in the *Financial Times* (Rachman et al, 2019). 'They are usually leaderless rebellions, whose organisation and principles are not set out in a little red book or thrashed out in party meetings, but instead emerge on social media. These are revolts that are convened by smartphone and inspired by hashtags, rather than guided by party leaders and slogans drafted by central committees." These 'leaderless rebellions' turn once-utopian dreams of a 'post-capitalist' society into pragmatic and achievable near-future goals (Chatterton, 2016). This can include the promotion of common ownership, cooperatives and the institution of a basic universal income. Here cities are not just sites for fighting against austerity or for making incremental demands for a more progressive capitalism but the 'terrain for epic struggle' linking anarchist and socialist principles with growing 'smart' capabilities (Carter, 2017). Outside urban centres, they provide the foundations for an ecologically and economically sustainable social order, using principles of the 'circular economy' to achieve 'radical social transformation in a resource-scarce world' (Hobson & Lynch, 2016). Just as importantly, such a blending of technology with ambitious political intent catalyzes fresh and feminist design methodologies for realizing 'post-work futures' associated with a radicalized version of 'full automation' (Baker, 2018).

However, underlying these decentralized and autonomous structures are centralized economic supply chains that can serve to reproduce exploitative market relations globally (Fuchs, 2018). This has resulted in a perhaps less publicized but every bit as important demand for 'rare earth' metals such as neodymium, dysprosium, praseodymium, terbium, gadolinium and lanthanum, mined to support these mobile innovations, as well as (ironically) strategies for 'green engineering' (Dutta et al,

2016). There is further tension between the radical impulses of these emerging mobile movements and the profit that can be extracted or dynamics that can be co-opted by the very corporations and interests they are resisting (Brandsen et al, 2018) – for example, a Conservative politician in the UK profiting from the food bank tragedy created by her own party though a platform app which charges food banks for the ability to choose which items of food they would like to be donated (Wyatt, 2019).

There is an urgent need, therefore, for a theoretically sophisticated and empirically grounded analysis that can shed light on the revolutionary potential of mobile technologies. While there is a widespread acknowledgement of the capacity of 'future tech' such as big data, social media, digital platforms and smartphones to utterly change social relations, there is significantly less engagement with its capacity to positively transform the very way we form our collective political subjectivities and sense of agency. Yet in the past half decade alone, these techniques have been fundamental to the creation of political, and increasingly economic, movements.

This book critically reveals the contemporary period as an era defined not just by mobile technologies but fundamentally by mobile power. It explores the increasingly viral character of social ordering and hegemony as well as the 'infectious' aspects of present-day domination. Yet it also presents the possibility of exploiting these technological resources for fostering 'contagious' new alternatives locally and globally. For this purpose, it shifts the focus from viewing these as technologies of governance and organizing to seeing them as new forms of collective democratic connection and leadership. It combines, in this respect, cutting-edge theories of power and post-human theory with in-depth empirical explorations of actually existing examples of guerrilla democracy. A key aspect of its originality is its linking of economic and political movements, revealing their productive tensions and potential points of solidarity. Emerging from this investigation is a new theory of 21st-century guerrilla democracy, which will help reveal the possibilities of waging hi-tech revolutions for progressively and radically transforming contemporary economies and societies.

Aim of the book

The aim of this book is to explore the potential of digital technologies to revolutionize political and economic organizing and for bringing about fundamental social transformation. The liberating promise of big data and social media to create more responsive democracies and workplaces has turned into a growing nightmare of election meddling, privacy invasion and 'fake news' and an exploitive gig economy. Yet recent events have once more highlighted the empowering possibilities of digital technologies for democracy and employment relations. The success of progressive movements such as Momentum, a grassroots movement of the UK Labour left that formed from the campaign to elect Jeremy Corbyn leader of the Labour Party, reveals how forms of digital guerrilla democracy can effectively create diverse political coalitions of voters that can be influential at both the local and national levels, a movement that looks set to remain influential despite the defeat of Labour in the 2019 general election. Likewise, precarious workers at platform companies such as Deliveroo and Uber, as well as at more traditional hospitality companies like McDonald's, Wetherspoons and TGI Fridays, have successfully used this technology to take successful strike action.

The new millennium finds us at a distinct and rather profound existential crossroads. We are at once experiencing a technological acceleration that is dynamically altering everyday life and at the same feel as if the existing status quo is as entrenched and permanent as ever. Even in the face of pandemics and uprisings, the ability to create a totally different society appears to be more science fiction than prospective reality. Yet scratching only slightly beneath the surface, another world is emerging, combining the latest advances in big data, mobile communication and augmented reality with radical values of equality and democracy. Simultaneously, insurrections against racism and police brutality are demanding and concretely pointing the way towards abolishing jails and state violence.

What this points to is a profound shift in the struggle for achieving radical social change. These technologies are not merely tools but rather indicate new types of subjectivity, agency and leadership, phenomena we seek to capture in our new concept of guerrilla democracy. These mobile political and economic subjects and practices are characterized by greater flexibility, faster communication and the ability to combine rapid direct action with a sustainable long-term political strategy. More precisely, new forms of political and economic agency are being created through human 'intra-action' (Barad, 2007) with technologies, highlighting injustices and their solutions. Significantly, these localized campaigns represent the radical possibility of upending an entrenched neoliberal status quo, building mass support among diverse populations for revolutionary transformations. While regressive forces spread disinformation and hate, guerrilla democrats foster hope and connection. They are at once localized in their impact and global in their ambitions. Emerging is a technologically sophisticated guerrilla democracy in which a mass network of diverse activists, individuals and communities can create the conditions for large-scale progressive insurrections, opening up previously closed spaces and topics, redefining the common sense of establishment politics and through such novel reconnections radically transforming and recreating their concrete existence. If hegemony has gone viral, so too can revolution.

This analysis is thus an original attempt to theorize a new social order and the possibilities of the political. It emphasizes the mobility of power, its paradoxical strength in being able to continually adapt and mutate to reflect and better change local host contexts. Hegemony, in turn, is progressively linked to the ability to diversely spread these discourses, rendering them infectious to a wide range of host populations. At stake in this work is how to go beyond the mere remobilization and dynamic spread of a social order and instead respectively politically reimagine and reorder the social. For this purpose, we focus on the ability of actors to inoculate themselves against these mutating hegemonic infections and embrace revolutionary, contagious alternatives through reconnecting with each other in new and radical ways. Contemporary democracy, thus, can transcend the narrow horizons of elections and liberal freedoms (while not eschewing them) to resituate the social around the collective pursuit of an emancipatory commons existence. What is key, in this regard, is the adoption of a novel ethos that rejects simply finding ever more 'innovative' solutions to prop up an unjust and unsustainable system for the disruptive creation of novel social realities. Yet the reimagining and reordering of the social also necessitates providing people with the concrete skills and networks to not only reimagine their social lives but fundamentally and contingently rematerialize them. This involves struggling against the 'liquifying' tendencies of our modern age – whereby social media and globalization are undermining historic bonds and identities – so that it is resolidified in ways that do not dangerously return to the nostalgia of essentialisms but exalt in the potentials of liberating 'glocal' alternatives. Guerilla democracy is, at its core, a fresh perspective on how we can begin reimagining, reordering, reconnecting, resituating, rematerializing and resolidifying our world together.

Mobile power

Mobile technologies are already rapidly transforming politics and society. The introduction of the internet and the smartphone has supposedly 'shrunk the world' and made communication possible at literally the touch of a button. It is the speed – the quickening pace of both our interactions and decisions – and our mobility – how boundaryless our movements increasingly are – that perhaps best reflect their impact. Information and movements now have the potential to go 'viral'– travelling over borders and to digital strangers in a matter of seconds. Emerging is a culture where individuals can check, comment upon and provide judgement on whatever is currently 'trending' in real time with seemingly anyone, anywhere in the world.

The leftist commentator Richard Seymour has recently commented upon this precise phenomenon in his book *The Twittering Machine* (2019). He describes it tellingly as a 'horror story', depicting an emotionally crippled world addicted to social media. He roots his analysis (at least in part) in the economic conditions of financial crisis and desperation in which this world was predominantly incubated. He offers an affective treatment of this dangerous 'twittering machine', placing the onus to an extent on users, who are able to gain a sense of connection from its use and exert a considerable and fairly constant amount of labour in maintaining this online existence. He proclaims that 'the twittering machine invites users to constitute new, inventive identities for themselves, but it does so on a competitive, entrepreneurial basis. It can be empowering for those who have been traditionally marginalised and oppressed, but it also makes the production and maintenance of these identities imperative, exhausting, and time-consuming' (Seymour, 2019, p 44). He ends this rather depressing treatment of our mobile age with a call to essentially 'turn off and tune out'– freeing ourselves from our largely self-imposed imprisonment to social media.

This perspective is certainly evocative and to a degree persuasive. Yet it perhaps risks overstating the threats of smartphones while downplaying their positive political contributions and possibilities. It also ignores the diverse motivations for people's participation in such 'viral politics'. Reporting on a study of social media use relative to the 2012 US presidential election, Penney (2016) notes that 'while some who engage in this activity enthusiastically embrace goals of persuasion, others opt for alternative conceptual frameworks, such as fostering citizenship by informing others and sparking deliberative dialogue, that seemingly avoid the manipulative connotations of political marketing' (Penney, 2016, p 71). Significantly, there are also genuine (if at times exaggerated) concerns about the creation of a so-called 'post-truth' popular culture, wherein facts have been replaced by trending opinions spread by manipulative algorithms (Peter et al, 2018). President Trump made upwards of 20,000 false claims during his time in office, it has been estimated, while the 'red scare' of liberals about Russian interference in the election reveals how quickly questionable claims can go viral and have real political effects. More optimistic are contemporary efforts to use these viral strategies to digitally spread progressive civic values (Pope et al, 2019).

Fundamentally, the mobile nature of the modern era is altering, if not power relations, then power itself. Indeed, power is traditionally understood in terms of control, domination and influence. Put differently, it respectively revolves around the capacity to rule, punish and shape people's views. The question popularly asked is how just this exercise of power is within a given context. Hence, democracy and liberalism are often heralded for their promotion of popular sovereignty, rule of law and the fostering of a 'marketplace of ideas'. Critical perspectives, especially those coming from Marxist and Anarchist traditions, have questioned the class basis of such paradigms of power as well as the normative worth of the very notion of sovereignty. Their critiques, in turn, open the space for reconsidering what power is, how it operates and what it can radically become. It appears we are at a historical crossroads where such technology will either expand the potential of freedom or lead to even more oppressive forms of neoliberalism.

However, the rise of mobile cultures and networks adds a new dimension to such critiques, being focused less on ruling territory and controlling discrete populations and more on shaping the spread of information and influencing networks that transcend conventional political boundaries. At play is an updated form of hegemony. For the Italian Marxist revolutionary Antonio Gramsci, writing while imprisoned by the fascists and unable to engage in practice as much as he would have liked, power was a dispersed phenomenon. It was a matter of social inscription and material domination, enacted across civil society and popular culture, shaping a population's 'common sense'. 'The state was only an outer ditch', for Gramsci, 'behind which there stood a powerful system of fortresses and earthworks' (Gramsci, 2007: 238). The task for revolutionaries was therefore one of counter-hegemony, to be fought in each 'fortress' and 'earthwork'.

In their landmark text *Hegemony and Socialist Strategy: Towards a Radical Democratic Politics*, Ernesto Laclau and Chantal Mouffe (1986) promote the concept of 'discursive hegemony', arguing that social relations are continually ordered and reordered through dominant ideas and associated regularized practices, progressing Gramsci's more class-bound and materialist account. Crucially, in their view, the strength of hegemony is found in the degree to which discourses remain naturalized and therefore unquestioned, with hegemony being enacted through language, in popular culture and via social identities alongside traditional politics. This is a rebooting of the dynamics of 'naturalization/denaturalization', so the political act is now the revealing of *any* social order as contingent – unnatural and inessential – and thus available to change.

Their theory chimes with notions of 'depoliticization' popularized at the end of the 20th century. Ferguson (1994) referred to this somewhat famously as the rise of the 'anti-politics machine' in which neoliberalism had rendered many areas once under political control now merely technocratic aspects of market rule. This extended from the marketization and hence depoliticization of nation states to that of global governance generally (Jaeger, 2007). Philosophically, such depoliticization is historically connected to the broader rejection of government accompanying the neoliberal revolution (Fawcett et al, 2017). The answer, it would seem, would be to repoliticize the social and in doing so work towards 'renewing socialism' while expanding the collective ideological imagination (Panitch, 2019).

Yet these desires, and such 'common sense' about the neoliberal composition of hegemony, are undermined by just how unbelievably political and dynamic the contemporary period seems to be. For all its criticisms of trolls and disconnection, it is close to undeniable that online culture is saturated by passionate political views and partisanship. Given that ideas can circulate so instantaneously, it is worth revisiting whether any singular belief or perspective can be considered dominant, let alone hegemonic. This resonates with theorists who have posed the question of whether we are entering a 'post-hegemony' age (Arditi, 2016), supposedly giving birth, in turn, to a novel manifestation of the traditional 'war of positions' between 'visibilities and invisibilities' (Cammaerts, 2015). Tellingly, this is most often expressed in the spread of a quite mobile and 'smart' type of populism, whereby ICTs, viral information, big data and popular discontent combine into a virulent anti-elite politics waged by the digitalized masses (Baker, 2016). Alongside, though less publicized, are mobile movements that draw upon and seek to refresh theories of radical democracy (Kioupkiolis & Katsambekis, 2016). Revealed in both types of mobile politics is a reconfiguring of contemporary collective action and 'hegemonic politics' (Kioupkiolis, 2018).

Fundamentally, power is shifting, becoming more mobile and less confined by conventional geographies or a demand to be coherent or homogeneous in either its ideology or practices. Instead it is characterized by a boundarylessness and pervasiveness, existing 'anytime, anywhere', flexibly adapting itself to local circumstances and amorphous digital networks of people. Perhaps the thinker who best captured and prophetically theorized this mobile transformation of power was Aihwa Ong. She referred early in the new millennium to neoliberalism as a 'mobile technology' whereby it 'is conceptualised not as a fixed set of attributes with predetermined outcomes, but as a logic of governing that migrated and is selectively taken up in diverse political contexts' (Ong, 2007, p 3). Importantly, 'because the focus is on forces drawn together, and the reconfigurations that emerge, there is no claim of determination by a global form. Although assemblage invokes nexus, it is radically different from concepts such as "network society" or "actor network theory" that seek to describe a fully fledged system geared toward a single goal of maximisation' (Ong, 2007, p 5). Consequently, neoliberalism is theoretically and empirically relocated from the 'nation state' to its various 'assemblages' and hence 'in contrast to popular accounts, neoliberalism is not conceptualised as a hegemonic order or unified set of policies' (Ong, 2007, p 8). Citizenship and sovereignty are also in the process of constant 'mutation' (Ong, 2006). To this end, citizenship is progressively a 'flexible' rather than permanent state, representing less an attachment to a territorially stable 'imagined community' and more an emerging cultural 'logic of transnationality' (Ong, 1999). Indeed, even the virulent resurgence of ethno-nationalism in the contemporary period is part of a global 'far-right' populist movement.

The proliferation of mobile power, in turn, has recast the aims and actualities of resistance. Smart technologies have made subversion a matter of connecting 'global assemblages', translating radical ideas and practices for diverse local conditions (Hannerz, 2006). Within the logic of the grassroots viral campaign, there is a need for resisting groups to be adaptive, flexible and innovative (Chenou & Cepeda-Masmela, 2019). These can often take the form of 'everyday struggles against digital capitalism' (Barassi, 2015). Concretely, this has also led to the development of radical technologies aimed at completely rebooting traditional forms of community empowerment (Firchow et al, 2017). Globally, these readical technologies have the potential to exploit new and more mobile digital communication for 'disrupting hegemonic power in global geopolitics' (Simon, 2019). In this respect, these hi-tech social movements represent the evolution of autonomous Marxist calls to build anti-capitalist counterspaces into novel manifestations of 'cyber-populism' (Gerbaudo, 2017). Yet they have also served to promote far-right populists such as the Dutch conservative revolutionary leader Thierry Baudet in the Netherlands, whose former Party, Forum for Democracy, used WhatsApp groups to spread its message among increasingly fervent and connected followers. 'WhatsApp groups have become important tools for political parties and for populists in particular. The groups are used to share political messages among young FvD militants and even to suggest a direct line between Baudet and his sympathizers', reports Maly (2020): 'The closed spaces of those groups not only enable so-called echo chambers, but they also facilitate more intimate conversations among party members and sympathizers as well as functioning as a teaching environment for new recruits.'

At play is an increasingly important and urgent 'viral' political struggle. It is a battle to see which ideas can circulate the most quickly, across the most digital and 'in-real-life' (IRL) networks, and which can best sediment, adapt and grow. These political contestations are waged as much on the streets as they are on social media platforms (Bonilla & Rosa, 2015). They must be flexible enough to speak to different demographics and compelling enough to attract the attention of a global cyber-audience. Nevertheless, there are serious concerns about how actually transformative and revolutionary these mobile actions are or can be (Daniels, 2017). For some, they point to an updated 'false consciousness' based on the 'illusion' of a 'digital commons' (Ossewaarde & Reijers, 2017). For others, such digital activism naturally tends towards political conservatism (Schradie, 2019).

It is absolutely critical, then, to explore how mobile power cannot just reconfigure politics as such but produce movements that are 'digital, political, radical' (Fenton, 2018). Or more to the point, to make revolution as mobile and viral as the dominant ideology and elites it is seeking to oppose and replace.

Viral orders

The first two decades of the 21st century have ushered in profound social, economic and technological changes. If the latter part of the 20th century was marked by the forces of marketization, financialization and privatization, then this one is being defined by the rise of digitalization, computerization and automation. To this end, it is predicted that humanity is on the verge of a major 'disruptive' shift in how it works and lives. Perhaps the greatest fear and hope is the ability of AI and robots to replace humans, causing mass unemployment and the creation of a society ruled by algorithms (Reischauer, 2018). Critically, this is reorienting traditional perspectives, and challenging and threatening capitalism (Fuchs, 2018). Humanity is also on the verge of radically updating contemporary existence, witnessing the evolution from a human to a transhuman world. (Benedikter & Siepmann, 2016).

Yet there remain questions as to whether the techno-shift represents a fundamental disruption to the current order or merely the technological upgrading of a neoliberal status quo. Emerging 'platform-based' employment, such as with Uber, remains by and large precarious and exploitative, heavily favouring 'employers' (they often refuse to call themselves that, preferring instead to insist that those who work for them are self-employed, evading the responsibilities they would otherwise owe). Digital networks and algorithms produce often grim real-life working conditions pointing to a complicated and potentially much less revolutionary contemporary reality (Laurell & Sandström, 2016). At the individual level, self-tracking practices associated with digital 'lifelogging' show the possibilities of 'cultural transformation' while also potentially reproducing self-disciplining regimes of capitalist efficiency and productivity (Selke, 2016).

It is important to remember here that technology emerges out of, and intervenes within, existing social relations. As Marx (1955) famously argued: 'The handmill gives you society with the feudal lord; the steam-mill, society with the industrial capitalist.' So, what kind of capitalist − and indeed subject − do digital technologies give us? This is one of the challenges of this book: to understand the potential and challenges that come with mobile technology. Marx, of course, was not arguing that either capitalists or workers were determined by technology. Instead, a critical understanding of 'technology reveals the active relation of man to nature, the direct process of the production of his life, and thereby it also lays bare the process of the production of the social relations of his life, and of the mental conceptions that flow from those relations.' The economic base, including technology, has a reciprocal relationship with the superstructure of society, with production as determining only in the last instance (Engels, 1890). Marx (1990, p 563) also held that technology could, and indeed had, played a key role in class struggle: 'It would be possible to write a whole history of the inventions made since 1830 for the sole purpose of providing capital with weapons against working-class revolt.' However, this process also laid the basis for future workers struggles. As Marx and Engels (1848, p 6) argued elsewhere: worker organization 'is helped on by the improved means of communication that are created by modern industry, and that place the workers of different localities in contact with one another.'

Ultimately, the revolutionary impact of these technologies will be overdetermined by political struggles and their often unpredictable economic development. What is perhaps more critically interesting is how this is reorienting the contours of politics, changing to a large degree its rules, character and operations. The struggle for equality and justice, the promise of a dramatic social reordering, is now waged as much on the digital terrain as it is on the traditional terrestrial one. While the spread of information – and disinformation – has always been a crucial part of any political movement, especially so in the age of mass media, it is now taking on a completely new tenor in terms of its intensity and importance. Populations are targeted, their preferences manipulated and their actions concretely influenced – often without their knowing so. Essential in this sense is the degree to which a specific ideology and political project can go viral, becoming a trending force that is at once widely attractive and locally customized.

The viral quality of present-day politics expands conventional notions of power and hegemony. Established perspectives emphasize the strength of a dominant discourse and its associated practices within a specific (though expansive) 'field of meaning', usually akin to a socially constructed political territory. This view is epitomized in the concept of 'logics' introduced by Jason Glynos and David Howarth (2007). They distinguish between 'social' and 'political' logics, representing, respectively, the naturalization of a certain order and its opening up to the possibility of reordering. Hegemony, then, is the continual cycling of these logics, as one discourse challenges and replaces another in dynamic, non-essentialist and not-easily predictable ways. This relation is captured in what Glynos and Howarth (2019, p 113–4) later refer to as a logic of 'discovery' and 'justification', one that structures our production of knowledge and social relations alike. Here, we exist (whether we are researchers of the social or its living subjects) in 'a kind of restless "spiral"– because as we move from one "moment" to the next, and back again, revising aspects of our account in light of adjustments made in other moments, we never return to the same spot ... pointing us back to the context of discovery"' (Glynos and Howarth (2019, p 4).

This approach further offers the ability to reveal the radical contingency underlying a given policy regime or power relation, and therefore also how the interplay between social and political logics help to produce and reproduce an existent dominant order (Howarth et al, 2016). As such, it is not simply that power is productive, as Foucault (1975) suggests, but also that it is dynamic and paradoxically political – a necessity rooted in the need to continually engage with, cover over and tame the inherent potential of the social to be otherwise than it is or proclaims to be. Significantly, this analysis, to a certain extent, defies conventional normative considerations. Put differently, while it challenges any notion of 'objectivity', it nonetheless is normatively neutral as a critical theoretical lens for assessing power and hegemony. Rather, its focus is on the complex and evolving establishment of order and domination. If there is a clear and present normative imperative underpinning this theory, it is to continue to privilege the radical contingency (the rejection of any essence) of social relations past, present and future. Consequently, it opens the space for alternative ethical approaches, ones focused on how affectively invested subjects are in sustaining a given order.

A key aspect of the 'political' then is the capacity to subvert existent hegemonic 'fantasies', thus allowing for new discursive relations and practices to emerge. This political ethics does not have to take the form of a complete social overhaul but instead the putting into question of prevailing perspectives so that new ideas or those currently marginalized can come to the fore. For instance, governments can better 'co-produce' public value with indigenous communities by de-emphasizing their perceived 'expert' knowledge and in the process co-constructing alternative and new discourses through combination and negotiation (Brown & Head, 2019). One example is the attempt to infuse existing scientific approaches with Inuit indigenous knowledge to understand and address environmental change in the Arctic (Daniel & Behe, 2017). Discursive agency, accordingly, is found in the capacity of individuals to critically identify a dominant discourse and allow for its practical rearticulation in the ordering of an established social order (Leipold & Winkel, 2017).

A distinction can then be made between whether a hegemonic order is undergoing innovation or disruption. Are dominant ideas and practices 'updating' themselves to reflect a dynamic social environment or are they being politically transformed into something relatively new? Of course, processes of innovation and disruption are rarely, if ever, mutually exclusive. They reveal how the social and the political always contaminate one another, in so much as every social ordering contains within it the seeds of potential political change and vice versa. Yet this theoretical perspective does serve as an instructive analytical lens for assessing the degree to which an aspect of the social, such as technology, is innovative or disruptive – hegemonic or counter-hegemonic. Laclau and Mouffe discuss this as the difference between 'moments' and 'elements', the former becoming part of a broader hegemonic narrative, the latter reflecting those social articulations that cannot be easily or fully integrated into such dominant discourses. It is the distinction between compatible moments of a hegemonic narrative and those discursive elements that have not yet been incorporated (and maybe never can fully be) into this hegemonic order. This contrast can be used to critically judge and deconstruct popular notions of technological innovation and disruption. ICTs are proffered as revolutionizing traditional politics through the creation of 'digital civics' (Vlachokyriakos et al, 2016). Yet it remains to be seen whether these technological upgrades are fundamentally altering or simply updating the current capitalist order (Massey & Johnston-Miller, 2016), whether they are innovative moments or disruptive elements. The promise of 'e-government' may thus be a rebooted fantasy of 'responsible' market governance, promoting an affective commitment to surface-level changes while the hegemonic discourse and status quo fundamentally stay the same (Schnoll, 2015).

Nevertheless, political disruptions can often occur, ironically, via less radical attempts at social innovation. The very demand for ongoing innovation reveals the incompleteness of hegemony, the need for any social order to constantly be 'improved' and update itself. Technology is a concrete manifestation of this ever-present political element. Practical innovations can lead to the discovery of novel social possibilities for ordering people and things within a given context. Hence, projects aimed at developing 'innovative civic technology for the public good' may start as merely reforming the present system and end up utterly transforming it (Golstein et al, 2016). This speaks to an increasing 'glocalization', and hence mobility, of the political, as such disruptions are commonly found in the adaption to and reconfiguration by local histories, cultures and institutions (Moulaert et al, 2016).

Reflected, hence, is the fundamental mobility of power underpinning and driving these social and political logics. The strength of hegemony and counter-hegemony is not their homogeneity but their heterogeneity, their ability to be flexible, dynamic and adaptive to wide-ranging social conditions. The always present contingency of any order emerges in the need for a dominant discourse to respond to and shape diverse contexts rather than establish a monolithic global order. The universality of hegemony lies in its overarching guiding principles combined with innovative capabilities for being mobile as necessary. This mixture of ideological coherence and practical mobility gives rise to a viral politics. Politics differs from the political, in this respect, in being the always present aspect of institutional and cultural change within a hegemonic 'field of meaning'. It is the capacity of and expectation for a status quo and ideology to update themselves and allow for proscribed contestation within acceptable limits (Bloom &

Dallyn, 2011). Accordingly, order is not so much imposed as continually decided and negotiated within a social order that is always in progress.

The introduction of the political, therefore, is one that must also navigate, accommodate and seek to transform such entrenched politics. The social and the political, accordingly, are viral in that they are constantly infecting, spreading and changing a host context and its population in ways that are both universal and tailored to local conditions. The establishment of social order is rooted in the capacity of discourse to effectively spread and mutate. The political, in turn, is the targeted disruption of this innovative order with the hope that it can be contagious in its reach and overall effect. Hence, a social articulation is one that pinpoints how an order can be sustained and replicated, while a political articulation is a forensic analysis of this viral order for its possible concrete disruption and radical alteration.

The return of guerrilla politics?

The notion of the guerrilla seems perhaps outdated in the new millennium. It evokes nostalgic images of heroic revolutionaries running to the hills to successfully – even if only temporarily – overturn global imperialist forces. It conjures up iconoclastic leaders such as Che Guevera, Josip Broz Tito and Ho Chi Minh, leaders who were able to inspire successful armed struggles against seemingly overwhelming odds with inferior forces and technology. Yet it also reminds people of a simpler political time, when the nostalgia of myth tells us that all that was required to break free from colonial chains and replace capitalism was to overthrow a corrupt leader and take over the government of a nation state. A half century of reaction, authoritarianism and revolutionary disappointment have made these ideas appear to be at best quaint and from a different, less politically jaded era – and at worst the misguided path to tyranny.

However, guerrilla thinking and practices have experienced a resurgence in popularity and significance in the new millennium (Laqueur, 2019). The figure of the out-resourced but more mobile and resourceful fighter speaks to a generation increasingly ruled by corporate monoliths whose size and power make head-on attacks seem futile (Kelly et al, 2019). These desires extend to novel strategies of 'guerrilla marketing' aimed at using unconventional methods to defeat larger and wealthier rivals (Levinson, 1984). They also, paradoxically, have been exploited by governments to solidify their rule and promote official ideologies, even at times against actual former guerrilla fighters, such as in Colombia with the FARC Rebels (Fattal, 2018).

The use of guerrilla techniques has, further, progressively emerged as a key resistance strategy in this period. Rosemary O'Leary (2019) has introduced the idea of 'guerrilla government' to describe contemporary efforts of subordinates to subvert, undermine and even expose the unethical, stagnant and exploitative practices of the governing organizations they work for. Such institutional guerrilla resistance can encompass attempts to fight against injustice as well as less radically seek to update overly bureaucratic public systems – thus mirroring the distinction between political disruption and social innovation. O'Leary notes that 'rather they choose to work behind the scenes. Guerrillas may cultivate allies among non-governmental agencies in their policy areas, slip data to other agencies and ghostwrite testimony for others. They may hold secret meetings to plot a unified staff strategy, leak information to the press and quietly sabotage the actions of their agencies' (O'Leary, 2019, pp 5–6). Guerrilla resistance, moreover, reflects the viral character of these guerrilla actions as they can spread quickly to different departments and governments as a principle by which those seemingly bereft of power can utterly transform the aspect of social order which they are tasked with maintaining.

These guerrilla-type actions can be drawn upon to invigorate present-day resistance movements and practices beyond those confined to official institutions. Notably, unconventional electoral campaigns deploying outrageous satire and methods that challenge social taboo – including candidates being in drag – have a history of subverting and temporarily upending traditional democracies (Bogad, 2016). It is telling that the popularity of 'electoral guerrilla theatre' is linked to the perceived legitimacy of formal democracies within a specific context, a point that Che himself highlighted as a necessary condition in his own initial analysis of guerrilla revolutions, declaring, 'When the forces of oppression come to maintain themselves in power against established law, peace is considered already broken' (Guevara, 2012, p 2). Less publicized, and certainly less dramatic, are efforts, often underground, of community members to provide 'self-provision' in areas that have been largely abandoned by governments through disinvestment and public neglect. A recent and compelling example is the taking over of deserted houses by residents in Detroit attempting to mitigate the human and social costs of neoliberalism (Kinder, 2016).

These modern urban guerrillas echo the actions of peasant farmers across the world who engage in 'guerrilla agriculture' through the illicit growing of food on lands that they have been excluded from due to processes of globalization, such as in the case of rural Ugandans (Cavanagh & Benjaminsen, 2015). Interestingly, this exclusion (unlike the example of neoliberal cities) is commonly driven by ethical desires for animal conservation. However, it again represents the turn to guerrilla tactics – ones that range from non-violent to explicitly militant dissent – by those who have been disempowered and marginalized by regimes of power. These guerilla farmers, 'far from passive victims of global economic and environmental change ... are frequently effective at carving out spaces of relative autonomy from both conservationists and the Ugandan state apparatus' (Cavanagh & Benjaminsen, 2015, p 725).

Such guerrilla tactics and ethos can also be exploited by governments to maintain their rule during periods of crisis and in the face of their own vulnerabilities. The most famous example of 'guerrilla governance' is post-Mao China, where the CCP was expected to succumb to mounting social and economic pressures to democratize and liberalize. By contrast, it has sustained its rule through engaging in 'adaptive governance' based on a flexible 'guerrilla policy style' (Heilmann & Perry, 2011). These official responses have extended to the daily attitudes and practices of an increasingly precarious workforce, also facing the pressures of corporate globalization. They are now expected to be proactive, adaptable and boundaryless in their career attitudes (Uy et al, 2015).

Theoretically, this resurgence of the 21st-century guerrilla – whether as an aspect of hegemony or counter-hegemony – gestures toward Laclau and Mouffe's original formulation of the concept of 'antagonisms'. These are conceptualized as those articulations which reveal the limits of a dominant discourse, thus exposing its underlying contingency and revealing the potential for its alteration and replacement. In their own words: 'Antagonisms are not objective relations, but relations which reveal the limits of all objectivity. Society is constituted around these limits, and they are antagonistic limits.' (Laclau & Mouffe, 1986, pp xiii–xiv). It is through such antagonisms that political disruption is made possible (Norris, 2002). Yet there is never a pure political articulation, it is always interspersed and emerging from an entrenched and innovative social context. At stake then is a continual battle to articulate given local events and experiments as either integrated hegemonic moments or antagonistic elements within a wider field of meaning (Thomassen, 2005).

More precisely, using the framework introduced in this analysis, the question is how localized guerrilla action can become a viral political movement for inspiring diverse forms of mass contestations and transformations. How can the subversive actions of individuals and groups be turned into networked collective movements (Rekret,

2014)? This theoretical concern is especially significant in the present age with the prospect of credibly moving towards a post-capitalist near future (Jones, 2019). The task, then, is how to transition and grow local guerrilla politics into a 'glocal' revolutionary struggle.

A central theme in this book is the radical and indeed revolutionary potential of what we term guerrilla democracy. Over the past several decades, a range of novel theories of "radical democracy" have emerged to enhance and even supplant both conventional ideas of liberal democracy and orthodox Marxist perspectives. These range from notions of 'agonism', popularized by Chantal Mouffe, to that of 'dissensus', most famously extolled by Jacques Rancière. They both promise a revitalization of the democratic through challenges to the status quo at its ontological foundations through, respectively, the radical promotion of values of pluralism and the 'redistribution of the sensible' through disagreement. Our theory and praxis of guerrilla democracy both expands upon and provides a revolutionary rebooting of radical democracy and politics generally. It emphasizes the capacity of individuals to build up localized resistances to 'infectious' hegemonic discourses and to replace them with contagious counter-hegemonic discourses. Instead of openness or disagreement, it highlights the possibility of establishing a liberating 'commons sense' through everyday networks dedicated to emancipatory forms of creative disruption. It does so through reorienting democracy and revolutionary change around the perpetual need to reconnect, reimagine and rematerialize our social existence.

Radical materialism

Guerrilla strategies and politics are most often associated with a relative lack of material resources. More precisely, the guerrilla historically emerges as much out of necessity as desire. It is a response to fighting an opponent with superior weaponry, wealth and human forces. Conventional approaches are thus deemed futile, leading to the adoption of these covert tactics. Fundamentally, though, it is grounded in the repurposing and rearticulating of existing material relations for the transformation of the social. More precisely, the guerrilla is engaged not just in hidden attacks and subversions against a status quo. They are forced, due to their position, to find new ways to use available objects, in the process disrupting their perceived purpose and opening the space for reconfiguring and redesigning a prevailing material hegemony. Consequently, guerrilla politics is one of literal 'de-objectification' and 'denaturalization' whereby counter-hegemony is rooted in a mobile and viral form of continual material disruption. In doing so, it concretely reveals the contingency of a social order at both the micro and macro levels and the practical possibility of a revolutionary transformation.

These insights echo emerging theoretical perspectives proclaiming the need for a 'new materialism'. In their pioneering text appropriately entitled *Introducing the New Materialisms*, Dianna Coole and Samantha Frost) write: 'For there is an apparent paradox in thinking about matter: as soon as we do so we seem to distance ourselves from it, and within the space that opens up a host of immaterial things seem to emerge: language, consciousness, subjectivity, agency, mind, soul; also imagination, emotions, values, meaning, and so on' (Coole & Frost, 2010 pp 1–2). Here, object and things are understood as having their own capabilities and agencies, that both restrain and expand those of humans. This perspective provides, accordingly, a 'new form of materialist philosophy in which raw matter-energy through a variety of self-organizing processes and an intense power of morphogenesis, generates all the structures that surround us' (DeLanda 1996).

Such perspectives, in turn, expand upon a poststructuralist tradition, recognizing the contingency and ultimately the social construction of all social relations. Discourses, to return to Laclau and Mouffe, form the 'ontology of the social', constituting its perceived necessity and the rationale for its order. Likewise, the materials within it have no essence but are constantly culturally constructed as social objects. The danger in this formulation, however, is that the signifier continues to reign supreme, power being located in linguistic articulation and conceptual domination that filters down into materialized regulation and oppression. Rey Chow (2010) addresses this concern presciently, observing that 'after post-structuralism attempts to lay claim to materialism/materiality are irrevocably transversed by an insistence on the determinacy of the signifier (understood broadly as language, action, practice, ritual, or gendered orientation and behaviour)' (Rey Chow, 2010, p 231). Poststructuralism, discourse theory and new materialism then find themselves to an extent at a theoretical and empirical impasse: Can there be a political disruption that neither privileges the material nor immaterial but rather the concrete reimagining and rematerializing of social existence itself?

At stake, then, is to not reduce discourse either to language or the immaterial, nor (to reduce) objects and material to reified social agents. On the contrary, it is to situate them both as constitutive agents of a viral socialized order made possible by regimes of mobile power, one that is constantly reproducing and reinventing itself. Jane Bennet (2010) comes close to articulating just such a project, proclaiming the need for 'narrating events (a power outage, a crisis of obesity) in a way that presents non-human materialities (electricities, fats) as themselves bonafide agents rather than as instrumentalities, techniques of power, recalcitrant objects, or social constructs' (Bennet, 2010, p 47).

This question can be rearticulated, though, to better reflect the fundamental mobility of power. Namely, what would politics be if we took it as a given that all existing materialities and immaterialities, all things considered human and non-human, were in a continual, contingent and overdetermined process of innovating or disrupting viral orders? Is that agency, then, not in any inherent or culturally imbued capabilities of a thing or idea but in its emergent contribution to such dynamic and ongoing social innovations and political disruptions?

These questions precipitate a novel understanding and practice of hegemony based not on stability but mobility – Gramsci's earthworks and fortresses float, evolve and adapt. The notion of dominance and domination is conventionally ascribed to the stagnation of social relations. It is as Foucault (1988) declares: "When an individual or social group manages to block a field of relations of power, to render them impassive and invariable and to prevent all reversibility of movement" (Foucault, 1988, p 3) By contrast, domination is found in its dynamism, its capacity for strategic updating and constant diversification. Its power is rooted in its ability to infest and infect all aspects of existence, not merely taming these spheres to its ideological demands but using them to discover new applications for its reproduction and growth. Materials, hence, do not have an essential agency any more than humans or ideas do. Rather, their vitalism is founded in their mobility, one which is both harnessed for a hegemony that is always viral and which is never exhausted by it or completely contained within it. They are actors in so much as they are moments or elements in the play of hegemony, which like all subjects have the ability to play both parts sometimes and often at the same time.

This infusion of materialism with mobility, vitalism and virality is perhaps especially resonant in this current epoch marked by the rise of digitalization, AI and big data. Witnessed is how what are traditionally considered material – people, places, things – are now being made into immaterial bytes of data the lives of which are lived as much 'in real life' as on the internet. Once-material labour is being augmented by the immaterial labour of data plundering and exploitation based on people's physical and virtual selves. Meanwhile, what was previously thought to be immaterial is becoming increasingly material. This process of social materialization ranges from the quantification and tracking of our deepest emotions to the greater recognition of the actual global economic relations that sustain this digital economy. In the near future, this supposedly sacred dividing line between the material/immaterial and its associated binary non-human/human will become even more blurred. The rise of transhumanism and the 'internet of everything' reveals a coming hybrid culture in which consciousness is no longer the exclusive domain of 'living things' but contained in all 'intelligent' objects.

The task, then, for a materialist guerrilla politics is to discover the disruptive political possibilities in otherwise innovative social orders. It is the engagement with the material world as a site for ongoing reconfiguration and repurposing aimed at fermenting 'glocal' antagonisms. They are 'glocal' in that they use local resources and conditions in order to reveal the viral possibilities of fundamentally altering a dominant discourse – slowing down its mobility and showing the potential for existing differently. Significantly, the task for a material guerrilla politics is the uncovering of the diverse and often unpredictable capabilities and intelligence of the objects and things that constitute our life worlds. It is in these immanent forms of radical experimentation and change, where alternative values are flexibly and practically adapted to a given context, that the seeds of revolution can materialize and spread. Its aim, again, is to profoundly reboot democracy as an ongoing viral struggle for political reconnection, reimagination and rematerialization.

The revolutionary promise of guerrilla democracy

The new millennium is challenging established notions of power and politics. Power is not merely productive and dominating but, perhaps more importantly, mobile. The power of power, its strength, if you will, is rooted in its adaptability and diverse applicability. Hegemony, in turn, is made possible through its viral potential – how rapidly and widely a dominant discourse can spread, infiltrate and shape a given context. The distinction between the social and the political – order contra transformation – is one based not in their dynamism but their purpose, direction, impact and affect.

The argument being made here about power and the political is meant to be both timeless and timely. Timeless in that it is highlighting a crucial aspect of order and transformation that spans generations and contexts. Timely in that new mobile technologies are making the mobility of power significantly more important. These insights allow for a theoretical reconsideration and practical reconfiguration of materialism and a materialist politics. Critically, what is significant is not the inherent capabilities of objects nor even their culturally constructed agencies. Rather it is their contribution to furthering social or political logics. In this sense, all things – including people and that which is considered immaterial – can be considered powerful materials. They are continually being used and adapted for the purpose of reinforcing a diverse and evolving hegemonic order. By contrast, they hold the possibility of challenging such orderings and revealing concrete possibilities for alternative social orderings.

In the contemporary period, these broader insights offer a significant lens for enhancing understandings of struggle and revolution. At stake in any counter-hegemonic movement is how it can transform radical materials into revolutionary agents. More precisely, what is required (both ideologically and practically) for prevailing social phenomena – existing as mobile moments of a dominant narrative – to develop into viral elements which can actively and effectively show the limits of these orders and provide the concrete basis for their dramatic reimagination? It is here that the mobile character of power and mobile technologies converge to help catalyze a new revolutionary actor. The greater capacity of individuals and things to be mobile – to use ICTs, big data and AI – for creating new networks of interaction across traditional geographic boundaries and demographic barriers, opens up opportunities to establish 'glocal antagonisms' and spaces of radical difference even in the face of entrenched global regimes of power.

Rosi Braidotti (2011, p 24) refers to this current period as one marked by the rise of 'nomads' in a rapidly diversifying capitalist world. 'Advanced capitalism is a difference engine in that it promotes the marketing of pluralistic differences and the commodification of the existence, the culture, the discourses of "others", for the purpose of consumerism', she critically observes. 'As a consequence, the global system of the post-industrial world produces scattered and poly-centred, profit-oriented power relations', she continues. If this is true, then what is key is the potential for such nomadism, these continual digital migrations, to evolve into sustained and purposeful guerrilla struggles – to take root and upscale. It is the transition from constantly innovating mobile subjects to disruptive agents of revolutionary change rooted in the perpetual 'glocal' processes of reconnection, reimagination and rematerialization.

The risk, though, is that such a guerrilla politics – the ongoing attempt to turn political interventions into viral movements for radical social reinvention – will become change oriented for its own sake. In particular, that it will come to reify the novel as itself an inherent good and the sole, or at least primary, basis for political engagement.

Indeed, the very mobility of power and hegemony should put such a politics historically to rest in so much as any dominant order is always in the process of updating itself, and as such is necessarily a mixture of the established and the innovative. Rather, it is imperative to match a politics of radical materialism with a critical historical materialism. It shares, to this end, the aims of Bennett's (2010, p 47) proposed 'vital materialism', which 'would run parallel to a historical materialism focused more exclusively upon economic structures of human power'. Yet this must not be a simple rote application of traditional Marxist theories to a new 'mobile' context. Instead, it should focus on how the mobility of power subverts and redefines such historical materialism so that it can critically inform a viral guerrilla politics. Specifically, this entails identifying the diverse material networks and relations that allow for a hegemonic ideology and status quo to reproduce itself and spread, as well as targeting 'mobile strikes' for their concrete disruption and reconfiguration. It also means a serious analysis and movement to turn 'glocal antagonisms' into global transformations – for viral interventions to become themselves new innovative social orders based on alternative ideological values and affective commitments.

Such a politics holds the promise, hence, of transforming prevailing notions of democracy and leadership. Critical scholars and political activists are already deeply involved with expanding current understandings and practices of democracy. At a time when basic liberal democracy appears increasingly under attack, these are perhaps more important than ever. The resurgence of far-right ideologies and populist movements reveal their limits and the need for their revitalization. The concept of guerrilla democracy builds on various ideas of radical democracy and in particular 'aversive democracy' proposed by Aletta Norval. What it adds to these is its explicit shift in focus from the procedural and ideological to the political and material. Put differently, its interest lies not simply in opening greater space for agonistic deliberation or an enhanced ability to expand hegemonic imaginaries. Instead it emphasizes the ability of actors to disrupt mobile social orders and the potential for establishing new ones locally and globally. In the process, it reveals continuously who is included in such efforts and who remains excluded and what this uncovers about these movements for change. Specifically, it is a continual articulation of who has the capacity to engage in guerrilla action and who does not and why, a critical assessment, in this regard, of who have the greater ability to become revolutionary agents rather than mobile subjects. Democracy, in turn, is made into an insatiable ideological, material and existential project of creative disruption. It is one centred on the diverse possibilities and concrete capacities to reconnect, reimagine and rematerialize hegemonic social relations locally and globally. Just as importantly, it represents an ongoing radical ethical commitment to use these guerrilla techniques and perspectives for doing so in order to establish more egalitarian communities based on 'commons' values.

It also requires a rethinking of what constitutes 'good leadership'. While this term is loaded with critical peril – containing within it the seeds of authoritarianism and managerialism at the very least – it nonetheless also holds the promise of enhancing a vibrant guerrilla democracy. Such guerrilla leadership should emerge from the grassroots as a collective, vibrant and democratic subject, as mobile and viral as its politics. Notably, it should be both distributed and fluid – not focused in any one person or group and diversely arising from different 'glocal' struggles. Here, established tropes of charisma, heroism and decisiveness fall to the wayside in importance. They are supplanted by the shared ability to disrupt and reimagine a social order in its everyday material realities alongside a commitment and openness to different perspectives and movements so that these efforts can go viral. As Bauman (2013, p 1) notes, we are living in 'liquid times' when 'there are no permanent bonds, and any that we take up for a time must be tied loosely so that they can be untied again, as quickly and as effortlessly as possible, when circumstances change.' Consequently, what is required is a liquid guerrilla leadership to meet these dynamic contemporary challenges and materially reinvent the world.

Conclusion

There is an urgent need for a theoretically sophisticated and empirically strong perspective that can shed light on the revolutionary potential of mobile technologies. While there is a widespread acknowledgement of the potential of future tech such as big data, social media, digital platforms and smartphones for utterly changing social relations, there is significantly less engagement with their capacity for positively transforming the very way we form our collective political subjectivities and sense of agency. Yet in the past half decade alone, these techniques have been fundamental to the creation of political, and increasingly economic, movements.

As outlined in this introductory chapter, this book seeks to make an original contribution to the emerging academic and popular literature on the relations of technology and society. It desires to shift the focus from viewing these as technologies of governance and organizing to see them as new forms of collective democratic leadership. It combines, in this respect, cutting-edge theories of power and post-human theory with in-depth empirical explorations of actually existing examples of guerrilla democracy. A key aspect of its originality, in this regard, is linking economic and political movements, revealing their productive tensions and potential points of solidarity. Emerging from this investigation we hope is a new theory of 21st-century guerrilla democracy, which will help extend understanding of contemporary politics and movements across disciplinary and practice lines. Concretely, it reflects the creative and disruptive ways these mobile technologies and newly politicized subjects merge to create a novel subjectivity, a post-human counter-hegemony to challenge entrenched power regimes both politically and economically. In this respect, it seeks to refocus radicalism into a revolutionary guerrilla politics that can resist infectious dominant discourses and foster contagious revolutionary alternatives for reimagining, reordering, reconnecting, resituating, rematerializing and resolidifying the world according to viral and perpetually expanding 'commons-based' values and practices.

2

Mobile Power

Guerrilla warfare is often thought of as something which emerged only in the modern era of revolutionary struggle. Yet, in truth, it has a long history stretching back to Sun Tzu's *The Art of War* (1963). Indeed it was prominently used in the US Revolutionary War in the late 18th century, where an outnumbered army was able to use a range of harassing attacks against invading British forces to successful effect (see Dederer, 1983). These same tactics would be adopted famously by Mao Tse-tung and the Chinese Communists, where Mao succinctly described the strategy: 'The enemy advances, we retreat; the enemy camps, we harass; the enemy tires, we attack; the enemy retreats, we pursue' (1965, p 124). Significantly, guerrilla tactics were viewed as more than simply a military technique. Rather, they were a way of being that emphasized values of adaptability, covert actions and resilience in the face of seemingly overwhelming odds. According to US Brigadier General Samuel B. Griffith, what makes guerrilla warfare and its practitioners so dangerous is that 'guerrillas are masters of the arts of simulation and dissimulation. ... Their tactical concepts, dynamic and flexible, are not cut to any particular pattern." (Mao Tse-tung & Griffith, 1964, p 26).

What lessons then, if any, would such a guerrilla ethos hold for present-day activism and social movements? At first glance, they may appear reserved for only armed insurrections or a rather duplicitous – indeed anti-democratic – mode of political operation due to their emphasis on simulation and dissimulation. Digging deeper, though, the contemporary relevance of guerilla tactics starts to emerge more fully. They speak to the possibilities of pursuing effective resistance and potential transformation in a social order whose domination is paradoxically marked by flexibility and innovation rather than stability and stagnation. While their rootedness in violence and duplicity may stand out, perhaps their true legacy will be in providing valuable insights into how to construct an insurgent revolutionary politics that is every bit as mobile – and often more so – as the power they are seeking to challenge and replace.

From remobilizing to reimagining

The second chapter of this book presents the theoretical basis for our broader critical analysis. It explores the rise of mobile devices as social technologies that have created novel cultural networks and political connections. This social reconfiguration reflects the changing character of contemporary power. To this effect, we draw on the pioneering insights of Aihwa Ong in relation to 'neoliberalism as a mobile technology'. We propose an original theory of mobile power, which focuses on how hegemonic ideologies currently battle for supremacy by flexibly 'customizing' themselves to local circumstances, publicizing their ideas so that they go 'viral', using analytics to guide effective action and forging innovative digital linkages across local, national, and global boundaries. Critically, doing so highlights the fundamentally mobile character of power, one whose stability and spread paradoxically rely upon producing social orders and subjects that are flexible, adaptable and dynamic. The strength of power lies not only (or even primarily) in processes of reproduction but rather in remobilization.

The key to resisting and transforming such power, then, is to halt this continual and insatiable process of remobilization and instead engage in fundamentally reimagining the social. This critical expansion of the social imagination, we will show, is not just a speculative exercise. Rather it is a necessary antidote to the inherent dynamism of the social, one which is continually in relative flux with constant local problems arising and needing to be innovatively solved. A commitment to reimagining, thus, is one premised on tracing out the mutating histories of contemporary regimes of power and concretely imagining how they could be otherwise. Consequently this will involve a continual effort to short-circuit social remobilization through sustained cultures and practices of political reimagination.

Rethinking power in the mobile age

The new millennium has witnessed the birth of an increasingly global mobile society. This extends from the proliferation of smartphones to the role such technology is playing in changing individual perceptions and shared social relations. A 2014 Brookings Institute report proclaimed that humanity was quite literally 'going mobile', reflecting a 'revolution in how consumers and businesses access information, and the far-reaching consequences of such uses, represents a fundamental turning point in human history. For the first time, people are able to connect with one another in a relatively inexpensive and convenient manner around the clock' (Bleiberg and West, 2014, pp 1–2). This broader shift has understandably led scholars, policymakers and activists alike to expound the promise of mobile technologies for similarly reinvigorating our democracy and civic society. Specifically, it is claimed that they help overcome the growing 'digital divide' for the promotion of equality and the public good (Mossey et al, 2019).

There is, though, a darker side to this mobile revolution. Popular critiques abound about how it causes human disconnection and alienation. Yet perhaps more politically salient and damning is its commonly less known and often intentionally hidden negative impact on the environment. Indeed, while 'information technology and communications consume about 2% of the world's energy, or roughly the same as the airline industry ... mobile networking represents between one half and one quarter of that total' (Lamonica, 2014). There are also similarly disturbing concerns about how the use of mobile technologies reinforces and can even expand existing gender inequalities and colonial power relations. Importantly, they assist in making such inequities themselves more mobile and flexible in the face of a rapidly changing and unpredictable contemporary sociopolitical environment. As Larsson and Stark (2019) presciently noted, mobile practices are not only gendered but 'deeply cultural', 'historically dynamic' and 'structurally informed'. At stake then is a critical investigation not just of how mobile technologies are supporting or challenging an existent status quo but of what type of power they are producing.

It is worth highlighting in this respect that power is, at its heart, always productive. Though it is popularized as a force of repression, its strength lies in its ability to create. 'What makes power hold good, what makes power accepted, is simply the fact that it doesn't only weigh on us as a force that says no, but that it traverses and produces things, it induces pleasures, forms of knowledge, produces discourse', according to Foucault (1982, p 225), 'it needs to be considered as a productive network that runs through the whole social body, much more than as a negative instance whose function is repression.' Traditionally, such production is linked to the advancement of a dominant discourse, a socially constructed way of understanding and acting in the world that has been naturalized and therefore rendered, if not unquestionable, then certainly unchangeable. 'Discourses are ways of talking, thinking, or representing a particular subject or topic. They produce meaningful knowledge about that subject', writes Stuart Hall (1992, p 277). 'This knowledge influences social practices, and so has real consequences and effects', he continues. Such discursive formations may benefit specific elite interests and groups, but they are not purely for their advantage or in their control. Instead they constitute what is accepted as 'truth', setting the conditions for possibility and action. As Hall further declares: 'Discourses are not reducible to class-interests, but always operate in relation to power – they are part of the way power circulates and is contested' (Hall, 1992, p 205).

It would be a mistake, though, to view such powerful productions themselves as either immutable ideologically or culturally sluggish. Rather, they are consistently marked by the creation and promotion of novel forms of social agency, granting individuals and communities supposedly new freedoms and spaces for action. As the anthropologist Sherry Ortner tellingly reminds us: 'Every culture, every subculture, every historic moment constructs its own forms of agency, its own modes of enacting the process of reflecting on the self and the world and of acting simultaneously within and upon what one finds there' (Ortner, 1995, p 186). Such agency, however, functions to reproduce dominant values and social understandings, part of the shared 'problemization' which economic, political and cultural relations are designed at a given historical moment to address. Hence, instances of power and resistance all too commonly 'refer to the same object, share the same style and support a strategy ... a common institutional ... or political drift or pattern' (Cousins & Hussain, 1984, p 84–5).

Nevertheless, if there is an internal consistency to this power and agency, there is always the threat of external pressures for change and competition being supplanted. As we have noted, Gramsci expounded a theory of hegemony for understanding this dynamic and uneven character of power. He envisions politics and social order as founded not simply in class struggle (which he ultimately still prioritizes) but in the ever-changing battle between groups for ideological and political supremacy. Hence, he conjures up a vision of a status quo periodically wracked by crisis, and if revolutionary conditions are ripe, liable to be replaced through a process of evolution, so that 'political forces which are struggling to conserve and defend the existing structure itself are making efforts to cure them within certain limits, and to overcome them' (Gramsci, 2007, p 178).

Equally significant is Gramsci's depiction of power as focused less on coercion and more on persuasion and naturalization. It is rooted (at least in its most modern forms of capitalism, in his view) in the construction of a 'common sense' which creates a shared world view among disparate populations. However, such 'common sense' is itself not stagnant or impervious to alteration. By contrast, while it may be grounded in the promotion of one class over another or in the perpetuation of a particular dominant economic system, its political and cultural manifestations can be utterly diverse and adaptable. Bates (1975), for instance, notes that Gramsci's theory of hegemony was formulated in part to account for the wide range of means by which capitalism is culturally propagated and politically governed across different contexts. In his well regarded book *Language and Hegemony in Gramsci*, Peter Ives highlights this productive tension within hegemony between spontaneity and discipline. He notes that hegemony is necessarily always 'conjunctural' in that it is composed of 'ever-changing combinations that are immediate, ephemeral and almost accidental' (Ives, 2004, p 76). He links it to Gramsci's own depiction of language as being divided between 'spontaneous grammar' and 'normative grammar' in which 'this whole complex of actions and reactions come together to create a grammatical conformism, to establish "norms" or judgements of correctness and incorrectness' (Gramsci, 2000, p 354). Consequently, as Ives observes, such normative grammar is 'not divorced from history; quite the contrary, it is predicated on it' (Ives, 2004, p 94).

More recently, this concept of hegemony has transformed into a whole theoretical and practical edifice for analyzing social relations and power. Perhaps the most notable theoretical perspective, in this regard, has been the work of Ernesto Laclau and Chantal Mouffe. As discussed in the previous chapter, they prioritize hegemony as the structuring force driving social order, portraying it as 'a space in which bursts forth a whole conception of the social based upon an intelligibility which reduces its distinct moments to the interiority of a closed paradigm' (Laclau & Mouffe, 1986, p 93). What power, hence, produces in their view is a singular and supposedly necessary set of social relations out of its contingent and diverse possibilities. Returning to Gramsci, he stresses the importance of uncovering the underlying discourses from which seemingly independent thought and action arise, observing that they are part of 'the ensemble of the system of relations in which these activities (and therefore the intellectual groups who personify them) have their place within the general complex of social relations' (Gramsci, 2007, p 8).

The task, then, in the view of Gramsci. Laclau and Mouffe, of any revolutionary politics is to construct a hegemonic movement that through its own unity of view and action can offer an alternative hegemonic discourse to the present one. In Laclau's words it must be 'to change the political direction of certain forces which have to be absorbed if a new homogenous political-economic historic bloc, without internal contradictions, is to be successfully formed' (Gramsci, 1971, p 168). While these theories of hegemony retain their sense of inspiration and are certainly practically compelling, they do not, however, fully account theoretically or empirically for how dynamic and flexible contemporary forms of digitally mediated power are and how mobile they have presently become. The social orders they produce are characterized by variation, flexibility and the demand for innovation. It is crucial, in turn, to radically reformulate understandings of power, resistance and transformation on this basis to meet these challenges.

Mobilizing hegemony and power

The concept of power is, of course, multifaceted and contested. Isaiah Berlin's classic formulation of 'freedom to' and 'freedom from' reflects its oft-intertwined positive and negative components – which are both respectively enabling and emancipating. By contrast, Steven Lukes's (2004) 'three faces of power' explores the various means by which actors or ideas can achieve domination over others – whether it be through coercion, agenda-setting or ideological control. As the previous section reveals, Foucault focuses attention on the productive aspects of power, the capacity of a discourse to produce and reproduce subjects and relations within a given time and place. Theories of hegemony, in this regard, highlight the continual struggle of discourses for dominance as well as their subsequent attempts at creating and regulating social order. Building on and expanding upon this tradition, we focus on the mobility of power – its ability to adapt, innovate and spread as quickly and widely as possible.

This more fundamental account of the mobility of power links to the concrete contemporary social impact of mobile technologies. Smartphones are already contributing to and challenging the very notion of what a place is and can be (Wiig & Wyly, 2016). The rise of 'smart' planning and governance add to this transformation, reconfiguring how people and spaces are understood and organized. There is a growing awareness on the part of policymakers and scholars alike of the importance of these diverse and large-scale 'mobility transitions' for societies. The danger is that, while harnessing new technologies, they will simply reproduce in innovative ways prevailing capitalist and colonial values. In a recent cross-national study of such mobility transitions, it was reported that 'two dominant logics emerged in the 14 countries [sampled], all of which operate under an increasingly neoliberal, capitalist global economy. These are: scarcity underlying mobility transition planning and austerity as a response to scarcity' (Nikolaeva et al, 2019, p 348). Optimistically, though, they observed an alternative logic, offering a different mode for designing and administering social relations and institutions using mobile technologies, noting that 'the third logic, commoning, is one that is emergent, often quiet, and defiant against the predominant logics of scarcity and austerity. However, it is a logic that demonstrates that spaces of alternatives and potential transformations are alive and well across the Global North and Global South' (Nikolaeva et al, 2019, p 348).

Examples of this 'commoning' logic are nascent but nonetheless abound. These include a cycling platform that allows for groups to form to use cycling miles as a means for crowdfunding social goals. These range in size, scope and activity from the commons-based artist social enterprise Block T in Dublin, which hosts over 70 creative studios composed of over 120 members who have engaged upwards of 800 artists and 150,000 visitors, to the Detroit Farm City Project, which has created a large commons-based park and garden in a blighted urban area, to the Opus La Mariscal in Quito, Ecuador, which has empowered community members to reclaim abandoned land in order to foster sustainable development and community wealth. These different initiatives are perhaps best epitomized by the 'labgov', which is a network of social policy 'labs' for experimenting with the transformation of 21st-century cities into spaces for commons governance.

It also encompasses No a la Costanera Norte ('Coalition against the Costanera Norte', hereafter named Coordinadora) in Chile, which was a bottom-up democratic group representing four diverse communities in Santiago to force governments not to make highway policies based on profit but instead on community needs. However, these inspiring instances of mobile-based emancipation are offset by the use of these same technologies for deepening human exploitation and mobile devastation. Significantly, the exploitative and dominating potential of mobile economies is not necessarily exclusively or even primarily oriented towards controlling an individual's economic transactions. Instead, it is a means for tapping into and influencing their 'immaterial values' at a deeper personal and collective level. Thus, 'to gain from immaterial values, businesses create different environments for "productive consumption" within a new "ecosystem" for integrated digital experiences', observe Kremers and Brassett (2017, p 659): 'In this context smartphones became ... device[s] to tap into its users' social lives and exploit their immaterial values.'

These developments require, therefore, a novel and more nuanced approach to understanding power generally and with regards to neoliberalism specifically. Aihwa Ong provides, in this respect, the most illuminating perspective for doing so – bringing to the fore how mobile and variable such forms of hyper-capitalism are and, in the process, shedding light on the degree to which the strength of power relies paradoxically on this light mobility. She declares that 'the very conditions associated with the neoliberal – extreme dynamism, mobility of practice, responsiveness to contingencies and strategic entanglements with politics – require a nuanced approach, not the blunt instrument of broad categories and predetermined elements and outcomes' (Ong, 2007, p 3) Accordingly, for her, 'neoliberalism is conceptualised not as a fixed set of attributes with predetermined outcomes, but as a logic of governing that migrates and is selectively taken up in diverse political contexts' (Ong, 2007, p 3).

The mobility and diversity of neoliberalism described by Ong should not be confused with either randomness or a lack of core principles. Instead, it is a recognition of how the central demand for maximizing profit via exploitation adapts itself to different cultural and historical environments. To this end, neoliberalism is a malleable technology and a portable problem, one that can be used and solved in distinct and at times divergent ways depending on the context. She argues, hence, that 'neoliberalism with a small "n" is a technology of governing "free subjects" that co-exists with other political rationalities. The problem of neoliberalism – i.e. how to administer people for self-mastery – is to respond strategically to population and space for optimal gains in profit' (Ong, 2007, p 4). The goal of neoliberalism, and its strength, then, is rooted in its flexibility and willingness to continually innovate. Significantly, this does not imply that it merely conforms to a socialized environment or that it utterly changes that environment according to its desires. Rather, its hegemony is founded on a continual process of integration, experimentation and, when necessary, compromise. Neoliberalism treats territories and societies less as places to conquer and more as spaces to uniquely infect and grow within. Consequently, 'neoliberal logic is best conceptualised not as a standardized universal apparatus, but a migratory technology of governing that interacts with situated sets of elements and circumstances" (Ong, 2007, p 5).

Ultimately, the power of this hyper-capitalist technology and logic of governance is grounded in its universal willingness to be locally aware and contextually effective. As such, its infection may not, for strategic reasons, spread beyond certain groups or areas within a society. It can be concentrated in specific populations when and if necessary for its overall survival and success. There is a top-down and strategic element to this, of course, with particular populations targeted purposefully for maximal reproduction and distribution of neoliberal ideology. For example, in 1980, Margaret Thatcher's government in the UK introduced the Right to Buy housing scheme, which gave tenants of public housing a generous subsidy to purchase their properties. The effects of this were twofold: first and foremost it drew a new wave of previously excluded people into the property marketplace (albeit mostly at the bottom of that market hierarchy), with its attendant mindset and patterns of behaviour; but secondly, it instituted a longer-term trend of these formerly public houses eventually becoming the capital of multi-property landlords' portfolios and reduced drastically the level of public housing stock.

The results of such selective neoliberalization are therefore twofold: first interpellating a new population of working-class people within neoliberal speculative and possessive norms; but second, further widening the gap between the profiteers of the system and the rest. The initial act – the strategic introduction of a policy – is but one element of a process that is adapted and continuously reproduced by a new population of neoliberals. For this reason, Ong refers to neoliberalism as simultaneously a 'mutation' and an 'exception'. It is continually shifting in its manifestations and multifaceted in its concrete instances, while focused on those people and places that best serve its purposes. As such, she contends that 'neoliberal calculations are introduced as exceptions to the prevailing political system, separating some groups for special attention, and carving out special zones that overlap, but do not coincide, with the national terrain' (Ong, 2007, p 6).

This analysis opens up new ways for approaching neoliberalism and power. In particular, dominant discourses such as neoliberalism are involved in a constant process of 'morphology'– changing their form in accordance with contextual expectations and needs. Peck, to this end, distinguishes between 'neoliberalism' and 'neoliberalization'. While the former represents an idealized vision of a free market society, the latter exists as 'a contradictory process of market-like rule, principally negotiated at the boundaries of the state, and occupying the ideological space defined by a (broadly) sympathetic critique of nineteenth-century laissez-faire and deep antipathies to collectivist, planned and socialised modes of government' (Peck, 2010, p 20). Accordingly, through neoliberalization, neoliberalism is both more and less expansive. Less so, in that it must respect local conditions. More so, as its possibilities for innovating and learning from such adaptations becomes limitless. Hence, neoliberalism in practice 'defies explanation in terms of fixed coordinates' and is a 'problem space' (Peck, 2010, p 20).

In this sense, neoliberalism is recast from being a disruptive force that must if possible be resisted, to being an interesting problem to be solved that requires both deep critical reflection and practical inventiveness on the part of infected populations. Returning again to the insights of Ong, she refers to neoliberalism as a 'technicalisation of politics' which 'recasts politics as mainly a problematising activity, one that shifts the focus away from social conflicts and towards the management of social life' (Ong, 2006, p 179). Such technicalization, though, should not be confused with mere conformity or a lessening of social vibrancy. The common misconception of neoliberalism as technocratic patently misses the innovation and resourcefulness required for this process of technicalization. It is perhaps mistaken to say that the human costs of neoliberalism are just ignored or that its social conflicts are placed out of view. Instead, they are, paradoxically, given greater view and attention, as issues to imaginatively solve – balancing, adapting and reconfiguring these potential problematic areas and cleavages into context specific solutions. The mutation and exception of neoliberalism is discovered, in turn, in the continual strategic articulation of how these concerns should be addressed and, just as importantly, by whom.

Critically, this adaptive technicalization of politics can itself become a political resource. Put differently, whereas neoliberalization can impose a range of structural and subjective conditionalities on actors, they can also be used to creatively solve problems (often that they have helped to cause) in quite radical ways. Tan (2019) offers an interesting and revealing contemporary case of exactly this subtle repoliticization of neoliberalization in her investigation of the 'new high-quality school project' in Shanghai. Here, the government was faced with chronic issues of educational elitism and a narrow pedagogical focus due to the competitive desire of parents to send their children to a small number of 'prestigious' schools. To counter this trend, policymakers created new 'high-quality schools' with a focus on 'holistic' education – which went beyond mere preparation for exams – and promoted them through discourses of 'school choice' and 'parent autonomy'. Accordingly, they exploited these neoliberal logics of personal freedom in order to try to alleviate existing and persistent inequalities. Tan notably depicts these strategies as connected to a broader phenomenon she refers to as the 'indigenisation of neoliberalism', whereby local actors innovatively use neoliberal ideas, logics and policies to realize a range of culturally specific and politically relevant ends.

These ideas speak to and help expand current notions of an 'actually existing neoliberalism'. Drawing perhaps their inspiration from the past concept of 'really existing socialism', these accounts stress the variation between neoliberal projects within different communities and countries. Brenner and Theodore introduced this concept as a contrast and antidote to those accounts which viewed neoliberalism as a global process of homogenous ideological and social change. They instead 'emphasize the contextual embeddedness of neoliberal restructuring projects in so far as they have been produced within national, regional, and local contexts defined by legacies of inherited institution frameworks, policy regimes, regulatory practices, and political struggles" (Brenner and Theodore, 2002, p 349). Based on this conceptual reframing, scholars such as Rowe et al view neoliberalism as characterized principally by 'enabling mutations' which allows its free market values to mutate and change in accordance with local conditions. For this reason, they theoretically insist on treating neoliberalism as a 'keyword' which must be critically studied in order to better understand 'the political, social, historical and cultural contexts in which neoliberalism travels and becomes variously nestled' (Rowe et al, 2019, p 158). This approach maps onto earlier studies by Ong and Collier to investigate neoliberalism as a 'global assemblage', one that 'enters into assemblages with other elements' (Ong & Coller, 2005, p 13). Adding to these insights, but from a quite different perspective, Anderson (2016) draws attention to 'neoliberal affects' focusing on the common 'atmosphere' and 'affective conditions'– such as feelings of crisis – which are conducive to and tend to invite neoliberal restructuring.

At stake then is the ultimate mobility of neoliberalism, its capacity to adapt and spread so that it can be 'actually existing' rather than a mere utopian (or depending on view, dystopian) social vision. It is the flexibility required to turn these hyper-capitalist dreams into a range of messy but effective realities. Crucially, this puts into greater focus what is actually being produced by power and, in turn, how hegemony actually operates. Specifically, power and hegemony are involved in continual processes of remobilization – encompassing the imperative to constantly reproduce discourses in light of concrete existing conditions and the struggle to mobilize alternatives for challenging and replacing such dominant ideologies and logics.

Remobilizing power

By highlighting the mobility of power, a number of key points about the general and historically specific character of power begin to emerge. While Ong brilliantly focuses on themes of mutation and exception, we highlight how this changes the meaning and implications of 'universalism' and by association 'colonization'. More precisely, there appears to be a universal demand to best take advantage of market forces (for example, privatization, marketization, and financialization) according to local factors. Every place faces its own challenges for doing so, existing as a unique 'problem area' to be continually solved and improved. There are then three levels of this universalization spanning and integrating the ideological, practical and subjective: Firstly, the shared recognition that such market values are socially imperative, if not always easily contextually adopted and embedded. Secondly, the concrete willingness and expectation of sharing good practices with other actors for their benefit. And finally, the responsibility to critically reflect on how best to maximize the market according to your specific and historical circumstances. Here colonialism morphs into interacting and overlapping (though necessarily unequal) networks of continual learning, experimentation, coordination and growth. The proliferation of mobile technologies for this purpose thus reveals the mobility of neoliberalism in this specific historical moment and the inescapability of power in this mobile evolution.

Crucial, in this regard, is disciplining subjects to apprehend the world as mobile market problem-solvers. They must themselves become the developers and designers of an ever-adaptable and improvable capitalism. Such transformations are already on display in the actual processes of current mobile technology creation. In order to mitigate feelings of technological alienation by consumers using digital gadgets such as smartphones, technologists are promoting a new productive 'ideology of AoD' (analogue-on-digital operating). The goal here is to make the experience of the digital feel analogue. In a recent study into such possibilities, Fujimoto explains that 'AoD provides sensory reality of "using tools" utilizing the analog-like methods in respect of operability and presentation' (Fujimoto, 2018). This is a timely example of the deeper reliance of power on processes of mobilization and remobilization, one that is reflected by, but ultimately transcends, emergent mobile technologies. Specifically, it is the evolution of dominant 'problemizations' into a means of producing capable problem-solvers.

At its core, this relies on the subjection of individuals and communities as inscripted and seemingly essentialized parts of a 'host population'. They must become aware of 'who they are' as an articulation of their own abilities and limitations based on their specific culture and situation. Their goal is to critically assess and practically overcome such circumstances. In the contemporary era, this is evident in attempts to develop technology that adapts to human needs without changing either its fundamental use or infrastructure. This is symbolic of the broader ways both scientific technologies such as AI and mobile phones as well as economic technologies like neoliberalism are continually involved in processes of alteration and updating based on the culture and limitation of their users. Equally important is their progressive inscription of users into this culture of improvability as part of emerging socio-technical economic networks. Horpedahl (2015) notes the rise of 'ideology Uber Alles' driving the use of blogging about Transportation Network Communities (TNCs) such as Uber and Lyft. This digitized community of users and service providers bears witness to a mobile culture that connects people not simply through social media platforms but through the desire to share personal experience for ongoing collective betterment.

Such connections echo and deepen insights into how new technologies such as big data and predictive analytics are reconfiguring human understanding and judgement in ways conducive to the reproduction of capitalism. Fourcade and Healy have introduced the idea of 'seeing like a market', contending that, based on the growing 'institutional data imperative to collect as much data as possible', there is a process of subjectification whereby 'individuals accrue a form of capital flowing from their positions as measured by various digital scoring and ranking methods' (Fourcade & Healy, 2017, p 9). The result of such continual quantification and self-tracking is the formation of a new market subject who bases their moral judgements – their sense of 'good' and 'bad' – in accordance with this datafied knowledge. Hence 'outcomes are experienced as morally deserved positions based on prior good actions and good tastes, as measured and classified by this new infrastructure of data collection and analysis' (Fourcade & Healy, 2017, p 9). While an epistemology of evidence-based calculation is certainly not itself novel (either for capitalism or historically), the marketization of these processes and judgements is both novel and profound, especially in the ways that 'the market has become a classifier. Personal records and the scores and categories derived from them are tradable objects' (Fourcade & Healy, 2017, p 11). Consequently, the habitus of capitalism is translated into a technologically mediated and ultimately mobile aggregate of one's tracked, archived and analyzed habits serving as the basis for one's economic and social worth. 'An ubercapitalised world is an economy of differentiated moral judgments where distinctions regarding good behavior become an economic structure of opportunity', note Fourcade and Healey (2017, p 24): 'As a result, the principle by which people become economically qualified or disqualified appears to be located purely within them. Everyone seems to get what they deserve.'

Significantly, it is not simply that we become trained to 'see like a market', it is also that the very acts of seeing and doing become continually and ever more deeply intertwined with such market logics. This 'seeing' is not a matter of simple or obvious ideological brainwashing or even a dogmatic acceptance of capitalist orthodoxy. Instead, it is acknowledgement of how capitalist values and practices – from competition to marketability – offer us the tools to flexibly navigate our increasingly precarious existences and perhaps even transcend them. This represents a contemporary version of the mobile subject, for whom adaptability is central. Knowing oneself, here, is a matter of becoming more deeply aware of how we are participants within and formed by a host context that does not so much overdetermine us as set the stage for our actions, survival and, if fortunate, personal and collective improvement. Thus, while our lives can be unpredictable, and we must always be flexible in meeting any challenge that confronts us, the underlying social structures appear quite transparent and unchangeable. William Davies presciently observed: 'While we view our own fates as subject to unpredictable buffeting by competitive forces, the "game" within which these forces operate feels utterly permanent. ... We must be ready for anything: but somehow this is never cause for hope of real change' (Davies, 2014, p 13) What becomes increasingly clear is how we are disciplined to see all things through this marketized lens of flexible problem solving, even our own personal happiness and well-being. As Davies observes in his later book *The Happiness Industry*, 'There is also a more disturbing possibility: that the critique of individualism and monetary calculation is now being incorporated into the armory of utilitarian policy and management' (Davies, 2015).

The implications of this affective disciplining, the linking of the market to individual utility wholesale, is the transformation of our very selves into a continual 'problem' to be improved via market ideas and practices. Here the focus of 'actually existing neoliberalism' is shifted from territories which must be adaptively conquered to populations that must be individually reprogrammed and constantly updated. This requires a critical self-knowledge rooted in an ongoing awareness and willingness to mine our own histories and contexts to discover how best to maximize our market value and realize our own personalized wellness. We become, quite literally, not just an object for capitalist exploitation but the project for its improvement and the site for its experimentation and growth.

However, this disciplining process is not one of omniscience. The greater availability and amount of personal and shared data, largely collected through the increasingly ubiquitous presence of mobile phones, does not necessarily expand an individual's overall social vision. On the contrary, it allows them to turn further inward, eliding deeper structural issues in favour of their own efforts at self-improvement. Yet it would be a mistake to conceive this simply as a process of quite literal internalization. Instead it represents an entire 'common sense', or using Gramsci's language, a 'normative grammar' for apprehending the world. It is one whereby everything is made into an abstract ideal from which actions can be quantified and tracked with regards to the progress a person, organization, community or state is making towards its realization. These become what Mitra (1998) has referred to as 'virtual identities', ones that are rendered visible via social media but only in so much as they reflect a vague idealization and system of personal commitments, such as to 'universal human rights'– for example, White people posting pictures of themselves kneeling in solidarity with Black Lives Matter rather than more systematically tackling racial inequality within their own institutions. This produces, in turn, a 'virtual invisibility' in which certain groups are ignored and unseen – dealt with and dismissed through the fleeting semiotics of internet visuals – so that the materialities of oppression, the actual complex experiences of 'citizens' are replaced by thin internet mediated 'transnational' identities.

Revealed is how our market vision is at once both dramatically more expansive with regard to our virtual connections and and more limited with respect to actual social possibilities. It can encompass a wide range of geographic and social contexts. Indeed, any and all emerging people, places and things can be rendered into marketized opportunities for profit and data-based well-being. It is also more mobile, in how flexibly and quickly people are able to react to diverse and dynamic environments by transforming them into unique problems to be innovatively solved and experiences that can potentially contribute to their broader professional and personal development. Yet it is also decidedly narrower in terms of the ideologies and possibilities it presents. Creativity is thus found in the ability to innovate without clear and rigid capitalist boundaries of acceptability. We must always keep them within our sights even as we try to see new ways to organize the social within their discursive limits.

At a deeper level of analysis, this phenomenon reflects the intertwining of the reproduction and remobilization of power. For dominant ideologies and practices to persist they must be mobilized – made into flexible sets of discourses and capabilities for subjects to draw upon as part of a 'host population'. Power must be constantly rendered into a mobile and adaptable form. Moreover, it requires a constant process of remobilization to account for the sheer diversity of the contexts and subjects it is seeking to inscribe and colonize. To Marxists, this need for power to stay mobile to survive and thrive will come as no great surprise, as, after all, the very operation of capital and the production of surplus value for capitalists, Marx tells us, relies on continuous transformation of 'money into capital into money' (M-C-M) (Marx, 1990). Yet what could not have been perceived by Marx at the time, rooted as he was in the political economy of factories and manual production, was how significant the creative manufacturing and reinvention of expressive and mobile worker-subjects would become to the production of value. Crucial to such remobilizing is the customizing of domination through, rather than upon, the production of a 'mobile subject', one who is able to critically and continually adjust these powerful forces to best reflect and work within their own personal circumstances.

Customizing domination

It is perhaps tempting to think of power and domination as mass phenomena. And to a very real extent they certainly and undeniably are. They affect people en masse over great geographic and cultural differences. Yet this bird's-eye view misses their utter specificity, or more precisely, their tendency towards and dependence upon a profound sense of personalization. Their success is found in matching their overarching principles and demands to the particularities of a context and subject. Power then is always a matter of ongoing accommodation, one that runs in both directions so that powerful actors, ideologies and processes must adjust themselves to the diverse realities in which they find themselves, while individuals and communities must adapt themselves to their domination. This accommodating aspect of power finds its greatest expression in the aforementioned mobile production of the problem-solving subject, who is able to transform the subjection of power into an empowering subjectivity and identity of self-development and transcendence.

The ability to 'see like a market' is both disciplining and aspirational in this respect. It both shapes how we process the world while also serving as an idealized vision of how we could and should see the world to maximize our success within it. Such marketized apprehensions are perhaps above all personalized, even as they reflect universal capitalist logics of efficiency, productivity and profit. This trend towards the personalization of power was presaged by corporate cultures that ironically harnessed values of individualism and autonomy as part of sophisticated strategies of managerial control. Far from the typical vision of the corporation as bureaucratic, colourless and anonymous, by the end of the 20th century most large enterprises were focusing on personal well-being and developing one's unique individual skills. 'Corporate Culturists commend and legitimise the development of a technology of cultural control', according to Willmott (1993), 'that is intended to yoke the power of self-determination to the realisation of corporate values from which employees are encouraged to derive a sense of autonomy and identity.'

This cultural shift has morphed into what Fleming and Sturdy have referred to as 'neo-normative control' whereby 'the celebration of difference and fun (exist) as expressions of self' (Fleming & Sturdy, 2009, p 580). For this purpose, 'this regime selectively enlists nominally private and authentic aspects of employee selves and is distinct from conventional culture and fun management programmes' (Fleming & Sturdy, 2009, p 580). This imperative to 'just be yourself' has been transformed into demands for discovering 'who you are' and how you can use your unique experiences, skills and desires to best navigate and succeed within neoliberalism and as connected to diverse processes of neoliberalization. Control in this mode is reframed as a mobile ethos and set of technologies for customizing it to the specific needs, desires and histories of the subject it is attempting to regulate.

Crucially, of course, the bringing together of freedom, calculation and personalization has long roots in the historical development of capitalism. As Foucault himself presciently notes, while the 'economic take-off of the West began with the techniques that made possible the accumulation of capital', it was sustained through 'a political take-off in relation to the traditional, ritual, costly, violent forms of power, which soon fell into disuse and were superseded by a subtle, calculated technology of subjection' (Foucault, 1988, p 220). Key to this process was the evolution from being subjected to 'market calculations' to the production of a self-disciplined 'calculating' subject. This represented a powerful 'history of how an individual acts upon himself, in the technology of self.' In the age of neoliberalism, mobile technologies have turned 'technology of the self' into a 24/7 call to be constantly vigilant as to how to best take advantage of constantly emerging market opportunities. Gill (2010) captures the dynamic spirit of the age, contending that 'managing the self in an age of radical uncertainty ... calls forth or incites into being a new ideal worker-subject whose entire existence is built around work' (p 259) Importantly, this mobile, 'always-on' ideal work subject 'must be flexible, adaptable, sociable, self-directing, able to work for days and nights at a time without encumbrances or needs, must commodify herself and others and recognise that ... every interaction is an opportunity for work' (p 249).

It is, of course, commonly understood, in this regard, that central to the ideology of the free market are values of individualism. Margaret Thatcher, one of the most notable and successful political acolytes of the neoliberal revolution, famously proclaimed, 'There is no society'. What is arguably less explored is how individualizing capitalist exploitation and control are rapidly becoming through new digital and mobile technologies. To this end, each person becomes a unique set of data and preferences for market exchange. This represents a process of constant collection and analyzing that encompasses the entirety of their existence in all its richness across a lifetime. Consequently, Schüll maintains that wearable 'smart' technologies exist as types of 'data-for-life' sensors that 'help consumers navigate the field of everyday choice making and better control how their bites, sips, steps and minutes of sleep add up to affect their health' (Schüll, 2016, p 317). In doing so, 'by offering consumers a way to simultaneously embrace and outsource the task of lifestyle management', these 'products at once exemplify and short-circuit cultural ideals for individual responsibility and self-regulation' (Schüll, 2016, p 317).

These mobile gadgets represent a profound ethos of personalization in their design and purpose as well as serving as an increasingly universal resource customizing an individual's neoliberalization. Revealed, in turn, is the mutually reinforcing form that this progressively digitalized 'market vision' takes, marked above all else by adaptability and customization. It is in this way that the market has become fully totalizing, exchanging the age-old desire to conquer the world with the seemingly infinite aim of profiting from humanity's diverse personal and ever-regenerating 'life worlds'. Importantly, one's complicity in these reproductions is built into their code – continual and personalized remobilization.

This has translated into the growing disintegration of conventional distinctions between consumers, workers and companies. Instead, people are now more and more walking, talking and internet-posting advertisements for products and brands that best match their own personal lifestyle 'choices'–their 'brand'. Here, 'as employees internalise the brand image of this external audience, they turn into brand representatives even in absence of face-to-face interactions with others and in their private lives' (Müller, 2017, p 895). Life, in this sense, becomes an ongoing and supposedly exciting journey of capitalist discovery. Emerging is a culture of 'everyday neoliberalism' wherein competition is intertwined with daily practices of self-tracking made possible through the innovative use of mobile technologies. Significantly, 'measurements produce and cajole as well as capture and envision' (Beer, 2015, p 2). The excitement of mobile technologies is rooted not just in their interesting capabilities for consumers but also (and perhaps fundamentally) in their serving as the very means by which people can quantify their experiences and thus personally uncover new and previously hidden aspects of their existence. 'We can see that the aim of a productive measure is to locate and illuminate hidden value, to find things in the data that cannot be seen otherwise and to exploit them', Beer (2015, p 10) critically observes: 'Metrics are seen to be productive in this regard, they are seen to make efficiencies, reveal truths and find value', he continues. The literal opportunity to have such power of prediction and data discovery in the palm of our hands is enticing and a key to contemporary self-disciplining. The use of predictive measures reveals the efforts to find unique value in our 'selves', using these metrics to discover our own special competitive advantage based on our personal histories and marketable talents.

This translates into new customizable modes of mobile control combining the thrill of self-discovery and improvement into a rapacious market desire for constant and ever-expanding profit opportunities. As Lupton contends, 'The concept of self-tracking has recently begun to emerge in discussions of ways in which people can record specific features of their lives, often using digital technologies, to monitor, evaluate and optimize themselves' (Lupton, 2016, p 1010). He explores, in this respect, the 'function creep' of such mobile control – encompassing the private and communal spheres as well as being simultaneously pushed, imposed and exploited. At its heart, though, it is a personal exercise in self-monitoring and disciplining. He argues that 'collecting data is a personal enterprise that is limited to the individual', so much so that, 'indeed, the very idiosyncrasy or uniqueness of many self-trackers' interests and consequent self-tracking data practices means that their data may not be interesting or valuable to others as it is not easily transferrable' (Lupton, 2016, p 106). Interestingly, such data-driven processes of personalization are not necessarily confined to single individuals. Rather, they become the exact way that a group articulates itself as a shared community with specific needs and desires, ones which can mix capitalist discourses and demands for marketability with democratic aspirations for greater inclusion and participation. Hence, coming back to the insights of Lupton, 'this representation of self-tracking portrays it as a civic duty in producing small data that are valuable not only or simply for personal use but also for others in one's community' (Lupton, 2016, p 113).

In order to mitigate, if not completely eliminate, these collectivizing (and potentially radicalizing) tendencies, it is necessary to produce and ensure people internalize, or at least accept, a sense of personal responsibility for using mobile technologies and their data in market-friendly ways. To this effect, the unwillingness or inability to fully capitalize on them – to make oneself more productive, efficient and a better person – is increasingly viewed as a moral failure. It reflects the deeper discourses of 'responsibilization' associated with processes of neoliberalization. According to Shamir (2008, p 1), 'Contemporary tendencies to economize public domains and methods of government also dialectically produce tendencies to moralize markets in general and business enterprises in particular'. This duty to be a good mobile capitalist is based on the assumption that mobile technologies and big data are necessary catalysts for our freedom and agency. It is a form of normative disciplining that is 'fundamentally premised on the construction of moral agency as the necessary ontological condition for ensuring an entrepreneurial disposition' (Shamir, 2008, p 7).

Consequently, arising is an innovative and flexible type of what can be termed 'user-led domination'. Its central feature is its paradoxical reliance on and exploitation of individual and community preferences for its strength. They are the materials and resources through which to further ensnare subjects into a complex but nonetheless subordinating process of mobile neoliberal control. This hi-tech disciplining is premised on a 'continually updating benchmark on which to judge us, revealing in real time our daily progress and our failures to fully maximise our potential' (Bloom, 2019, p 48). The power and domination of the market is made possible and strengthened through its personal mobility. It is personally tailored to individual and community preferences, histories and real-time actions for uniquely predicting and shaping their future. Revealed is the progressive integration of mobile power with mobile technologies for the customization of domination.

Reimagining power

The mobility of power relies upon, perhaps more than anything else, the exploitation of desire. It is a means of identifying preferences and finding ways to capitalize on them. It is also a process of shaping short-term wants and long-term aspirations. Here the self becomes an object for continual self-improvement, the very thing that is constantly in production and requires creative applications for its betterment. There is thus an almost mystical quality that discourses and technologies of mobility imbue into the subject, creating fantastic visions for people that hold out the promise of limitless possibilities if only they are 'smart' and disciplined enough to discover and turn them into realities. In this way, smartphones are more than mere gadgets that make our existence more convenient; through their apps they become a digital doorway to 'wondrous possibilities' (Tucker, 2017, p 27). They are akin to hi-tech forms of contemporary magic which from the push of a button 'offer access to delicious food, comfortable hotels, quick transportation and other pleasing commodities' and 'remind us of the genie that emerges from a bottle in the Arabian Nights' (Tucker, 2017, p 27).

Theoretically, this points to the deeper role that desire and fantasy play in dynamically constituting this increasingly customizable market subject. The psychoanalytic theories of Jacques Lacan provide a useful framework for understanding this affective dimension of power and domination. He focuses on how socially created fantasies serve to structure the subject, creating and grounding the self in an ever-present but eternally disappointing quest for psychic completion through them. The presence of fantasy permeates social relations, serving as the very elusive discourse and object of desire that helps to bring an imagined community together. According to Žižek, 'The bonds linking together its members always implies a shared relationship to the Thing, toward enjoyment incarnated' (Žižek, 1993, p 201). Specific to questions of control, these inscriptive fantasies provide individuals and communities with a sense of affective enjoyment and psychic attachment to the very ideologies and systems that they are not only subjected to but often oppressed by. Returning again to the insights of Žižek: 'What psychoanalysis can do to help the critique of ideology is precisely to clarify the status of this paradoxical *jouissance* [the specific Lacanian word for an enjoyment rooted in something that is perpetually lacking] as the payment the exploited, the served received for serving the master' (Žižek, 1993, p 48). Crucially, fantasy reveals the paradoxically expansive rather than restrictive character of domination. Just as Foucault stressed the productive as opposed to repressive aspects of power, so too it is important to recognize that the ability to control and exploit often rests on opening up possibilities *contra* closing them down. Indeed, fundamental to the appeal of neoliberalism is the fantasy that anything is possible with hard work and a willingness to sacrifice everything (your time, health and personal relationships) to achieve your dreams. Nothing is impossible, it would appear, if one adopts the right attitude and work ethic, the 'sky's the limit' (Bloom & Cederström, 2009).

Historically, this gestures towards the strategic linkages between capitalist exploitation and enjoyment. In contrast to critical perspectives that stress the overtly disciplinary aspects of market identity – ones premised in Weber's highlighting of the Protestant work ethic, for instance – Hennessy emphasizes how 'pleasure became a keystone of sexual liberation politics in the mid-twentieth century when bodies and their capacities for pleasure emerged as new sites of capital investment and the basis for a counter-narrative to disciplinary norms and practices' (Hennessy, 2017, p xxiii). The coming of the new millennium and the ascendancy of neoliberalism as a supposed 'end of history' were met with a mix of surrender to the impossibility of creating a more egalitarian and just world matched only by an expanding and enhanced ability to fulfil one's varied desires as a consumer, and a channelling of the affective struggles for liberation of the late 1960s and 1970s into the logic of the market. 'Gone is any official speak of egalitarian futures, work for all, or the paternal government envisioned by the various freedom movements', note Comaroff and Comaroff (2000, p 299): 'These ideals have given way to a spirit of deregulation, with its taunting mix of emancipation and limitation.'

What emerges from this positive mode of capitalist power and inscription is its simultaneous homogeneity and heterogeneity. It is at once demanding that individuals adhere to the basic rules, practices and even values of being an active consumer subject while also giving them rather substantial scope to tailor such subjection in accordance with their personal preferences and needs. This speaks to the distinction Lacan makes between 'the Law', on the one hand, and 'Fantasy', on the other. The former is a universal mandate meant to be accepted and followed by everyone – constituted through formal and everyday language, or the symbolic, in Lacan's terms – while the latter is an individualized desire within this broader social horizon, a realm of imagery and feeling constituted through the lacks and gaps impossible to cover over with a system of language that shows us how to act and feel (Lacan, 1977). One of course feeds the other. In this case, capitalism and its values of marketization, privatization and profitability remain the Law which allows for a diverse set of individualized fantasies to emerge and flourish.

This perspective helps to deepen understandings of the complex ways that power, and as such domination, is not only ultimately productive but mobile. As opposed to thinking about power as simply reproducing the same subject and social relations, it is more accurate to view it as creating the very conditions of the social possibility of such production. Foucault himself contends that what is critical is how 'forms of repression and constraint have acted' so as to reveal to people 'the frontier possibility of self-determination' (Foucault, 1989, p 452) A dominant discourse acts, in this regard, to set the boundaries within which the self can emerge, develop and fantasize. It exists as the 'limit-experience' of existence, 'an experience that undermines the subject ... because it transgresses the limits of coherent subjectivity as it functions in everyday life, indeed threatens the very possibility of life – or rather the life of the individual – itself' (Jay, 1995, p 158; also quoted in Tobias, 2005). Thus, just as this limit-experience is a closing, it is also an opening. It provides the coherence necessary for people to make sense of, explore and change their given social world within these delineated boundaries.

For this reason, scholars such as Tobias (2005) have made compelling arguments that, for Foucault, there must be minimum material requirements in place if people are to experience freedom, also a basic premise of Marx, who situates the subject firmly as a subject within nature's 'metabolism', who must have sustenance, health and shelter in order to pursue non-alienated being, or rather, who will never be able to escape the basic drives to produce in order to live (Marx, 1990). A parallel reading would be that power functions by creating the necessary material and ideological conditions of possibility for people to become 'desiring subjects'. It is, to use Lacan's terms, the Law that permits individuals and communities to fantasize. Just as importantly, this 'minimum requirement' is expressed in the construction of a host context that one can operate within. The Law in this regard, which Lacan tellingly compares to 'the order of language', is precisely that which must be adapted to and pushed against. Through fantasy it is in a constant state of mobilization and remobilization, as dominant ideologies must be customizable to specific host cultures and the varieties of individuals.

Enjoyment is found not in transcending or traversing beyond these power regimes but rather in effectively adjusting them to one's own situation in a way that feels agentic and reaffirms their 'ontological security' as a coherent social subject. This discussion raises an interesting question relating to material conditions and barriers of entry to neoliberal law and fantasy. Although in some senses the barriers to entry are low – the cost of a mobile phone with some internet access over and above the basic means of sustenance and security are reasonably low – nevertheless we might observe that a great swathe of the world's population will not enjoy the privilege of full absorption or acceptance within the realms of neoliberal law and fantasy. For them, existing at the margins, a preoccupation with life and survival predominates. For the refugee, the unemployed, the partner fleeing domestic violence, the welfare claimant, the gig worker and the agency worker necessarily will not be full participants in mobile neoliberal fantasy and theirs are lives to be managed (Mbembe, 2003) – of course through the power of sovereign rule and webs of governmentality (Agamben, 1998) but also through an outsourced mobile network of the perpetually enraged xenophobic and bigoted consumers of reactionary media who take it upon themselves to scapegoat and 'spontaneously' (Gramsci, 2007) regenerate neoliberal discourse and norms. Much as Marx turned to the universal subject of the proletariat for leadership against capital, might we therefore re-envisage an emergent constellation of mobile, precarious subjects for leadership in these times of outsourced and distributed neoliberalism, those at the margins who can more readily identify the fractures in the system? We shall return to this question, but for now the dynamic of who is interpellated and who is to be managed is a point to be noted.

With the emergence of neoliberalism, and for those privileged subjects included in its matrix, it has evolved into a moralized duty and desire to use one's unique talents and skills for 'improving' and maintaining organizations, communities and personal well-being. Gunder (2016) presciently observed, in this regard, that neoliberal governance 'places a burden on planning to often take "responsibility" for the failure of market-led governance to deliver its policy promises of betterment, security and future enjoyment'. Here, mobile technologies merge with mobile power, as we are continually able to keep track of our success as 'problem-solvers'– whether at a personal or community level. What is absolutely paramount is how such responsibility for covering over market failures morphs into mobile fantasies of individual and collective progress.

Conclusion

This chapter introduced two of the central concepts of the book – 'mobile power' and 'remobilizing power'. We argue that regimes of power draw their strength from their ability to be adaptable to a range of diverse contexts. More precisely, they must be constantly 'remobilized' to flexibly accommodate a wide range of cultural and historical circumstances. This draws on an emerging understanding of power as not simply repressive or productive but instead dynamic and customizable. Yet the argument of this book takes these insights one step further. The contention is that power – encompassing dominant ideologies, practices and actors – requires and is often at its most potent when it transforms people and places into 'host subjects' and 'problem-solvers' to innovatively adapt these discourses to their specific situation and context.

This fundamental though often underexplored dimension of power is perhaps especially relevant in the contemporary period with the growing import of mobile technologies and relationships. The rise of ICTs, in particular, reveals the ultimately mobile character of power – one in which dominant regimes can be personally applied and updated to one's various contexts and domination can be made increasingly customizable. It allows more and more people to be mobile market-based 'problem-solvers' literally at the touch of a button based on almost instantaneously updating real-time information. The next chapter will explore how this has given rise, in turn, to a 'viral' political culture.

3

The Spread of Viral Politics

In an era that was meant to signal the supposed 'end of history', it is perhaps worthwhile to think back to a different 'age of revolutions'. The late 18th century was marked by profound political conflict and mass movements to radically transform society. Here the fight for universal liberal rights and the values inspired by the philosophical Enlightenment mixed with the blood of violence and armed rebellion. From the relatively comfortable vantage point of history, the events and their radical implications appear obvious and easy to discern. Yet, at the time, these revolutionary currents were as much rumours as they were facts. They were murmurs of possibilities, viral discourses of fact and fiction, hope and fear, spread within communities and across otherwise separate populations.

This retelling of history reveals surprising truths about the complex realities of these epochal social changes. The American Revolution is now retrospectively celebrated as an exemplar of the struggle for independence and liberty. Yet at the time its radical sentiments were both a source of excitement and worry for those involved. The initial seeds of rebellion, for instance against the Stamp Act in 1765, more than a decade before the Declaration of Independence, were a source of inspiration and worry for the White colonists. While they opened up, even if only briefly, the possibilities of liberty, they were just as concerned that these desires would spread to Black slaves, inspiring their own revolt (see Nash, 2005). When the actual revolution arrived, rumours continued to swirl in directions that profoundly challenge dominant narratives of today. The British promised the slaves freedom if they were to fight against the colonists, an offer that, in an age before mass communication, circulated unevenly, as much in whispers as in official pronouncements. This led those in bondage to the very revolutionaries proclaiming to be freedom fighters to make a difficult decision, as the promise of liberty for slaves 'had reached a crossroads

... with one large contingent casting their lot with the British and the others hoping against hope that white Americans would honor their founding principles by making all people free and equal' (Nash, 2005, p 427).

At the end of the century, these same ideals would inspire the Haitian Revolution led for and by slaves. In the newly created United States, this produced renewed fears among the free White citizens that their own slaves would hear of this victory and rise up against their American masters (Klooster, 2014). In Haiti itself, the revolution was sustained through the population's ongoing discussions and political gossip. Indeed, 'Caribbean residents engaged in regional news networks that brought – rather than liberation stories – tales of retrenchment, hostility, and dynamic imperial threats' (Eller, 2017, p 653). The spirit of the revolution was maintained through these daily discussions and stories, ones imbued equally with optimism and the need for constant vigilance against colonial invaders, 'passed from hand to hand, read aloud in taverns and in plantation homes, discussed and debated as to their veracity' (Taber, 2017).

From viral hegemony to counter-hegemonic reorderings

These examples speak to a more fundamental truth concerning power and politics. While they represent a time apparently far different from our own with our almost instantaneous information sharing and communication, they nevertheless reflect something perhaps timeless about the flow and possibilities of social and political change. This chapter explores how the strength of hegemony depends on how deep and wide a discourse can spread and at what speed. Its success is linked not only to the coherency of its rationality or the influence of its main supporters. Rather, it relies upon a capacity to move flexibly and quickly within a diverse range of contexts and situations. Revealed is a new logic for understanding social order and transformation, one that intermingles with but is also distinct from the social, political and ethical logics already discussed (and which will be explored in greater depth later). It is the introduction of viral logic, the critical interrogation of the degree to which dominant discourses and those which challenge it can spread, expand and shape existing people, places and things.

Critical, in this respect, is the challenging of viral hegemonies with counter-hegemonic reorderings. A dominant discourse relies upon encompassing both physical and digital networks. These networks may appear fundamentally different or even in opposition, yet they locally and globally entrench power relations and exploitative material systems. Hence, the battle between the police and protestors reflects a relatively stable social dynamic of traditional (but necessary) sovereign resistance, which itself can spread beyond its own borders and come to represent other similar struggles around the world. However, the capacity to use such movements to create new spaces of freedom or to promote alternative visions for imagining 'community safety' reflects the incipient transition from urgent resistances to disruptive revolutions. More precisely, it reflects the capacity of people and things to dramatically reorder their present realities in search of emancipating alternatives.

Beyond global hegemony

Thus far this book has focused on the mobility of power. While conventional accounts tend to emphasize its repressive, stabilizing or productive dimensions, we highlight its expansive, adaptive and innovative aspects. At the heart of this theoretical reconfiguration of power is an understanding how dominant discourses are able to infiltrate and successfully thrive within wide-ranging cultural, political and institutional contexts. It is necessary, in this regard, to explore the different logics – or prevailing rationalities – that allow for the reproduction of a dominant discourse in such diverse environments. David Harvey, for instance, has referred to two 'logics' of capitalism – the 'logic of capital' and the 'logic of territory', representing 'a contradictory fusion of "the politics of state and empire"' (Harvey, 2003, p 30; Wood, 2006, p 10). While Harvey is interested specifically in illuminating the imperial tendencies of capitalism, this logical exploration also sheds light on the inner workings of the spread of power over time. In particular, it highlights the presence of a universalizing discourse in the logic of capital and an internally culturally specific one in the logic of territory. This dynamic is similarly captured in Mercille's distinguishing of contemporary ' "geopolitical" and "geoeconomic" logics of power' in which 'the former logic arises out of capitalism's tendency to expand geographically and the latter out of politicians' need to maintain credibility internationally as well as from pressures generated by domestic public opinion' (Mercille, 2008, p 570).

Just as importantly, these logical tensions do not just apply to the global/state relation but rather form a general dynamic for guiding the mobile ordering of institutions and society. In the contemporary period, for instance, 'organisations in market settings face complex institutional contexts to which they respond in different though patterned ways' (Greenwood et al, 2010, p 521). Such insights point to the dynamic 'spatial' dimension of hegemony. At its most basic level, this involves the ability to organize a given social space – whether that be an urban slum, a rural village or a white-collar workplace. Yet digging deeper, it highlights the necessarily adaptive demands placed on dominant discourses and actors as well as those placed upon the populations and places they are seeking to subjugate. Any place is transformed into a hegemonic space precisely in its forcing regimes of power to accommodate its contextual particularities and vice versa, as it too must be adjusted to fit the needs of this hegemonic force.

The traditional reading of hegemony and change is defined by crisis. Specifically, it is via 'organic crises' that dominant social and economic relations can be fundamentally challenged, transformed, and replaced, existing as 'moments of crisis of command and direction when spontaneous consent has failed' (Gramsci, 2007, p 12). While undeniably events such as war or public health pandemics can be the catalyst for profound reorderings, it is perhaps dangerous to overemphasize the role of crises in understanding radical historical shifts. Indeed, as Fusaro (2019) has recently theorized in his book *Crises and Hegemonic Transitions*, often during crisis the battle comes to be over who is the hegemone rather than over any possibility of instituting a radically new social order. Global hegemony, in turn, is indicative of the political construction of the 'world' as an imagined community for influence and domination.

This reflects two different though not necessarily mutually exclusive accounts of hegemony. The first is the one proposed by theorists such as Laclau and Mouffe, which to a degree treats the concept as ontological, a relatively permanent feature of social relations *tout court*. This is, at least, the conventional reading given to their thoughts and one which drives more critical discussions of hegemony. To think politics and the political outside this play or battle for discursive supremacy borders on the utopian. By contrast, recent interventions have, intentionally or otherwise, gestured towards an alternative reading of hegemony wherein the relations of power to ordering are historical and themselves socially constructed. In this respect, the social is hegemonically framed, if you will, for hegemony – turned into a 'field of meaning' whose primary emphasis is on conquering and relative monopolization.

Required, then, is not just a critical interrogation of the various discourses striving for hegemony but a deeper analysis and clarification of what type of hegemony they are seeking to attain. It is worth taking a brief pause and tracing out what type of hegemony capitalism, and more broadly modernity, has primarily relied upon. It is overwhelmingly that of conquest and exploitation, one premised on both forces of coercion and persuasion. The intricacies of liberal thought and democracy reflect this underlying hegemonic assumption. On the one hand, it directs questions of political ethics to those of either inclusion within a dominant ordering or toleration and management of life on its interstices. On the other hand, it frames politics as a matter of either outright political victory or negotiated power sharing. Underpinning this politics, in turn, is an abiding commitment to power as sovereignty – either over a territory, organization, community or oneself. As such, the watchword of both power and politics is control, manifested in either ideological hegemony, direct rule or a combination of the two.

The notion of mobile power introduced in the previous chapter contributes to what we can call this sovereign mode of hegemony. While not necessarily at the forefront of these processes, it does provide an element of diversity in the otherwise rather homogenous tendencies of sovereignty and control. Rather than drawing its justification from the universalizing and objectifying claims of 'divine right', democratic process or scientific management, it highlights the importance of difference for strengthening such domination. This has particular import when revolving around efforts at exploitation, as spaces and people transform from interchangeable masses into particular places and populations whose value must be uniquely extracted. Mobility, therefore, is a necessary part of this global conquest, giving these hegemonic regimes of power the appropriate flexibility to overcome cultural discrepancies while still adhering to universal goals and values.

The spectre of globalization, though, has also made this type of hegemony, if not obsolete, then certainly insufficient. The very invocation of the 'world' or the 'international' already implies that which cannot be so easily universally managed. It entails a profound sense of difference which will have to be concretely acknowledged and diversely ordered. While the lineages of colonialism and empires can do much to explain competing political entities, they only touch the surface of the multitude of manifestations that something thought to be as universalizing as capitalism demands. Different industries require different rules and regulations, different regions require different economic and political plans, different individuals require different types of motivation.

This dimension is only intensified by the rise of ICTs and other forms of 'world-shrinking' technologies. Their very presence does much to connect the 'globe' and render it a smaller space for hegemonic conquest. In principle, this could provide the basis for an easier, more manageable and coherent form of international sovereignty. Yet it also reveals how profound the differences are between these geographic and cultural contexts and the need for proper strategies to effectively deal with such diversity. It is not a coincidence that in the midst of globalization there is also a renewed stress placed on 'multicultural management'. Even while making things more materially interconnected and culturally linked, this process has highlighted the significance of difference as an ordering principle within the broader ideological hegemony of hyper-capitalism. Whereas principles of marketization, privatization and financialization are meant to be universally adopted, it is formally recognized that each nation and region can have their own means for doing so.

It is precisely here that mobile power becomes so important for the survival, reproduction and ultimate success of neoliberalism. Whereas the post-War Bretton Woods world was premised on a mixture of international capital regulation and unequal alliance building between great and lesser powers, the end of the 20th and beginning of the 21st centuries revealed the need for marketization to be both collectively internalized and progressively self-managed. This does not deny the still-present requirement for imperial military control (both in terms of its coercively dealing with various economic and political threats as well as its being a major industry and influencer in its own right). However, it does reflect that capital control was both deepened and devolved under this emergent neoliberal regime of power. Deepened in that not only were people and places meant to be exploited for their value but they should also come to accept these market logics as authentic, fundamental and inevitable. Devolved, though, in that these same actors (whether individuals or nations) were tasked with being entrepreneurial, exploring and taking 'personal' responsibility for maximizing their own value extraction.

Mobility, in this respect, became itself an ordering principle for sustaining this evolving type of global hegemony. Sovereignty, while not discarded, was deprioritized or more precisely repurposed for disciplining processes of market-based 'responsibilization'. Accordingly, the recognition of difference developed into a set of individual and collective social technologies for its insatiable exploitation. Spatial hegemony was less about 'crowd control' than it was about discovering capitalist opportunity. As new territories for capitalist conquest soon dwindled, this colonial impulse turned to fresh frontiers of personal value extraction – as each individual, community and nation was uniquely positioned as a source for market advantage and profit.

This provided the impetus, in turn, for greater data collection and tracking – made possible via advances in mobile technologies and communication – for aiding this growing demand for 'self-exploitation' (Cremin, 2010).

Global hegemony thus has catalyzed a different type of hegemony, one premised less on conquest and more on mobility. At stake is the ability of dominant discourses to infect a host context and of actors within this context to critically reflect and craft their own solutions for optimizing their economic value. Simultaneously, as will be explored more in the next chapter, this requires a renewed resilience on the part of these subjects to deal with both a volatile marketplace and the severe social and even biological costs of this hyper-capitalist transition. For this reason, established logics of stability and change (social and political) are no longer sufficient for critically explaining this more dynamic, insidious and distributed form of capitalist control. Called for instead is an illumination of how knowledges are produced, adapted and come to diversely dominate different host contexts. Consequently, it can be said that in the age of mobile power, traditional global hegemony has gone viral.

Introducing viral logics

The complex character of contemporary social ordering and hegemony is enhanced by mobile power. It is worth again clarifying theoretical terms by distinguishing social ordering generally from the specific political condition of hegemony. The former reflects the fact that any set of relations will be meaningfully and to an extent practically organized. There is a regulative and more or less predictive quality to the social. The various daily actions that compose our existence are, in this regard, conventional – formed at a minimum through a combination of personal history, cultural expectations and bounded rationality. The latter phenomenon of hegemony, by contrast, is the attempt to direct this ordering for the purposes of establishing and maintaining dominant ideologies and power relations. It is political, in the strictest sense, in that it seeks to purposefully activate the contingency of social relations. Yet it is *paradoxically* political in so much as its recognition and use of contingency (the changeability of the social) is performed in the service of naturalization. Indeed, the political, as it is expressed in and through hegemony, is ironically constituted via a process of socialization. Accordingly, it is the ongoing and always incomplete transformation of social dominance into political domination.

The dynamic quality of contemporary hegemony, however, requires a substantial theoretical reconsideration of, respectively, both social ordering and political domination. A useful starting point for this analysis is a revisiting of the critical logics of hegemony first proposed by Glynos and Howarth (2007). Logics, in their view, comprise 'the grammar of assumptions and concepts that informs a particular approach to the social world: a way of formulating problems, addressing them, and then evaluating the answers that have been produced' (Glynos & Howarth, 2007, p 8). The conventional use of logics, even critically, can fall prey to a rather simplified understanding of hegemony premised on the opposition of stability to disruption. 'The social dimension captures those situations in which the radical contingency of social relations has not been registered in the mode of public contestation', argue Glynos and Howarth, 'whereas the political dimension refers to those situations in which subjects responding to dislocatory events reactivate the contingent foundations of a practice by publicly contesting and defending the norms of that practice' (Glynos & Howarth, 2007, p 14).

Critical to this analysis is the dual role that these logics contribute to the interrogation and explanation of power. They are both ostensive and performative in this respect. On the one hand, they have a specific purpose and reflect a particular problematization central to power. This could involve questions of ordering (for example the social) or disruption (the political, for instance) or the affective enjoyment we gain from hegemonic discourses (for example the ethical). On the other hand, their actual existence, or performance, can lead these logics to have quite different and unpredictable implications which exceed their ostensible purpose. Hence, the originally quite socially oriented 'war on terror' – one premised on how to best 'fight extremists'–could open up deeper existential debates about the dangers of Western militarism and an affective reidentification with resisting such imperialism.

It is therefore necessary to view these logical interactions as complex, contingent and always evolving. Howarth touches precisely on this rich interaction between logics in his own discussion of the relation of hegemony and policy formation. 'Power is also evident in the sedimentation of social relations via various techniques of political management, and through the elaboration of ideologies and fantasies', Howarth notes, 'where the function of the latter is to *conceal* the radical contingency of social relations and to naturalize relations of domination.' (Glynos & Howarth, 2007, p 309). For this reason, Glynos and Howarth (2007) speak of an 'assemblage of logics', which combine the social, political and 'fantasmatic' within the evolving play of hegemony. They nevertheless remain wedded ultimately to the, admittedly messy, dichotomy between processes of 'stabilization' and 'concealment' versus those of 'disruption' and 'revealment'. A mobile perspective on power, however, focuses attention on their continual interaction as part of any complex and dynamic social ordering. It is perhaps more illuminating to interrogate, therefore, which elements of the social are revealed as contingent and which are naturalized and to what critical ends. This would also permit a more nuanced investigation of the conjectural character of fantasies – how they combine both a social and political ethos for a more complex type of psychic enjoyment and affective identification.

The complex logics of order both enhance and are enhanced by mobile perspectives of power. The conventional use of logics, even critically, falls prey to a rather simplified understanding of hegemony premised on the opposition of stability to disruption. Indeed, paradoxically, 'political pluralism stabilizes social relations and determinations of the self around fixed points of contestation' (Bloom & Dallyn, 2011). What this reveals is the ongoing and eternal mutual implication of the social in the political and vice versa. Every dominant social ordering will have an element of the disruptive, an aspect that is made available to change and encouraged to adapt. Likewise, every challenge to this status quo will at least partially depend on creating a stable social order. At stake, then, in hegemony is the analysis of the integration of this socialization and politicization.

This is not to completely reject the classic distinction between socialization and politicization. Indeed, while the social and political may always be to some degree intertwined, how they are combined is a matter that can remain relatively open or closed to questioning. Nevertheless, it would be a mistake to once more retrench hegemony to reflect this distinction. Significantly, hegemony has what can be termed a 'viral deficit' based on a failure to fully account for the contextual flexibility and mutability of discursive orderings as well as how quickly they can spread across otherwise different cultural, political and economic contexts. Far from being stagnant or even necessarily comparatively stable, they are perhaps better viewed as infectious ideologies and practices that can move within and between geographic borders and adapt to diverse social settings. What makes hegemony distinct though from simply a random collection of discourses, 'what makes hegemony hold good', to paraphrase Foucault, is its ability to transform dominant values and practices into 'problems to be solved'. It is the transformation of a political question into a social problem to be innovatively approached and resolved in ever-newer, creative and context-specific ways.

In order to illuminate this fundamentally dynamic quality of hegemony, there is a need to introduce a new type of logic to complement those associated with the social, political and ethical – that of 'viral logics'. This logic refers specifically to how adaptable and infectious a discourse is within and between contexts. This logic is marked less by inscription and more by creativity and competitive pressure. Tellingly, Glynos and Howarth draw heavily on the Foucauldian idea of 'problemization' within their theory of logics. What viral logics point to is how hegemony, the very basis for social ordering, is founded and reproduced at least in part through the articulation of ideologies and practices as 'problems'. The issue, in this regard, is less about the concealment and revealment of contingency and more about the ability of different discourses to effectively spread both within and between contexts while slowing down and stopping the spread of others. Both hegemony and counter-hegemony are thus matters of contagion and inoculation, problematization and the demand for innovation.

To a certain extent, the rise of mobile technologies has highlighted and expanded this viral politics. Personhood is increasingly a socially mediated branding of the self, carefully 'authored' by individuals and cultivated over various social media platforms. This version of 'Me, Inc.' (see Makovicky, 2016) permits contemporary subjects to both feel in control of their 'selves' while also continually conforming them to constantly shifting real-time expectations and views. At a broader level, this speaks to how 'actually existing neoliberalism' has embedded itself unevenly and at times unpredictably across a number of overlapping 'geographic scales', catalyzing an ongoing process of 'creative destruction' in spaces ranging from the household to cities to nations to the global (Brenner & Theodore, 2002). These perspectives help to resituate both capitalist reproduction and hegemony generally as a set of enabling practices that reinforce an existing status quo and in the longer term promote particular types of capabilities and agency. Porter, hence, writes implicitly of the viral aspect of global finance spanning an entire millennium, noting that 'finance plays a key, but poorly understood, role in the rise of hegemony and in the stimulation of long waves of economic growth in the world economy … finance as an industry which produces institutional mechanisms for organizing economic activities and transferring value over extended stretches of time and space' (Porter, 1995, p 387).

Theoretically, this emphasis on virility builds upon and ultimately serves to reconfigure established political logics of 'difference' and 'equivalence' first proposed by Laclau and Mouffe. The former depicts the incorporation of alternative values, ideas and practices into a dominant set of social relations, while the latter signifies the direct contest between hegemonic and counter-hegemonic forces. Despite their stated differences, both of these logics point to the dynamism at the heart of hegemony, conceptually trying to capture the complex and evolving ways that dominant discourses are established, challenged and replaced. In the words of Laclau and Mouffe: 'Social actors occupy differential positions within the discourses that constitute the social fabric. In that sense they are all, strictly speaking, particularities. On the other hand, there are social antagonisms creating internal frontiers within society' (Laclau & Mouffe, 1986, p xiii). Particularly relevant for this analysis are how strategies of difference and equivalence – incorporation versus confrontation – represent different approaches for discursive infection and inoculation. They are contrasting, though not mutually exclusive, ways for a 'living host' social context to welcome and shield itself from such a hegemonic contagion.

Yet these viral logics reveal something perhaps more fundamental concerning the relation of discourse to deeper questions of power and hegemony. The very idea of the social becomes itself discursively articulated around the possibilities and threats of viral infection. The well-rehearsed insights into how, commencing at the latest during the Enlightenment and in the West, society became equated with a 'healthy body' reflect this underlying association of the social with notions of health, adaptability and infection. The biggest issue was which elements are most copacetic for an existing 'body politic'– which can it absorb and which threaten its very survival. Foucault's rightly celebrated ideas of 'biopower' further gesture towards this equally significant basis of 'viral politics'. The focusing of power on 'populations' permits a rather forensic analysis by those in power of how to best orient institutions, laws and interpersonal relations to accept, manage and if necessary treat various social contagions. Globally, the history of colonialism, thus, is in part a reflection of this legitimate threat of viral invasion and the attempts to build up individual and shared resistances to it. What discursive perspectives further bring to these discussions, then, is the broader social construction of an 'actually existing' context as a potential 'living host'– a perceived organic collection of conventions, regulations and institutions that must be inoculated against or opened up to 'viral infections' from within and outside.

The rise of viral hegemony

The use of the term viral has increasingly entered into the popular mainstream. Once concerned almost exclusively with matters concerning viruses, it now signifies the rapid spread of information – usually through social media – within society. However, as this analysis has sought to show, it also still has quite a bit of symbolic value for illuminating power and hegemony. It reflects the capacity of a discourse to 'infect' a 'living host' community, one that has its own complex history, culture and political realities. To this end, power is fundamentally mobile – moving between and adapting itself to such a host. Hegemony, moreover, is thus both constantly mutating and transformational – a dominating discursive social virus that can survive in diverse sociopolitical environments and dramatically reshape them over time. This viral quality of domination reveals the overriding importance of 'politics'– the liminal space that exists and is constantly at play between the poles of the social and the political. Emerging ever stronger is contemporary viral politics, in which different 'infected' contexts vie against each other and learn from one another as to how to best strengthen and resist a dominant ideology and its underlying power relations.

Required, in turn, is a significant decolonization of current conceptions of hegemony. Recent scholarship around hegemony – particularly those associated with the ideology and discourse tradition inspired by Laclau – has admirably extended its critical gaze to international contexts ranging from post-Apartheid South Africa to the current struggles for the liberation of the Kurds (see Gunes, 2013). However, bearing these exceptions in mind, it tends to share a specific and quite Westernized view of the basic composition of domination and social ordering. In particular, it is rooted in an idea of a hegemon, a dominating actor which can disproportionately influence a social environment. Theories of discursive hegemony do well to depersonalize this hegemon – speaking instead of 'subject positions'– yet continue to fixate on a dominant idea and way of doing things.

This fixation has its historical roots in the rise of a dominant 'West' starting in the 16th century, which has come to be widely accepted as itself the origin of capitalism and modern world systems. Nevertheless, its actual beginnings are found in the 13th century where early capitalist rationalities of competition and surplus value spread across the world without a clear or definite hegemon. Abu-Lughod describes this period and its importance in his groundbreaking book *Before European Hegemony: The World System AD 1250–1350,* writing that our current world system 'has persisted for some five hundred years [when] the West was clearly hegemonic' and that yet 'to understand its roots it is necessary to examine the period before European hegemony' (Abu-Lughod, 1989, pp 4–6). Significantly, he notes that prior to this Western-dominated world system, hegemony as it currently exists was profoundly different. 'The world economy of the 13th century is not only fascinating in itself', he notes, 'but because it contained no single hegemonic power, [it] provides an important contrast to the world system that grew out of it: the one Europe reshaped to its own ends and dominated for so long' (Abu-Lughod, 1989, pp 4–6). Consequently, he presciently concludes that this 'contrast suggests that characteristics of the world system are not invariant. There is no unique way for the parts to be organized' (Abu-Lughod, 1989, pp 4–6).

What these historical insights theoretically gesture towards is the dispersed and multipolar character of hegemony, which is often overlooked due to the overriding focus on the underlying presence of a hegemon – whether that be in the form of an actor, a discourse or both. It is more appropriate and valuable to examine how certain ideological values and processes – such as marketization or multiculturalism – become social imperatives for individuals and groups to effectively implement, improve upon and if necessary innovatively cope with. This also helps illuminate how our version of hegemony, the transition from social ordering to political domination, is itself hegemonic. It leads to an assumption that global values and hegemons are natural, the permanent norm of power wholesale. Revealed, in this regard, is another dimension of the force of hegemony, if you will. Its most obvious forcefulness – understood here to mean its 'grip' and persistence – is its being able to render itself simultaneously as a natural or inevitable feature of the social and as a dynamic problem to be 'solved' and improved upon. However, at a somewhat deeper and longer-term level, this discourse is cementing the historical character of hegemony. Here the specific contemporary content of hegemony may be somewhat interchangeable but its underlying rationale is more or less historically entrenched. Accordingly, political domination consists at once of the 'play' of hegemony (along with its attendant rules and structuring ideologies) and the underpinning grammar or game of hegemony upon which it is ultimately based.

A major contention of this book is that mobile power and viral logics are profoundly transforming both the play and game of present-day hegemony. As such, these viral logics reveal something perhaps more fundamental concerning the relation of discourse to deeper questions of power and hegemony. However, it would be misguided to assume that 'mobility' and 'virality' are continuously predominant in the operation of power and hegemony. This discussion was meant to highlight that they is necessarily always a dimension of social ordering and production as well as political domination. Nevertheless, in the past – in the broad age of Western colonialism and the 'world system'– they were a component rather than primary force. In particular, this period of hegemony was marked more significantly by efforts of sovereign and ideological conquest – a potent mixture of coercion and persuasion. The current historical conjuncture, though, is illustrating a new era of hegemony wherein mobility and virality are much more at the forefront. It is one increasingly defined, respectively, by the ability of power to be continuously socially remobilized and of hegemony to forge political reconnections.

There are three dominant aspects to this progressively viral framing of the social, and as such of power and hegemony. The first is *mutability*, the ability for a 'host' context and existing discourses to be flexible and adaptable. Most obviously, this can refer to the openness of a given culture to change or how malleable 'universal' ideas are to local realities. At a deeper level, it also points to the capacity of an ideology or regime of power to opportunistically update itself over time. Lima's (2020) recent study of 'sustainable citizenship' is illuminating in this regard as it reveals the ability of the notion of citizenship to respond to present conditions in support of conservative social, political and economic ideologies once thought outdated.

The second is *transformationality*, based on the capacity of a host to be fundamentally changed in conformity with a viral ideology and set of practices. This does not necessarily imply either normatively or empirically an embrace of a status quo or domination. Indeed, it can depict a quite disruptive and revolutionary situation. The contemporary establishment of the new Sparks Laboratory is a case in point as it is 'part of a growing design practice in which curious narratives act as the research mechanism for addressing complex issues' (Alipour Leilie et al, 2017, S4344). The laboratory is itself inspired by 'a proliferation of utopian visions of driverless technology, post-work economies, and ubiquitous artificial intelligence' (Alipour Leilie et al, 2017, S4344). Yet it is also reflective of how host contexts and populations must be constantly engaged in transformation – whether, as will be shown in the next chapter, of the innovative or disruptive kind. What is crucial to stress at this point is that the 'viral' subject of hegemony is one who is first and foremost a 'problem-solver'– entrepreneurial and creative in their capacity to identify particular problemizations and seek their local solutions.

The third and final aspect of viral politics is that of *immunity*, or the lack thereof. At stake here is the degree to which a host can inoculate itself against viral discourses and vice versa. It gestures towards issues of control and management, the extent to which a society can direct processes of change and minimize their costs while maximizing their benefits. The ongoing reconfiguration of public administration is an example of a deficient immunity on the part of traditional government power holders as 'new approaches not only challenge the government's direction, but even place it in the back seat, or in the boot of the car' (Steen et al, 2019, p 63). Accordingly, 'implementation comes to take primacy over planning, as key decisions are taken during the delivery of services' and, even more so, 'significant changes are initiated, not by governments, but by a shapeless and multifarious movement that cannot be easily captured or channelled' (Steen et al, 2019, p 63). Absolutely critical is that, while there may be global discourses, the emphasis is on processes of creative implementation combined with an ethos of harm reduction.

Viral logics and hegemony, therefore, provide a radical new lens for critically examining power, social ordering and change across time and within evolving contexts. They represent the dynamic spread and response to prevailing and emerging discourses, an eternal process that has gained renewed strength and vibrance in an era of mobile communication, technologies and social networks. Hegemony revolves around, in turn, the articulation of people, spaces and things as part of a living host context that must adapt or resist contagious ideas and practices arising internally and threatening to invade from the outside. The realities of mobile power are then ongoing critical questions of how mutable, transformational and immune a specific host context and infectious ideologies are at any given time and with regard to one another.

Hegemonic reorderings

Thus far, this chapter has introduced and argued for the fundamental importance of viral logics for theoretically and empirically understanding power and hegemony. In this regard, it can be considered relatively 'timeless' in its analysis and insights as it reveals virility as a constant companion to domination and resistance. Yet this foundational aspect of social ordering has taken on special relevance in the contemporary period. The growing ubiquity of mobile technologies has made the ability of information to go viral a vital part of the present-day popular imagination and a daily feature of 21st-century existence.

Witnessed are the multiple levels on which hegemony is viral. It is a fundamental logic of any power configuration, reflecting in particular its temporal capacities to spread, adapt and transform diverse contexts. It is also a discursive formation for articulating a field of meaning as a host population for these wide-ranging viral infections. Finally, but no less significantly, it can itself be a hegemonic discourse for shaping social and political relations. In the current era, the notion of going viral captures the contagiousness of ideas and how important this dimension of power has become. The ability for products and concepts to be rapidly 'passed on' through digital word of mouth and social media, thus exploding in popularity, is referred to as a 'viral loop'.

Significantly, these viral loops or networks help to reconfigure and in many instances strengthen conventional social bonds between like-minded individuals, creating 'in-real-life' communities that are rooted within traditional geographic borders and virtual ones which transcend these physical barriers. In this sense it is a combination of the old and the new in which 'community structures, particularly reciprocal ties and certain triadic structures, substantially increase social contagion' (Harrigan et al, 2012, p 470). Critically, the reasons for this 'increased social contagion are, first, that members of communities have higher similarity (reflecting shared interests and characteristics, increasing the relevance of messages), and second, that communities amplify the social bonding effect of retransmitted messages' (Harrigan et al, 2012, p 470).

This illuminates, in turn, the importance of connection and reconnection for viral hegemony. Indeed, it is increasingly proclaimed that we have entered into the age of networks. No longer are populations and communities primarily defined by human interaction or even 'imagined' relations. Now they are marked by digital communications and shared predictive preferences. Human belonging is found in the present time as much on Facebook and Instagram as it is in 'in-real-life' contact. For sure, there is much to despair over and fear from this historical turn of events. It can ironically lead to profound feelings of disconnection and alienation. Yet it can also allow people from different backgrounds to connect and experience a sense of kinship, even if only virtually. Equally significant, though perhaps too often overlooked, is that it has bred a particular modern way of viewing and engaging with politics, as evidence reveals that those who are more active on social media sites like Twitter tend to be more politically engaged and simultaneously more distrustful of elites (See Bode & Dalrymple, 2016).

The next chapter will go into greater depth on the critical importance of such networks and processes of networking. What is crucial, however, at this point of the analysis, is to stress the connective aspects of power and hegemony. Previously, we discussed how power must be continually mobilized and remobilized. Similarly, hegemony (especially in its more viral forms) requires constant connection and reconnection. Revealed, consequently, is the dual rise of the hegemony of networks and networks of hegemony. The latter describes how different networks combine to promote a hegemonic discourse. The former refers to the dominant ways in which social relations are being articulated and operationalized via discourses of networks. These are primarily rooted in the digital sphere but also extending to in-person encounters. We are now less part of coherent communities and discrete ethno-national populations than we are linked up to diverse interconnecting networks of shared preferences and common platforms.

Both of these combine to reflect a more mobile and viral form of hegemony. New big data methods, such as sentiment analysis of social text, for instance, are being used to 'nowcast' elections – thus producing rapidly changing, real-time 'common sense' that can equally spread rapidly across different networks and adapt to their culture as well as permit alternative ideas to enter into the mainstream and spread in similar ways. These developments speak to the rise of 'platform power', which according to Culpepper and Thelen (2019, p 288) "inheres in companies of economic scale that provide the terms of access through which large numbers of consumers access goods, services and information'. Yet platform power can also permit new actors and ideas to deconstruct, disrupt and challenge this alliance for the creation of less consumer-based and more political identities.

At stake, then, is the emergence of viral agency expressed most notably through the ability to strengthen existing connections and forge new ones. Crucially, just as each society is in a state of constant rearticulation as a living host, so too does each historical epoch discursively put forward its own form of viral agency – how they predominantly perceive, implement and hold accountable people's relationship to time and the spread of ideas and practices. For modernity, it is a time of viral self- and social creation, wherein each individual and society are the supposed creators of their own destiny. It is a 'situation where human beings commit themselves to determine their own lives, their relations to others and their ways of "being in the world"' while political modernity is a commitment to the 'self-determination of the life in common with others, to the rules of the life in common" (Terrier & Wagner, 2006, p 10).

This proposition has been radicalized by thinkers such as Chantal Mouffe, who proclaims that 'therefore the challenge to rationalism and humanism does not imply the rejection of modernity but only the crisis of a particular project within modernity, the Enlightenment project of self-foundation' (Mouffe, 1989, p 34). In this spirit, 'self-foundation' is transitioning from a project of individual identification and progressively towards one of multiple collective formations. What is more and more key is the groups you are part of, the networks you have joined and that connect you with others, the preference-based demographics you fall within and the multiple representations of the self that arise from these connections.

Hegemony, consequently, goes viral precisely in its ability to use its mobility to infiltrate and flexibly adapt to these diverse but overlapping networks. Its force is grounded in its capacity to navigate and shape these connections while also creating new ones based on its values and contingent political needs. There is then a shift in the game of hegemony from conquering and homogenizing a place and population to influencing and reconfiguring its various social networks. The grammar of hegemony, its meaningful domination, is found, as such, not in overdetermining the terms of social existence in any obvious or necessarily coherent way. Rather, it is in being able to adopt the numerous vocabularies of differing physical and virtual communities to its own desires and purposes. Fundamental to its reproduction and success, hence, is the move from constantly remobilizing power to reordering hegemony when and where necessary.

Viral times

Shedding light on the foundationally viral character of social ordering allows for a rethinking of the temporal dimensions of hegemony as well as its contemporary composition. Discussions of hegemony often focus on the ideological and practical – the dominant discourses which regulate beliefs, meaning and actions. When temporality is brought into the discussion, it is most commonly in the form of repetition. Namely, how these regulative ideas and practices are replicated within a given field of meaning. More broadly, the theoretical recasting of hegemony by post-Marxists away from economic determinism risks a type of repetitive history defined by eternal battle between competing discourses for hegemony. The French philosopher Gilles Deleuze – though neither identifiably post-Marxist or a theorist of hegemony – captures this idea in his discussion of the paradoxical relation of repeatability and newness: 'We promote something new only on condition that we repeat – once in the mode that constitutes the past, and once more in the present of metamorphosis', he observes. 'What's more what is produced is nothing more than repetition' (Deleuze, 1968, p 90). All such instances of difference, of novelty, are in this process ultimately extinguished.

A critical turn to challenging such a modern viral politics is to directly question and find ways to materially manifest a less repetitious notion of time and social change. In particular, virality in the modern era is most dominantly rooted in the efforts to establish one way of life over another, to fight for a singular present leading to a certain and predictable future. It is a repeatable pattern where novelty is less in the establishment of a different way of materially and socially existing and more in who is the current victor of the seemingly permanent game of capitalist and liberal democratic competition. Löffler introduces, by contrast, a notion of 'post-capitalist' time that allows for a different way of being than the limiting temporality of capitalist modernity. 'The homogenous continuum of the unilinear time Gestalt is dispersed into multiple realizable lines of development', he proclaims. 'The informational rendering of systems allows for an extrapolation of their developments and the conception of various scenarios of their future being' (Löffler, 2018, pp 38–9). Consequently, time transitions from a linear or cyclical inevitability to a set of possibilities. Crucially, for Löffler 'this results in the constitution of a spectrum of possible futures that depend on the factors in the initial conditions and their weighting. ... Their objectivity is constituted by how much value we are willing to assign to the worlds we want to produce' (Löffler, 2018, pp 38–9).

While this presents a worthy radical project, it is still imperative to better understand the rich temporal dimension of hegemony. Especially as it is dangerous to quickly distinguish homogeneous 'capitalist time' from a more multiple and imaginative post-capitalist one. The viral aspect of both social ordering generally and hegemony particularly is witness to the simultaneous heterogeneity of temporalities (the mobility of time) and more recently the diverse spread of such temporalities across different networks. As such, it is critical to highlight the ways powerful actors can use technologies to establish dominant modes of temporality. A present example is the attempt by executives of tech corporations to exploit growing digitalization for their own monopolistic economic purposes (see Staab & Nachtwey, 2016). Key to this rebooted 21st-century monopoly capitalism is the exchanging of a traditional 9-to-5 temporal regime with one wherein individuals must always be updating their information in 'real time' and be willing to work 'anytime, anywhere'. This transition can be read with and against Marx's account of the working day and the operation of the capitalist extracting surplus value from the worker, 'vampire-like, [living] only by sucking living labour, and [living] the more, the more labour it sucks' (Marx, 1990, p 405). For Marx, the surplus value gained by the capitalist from labour could be envisaged in surplus labour time over and above that accounted for in the wage, which was itself determined by generalized social standards of 'civilization' or the degree to which labour successfully struggled to improve pay and conditions. Marx himself recognized that calculating surplus value was not as straightforward as dividing a day between the portion of it for which the worker is reimbursed for the labour power expended and a portion of the day dedicated to surplus for the capitalist. Rather, surplus value might co-exist all through a labour process, and this must be the case even more in contemporary forms of work that rely less on manual labour and more on networked knowledge and emotional labour. Time, labour (salaried and domestic) and value become more liquid, as anyone working from home during the COVID-19 pandemic would testify. This profound temporal shift has resulted in what Crary refers to as '24/7 capitalism' by which '24/7 markets and a global infrastructure for continuous work and consumption have been in place for some time but now a human subject is in the making to coincide with these more intensely' (Crary, 2013, pp 3–4).

This obviously speaks to the deep viral logics at work in hegemony. The ability of a discourse to spread quickly can prevent others from rising up. In this respect, any hegemonic viral logic is simultaneously a process of infection and inoculation – fostering certain discourses within a host while making it resistant to others. Turning once more to themes of capitalist time, Leyshon and Thrift observe that 'the speed of capitalist globalization ... act[s] as a barrier to intervention because of its opacity and the likelihood of unintended consequences.' In particular, globalized capitalist forces 'smother smaller concerns which cannot raise sufficient capital. They cancel out the promises made to weaker investors. They blot out faith in the future' (Leyshon & Thrift, 2007, p 97).

Subjects can transform to match a certain temporality, learning to regulate their existence in conformity with the hegemonic time required of them. The emergence of the contemporary 'iTime' linked to mobile technologies reflects this temporal disciplining. 'iPhones create iTime and fundamentally alter the boundaries between public and private and day and night', according to Agger

(2011, p 119): 'We are now online anytime/anywhere, requiring new theoretical understandings of time and place.' He views this as a universalizing process, one that runs across generations, as 'this starts with the young, who are inseparable from their phones, and has now spread to their parents.' Tellingly, resistance consists in retaking temporal control of our lives, for 'in a good society, we would be the masters of technology, retaining the connectivity and global reach of our smartphones, but not enslaved to them as many of us are today' (Agger, 2011, p 119). Such statements are affirmations of Marx's ultimate ambitions for technology, which may have been developed to maximize, grow and spread capital but can yet be repurposed to hasten egalitarian and worker-led purposes.

Nevertheless, it is fundamental to remember that viral logics are as mobile as any other aspect of hegemony. They adapt to the needs of a given context – as indeed domination often requires a diverse range of temporalities for its survival and expansion. Similarly, each depends upon different temporalities at different times and for different purposes. A mistake continually made by those analyzing capitalist time, thus, is that it is singularly regulative. This follows from the landmark historical analysis offered by E.P. Thompson, which presciently connected the capitalist disciplining of labour to the social standardization of time, noting that 'indeed a general diffusion of clocks and watches is occurring (as one would expect) at the exact moment when the industrial revolution demanded a greater synchronisation of labour' (Thompson, 1967, p 69). While certainly a compelling critique of capitalism's development, this ignores just how diverse this temporal disciplining actually was and still is. Rather than just relying upon one temporality (that of regulative timekeeping and daily scheduling), it drew upon diverse forms of disciplined time encompassing processes of standardization, regularity and coordination across zones and norms of time (Glennie & Thrift, 1996). These could be faster, slower, fixated on the short term or planned for the long term depending on the situation. Glennie and Thrift (1996, p 285) thus note that 'the identification of diverse time structures in everyday life is more than an empirical point, because it highlights the extraordinary taken-for-grantedness of Thompson's time-discipline … in particular it is usually used in the singular, whereas we see time-discipline as a multi-faceted concept whose elements ought not to be conflated with each other.'

Under neoliberalism, this disciplining and management of diverse temporalities has become increasingly individualized and personalized (and hence also the extraction of surplus value from the worker). More precisely, it is a matter of individual responsibility (whether that be in the form of a person or cohesive group) to find the right 'time' for oneself. David Harvey refers, in this regard, to the 'time-space compression' that is increasingly defining late capitalism, one which both 'shrinks the world' and opens up a range of different profitable trajectories for individuals and communities to pursue. For this reason, he argues that we are leaving modernity for 'the postmodern condition', one characterized as much by plurality and choice as it is by singularity and historical necessity. This expansion of historical possibilities (or at least potential expressions of capitalism) results, in turn, in the creation of the 'enterprising' temporal subject, whereby arises, 'at the start of the 21st century, in the globalised risky labour markets of the over developed economies, the cultivation of the self as an enterprise that should give meaning, purpose, and direction to a life" (Kelly, 2016, p 4). Consequently, neoliberal subjects are made responsible for 'synchronizing' their time so as to maximize its overall value. This can include the 'balancing' of various spheres of their existence – ranging from individual time to family time to historical time – for this purpose (see Hareven, 1991). It also allows for the turning of 'social time' into 'political time'– creating the opportunity to question dominant temporalities and experiment with new ones. Adam thus speaks of social time as a reflection of the fact that temporality is socially constructed and as such multiple, permitting 'the transformation of dualisms into multiple dualities' (Adam, 2013, p 278).

However, one of the defining features of present-day capitalism and society is the incorporation and exploitation of these multiple temporalities. Marx's vampire, rather than taking time out while the worker sleeps and takes care of home, becomes a permanent appendage to the contemporary cyborg subject. As Beck (1992) prophetically observed, digital technologies were forcing capitalism to undergo a 'desychronization', so that time could be customized to exploit diverse contexts and populations. In the case of neoliberalism, its hegemony was rooted dually in its mobility and virality. It transposed the insatiable thirst of capitalism to discover fresh markets into an infinite demand for innovatively adopting its core tenants of financialization, privatization and marketization in ever new ways and places. Leyshon and Thrift observe, hence, that 'the bedrock of financial capitalism is not the spectacular system of speculation but something more mundane; that is, financial capitalism is dependent on the constant searching out, or the construction of, new asset streams, usually through a process of aggregation, which then – and only then – allows speculation to take place' (Leyshon & Thrift, 2007, pp 98–99).

It is precisely here, in this process, that the virality of time and its reliance on connecting and reconnecting meet and reinforce one another. It is rooted in the capacity of individuals to experience, discover and spread a variety of profitable temporalities. Put differently, it is the ability to diversely exploit time, one made possible through the forging of new social connections, whether virtually, physically or both. And indeed, fundamentally, hegemony has always relied upon the viral spread of diverse temporalities for its reproduction and success. Required instead, then, is not simply the multiplication of time but its ideological and material politicization. This would open the way for new experiences of time that could help build up resistance to dominant temporalities. 'Such a task implies the calling into question of everything that pertains to time, everything that has formed within it', in the view of Foucault (1973, p 332) 'everything that resides within its mobile element, in such a way to make visible that rent, devoid of chronology and history, from which time issues'.

Returning to the present, the speculative aspect of capitalism therefore shifted from focusing simply on future profits to a broader cultural effort to imagine how it could be imaginatively embedded in rapidly changing and multicultural temporal worlds and lifestyles. It was also critical to invent and exploit novel possibilities for the spread of this heterogeneous capitalist society – one which was both utterly inscriptive in terms of its ideological demands and relatively open with regards to its concrete realizations. Consequently, Hassan links these radical changes to the contagious spread of ideas and practices within an increasingly networked society, noting that 'communication and information technologies ... have become an integral part of almost every institutional practice in the industrialised world and beyond' (Hassan, 2007, p ix). However, it is exactly our historical proximity to these dramatic transformations that makes them simultaneously so easy to adapt to and so difficult to control. Indeed, he declares that such 'revolutionary social changes have a habit of sneaking up on us. They are easy to detect from a temporal distance but much harder to identify while they are happening, in the processes of change and their effects' (Hassan, (2007, p ix). Consequently, the speed of technological change must be critically understood 'in relation to the much older and slower, if equally pervasive, processes of global change associated with social relations, technologies, and economies of time' (Hassan, (2007, p ix).

Reordering hegemony

The viral logic increasingly at the heart of hegemony is profoundly changing the character of domination. In the previous era of the Western world system, its defining feature was one of sovereignty – of either a direct ruling or ideological nature. It was perhaps above all else focused on shaping social order to reflect the needs of a dominant set of power relations as well as prevailing values. Of course, this attempt at homogenization was always complemented by a required mobility – the capacity of a discourse and the power regimes it supported to adapt to various 'living' contexts. And indeed, virality was crucial for this spread of a more conventional form of hegemony, in so much as ascendant discourses, whether they be Christianity or the free market, spread globally. Yet what marks this age of hegemony as different or at least distinguishable from what preceded it is that mobility and virality have now come to structure the underlying grammar of hegemony; not just how it is played, but the very game itself. Of overriding significance now is the ability of ideas and powerful actors to flexibly infiltrate diverse social networks while forging ever-newer connections to influence and exploit.

It is worth going back to the complex perspective of productive power first offered by Foucault to theoretically and practically begin to illuminate this shift in the dominant operation of power and form of hegemony. In a somewhat rare moment of conceptual overview, Foucault (1982, pp 786–787) describes power as being composed of three 'domains' or components, those of 'power relations, relationships of communication, and objective capacities'. He is careful, though, in noting that these are not fully distinct or separate but rather 'it is a question of three types of relationships which in fact always overlap one another, support one another reciprocally, and use each other mutually as means to an end" (Foucault, 1982, pp 786–787). We should be cautious about over-relying on this single passage from the entirety of Foucault's work to make any general statement concerning power. Nevertheless, it is a useful lens for understanding the transformation of power and hegemony from monopolization and sovereignty into mobility and virality. In the previous era, an ethos of mobility and the possibility of viral discourses were a resource, 'an objective capacity' for supporting and ultimately reproducing sovereign discourses and power relations. Communication and the technologies associated with it were similarly oriented towards the construction and shaping of this homogenous (though never completely so) population – reflected in the rise, for instance, of 'mass media'. By contrast, the contemporary period is progressively characterized by elite power relations that are more dispersed (made up principally of complex networks of oligarchy) and the capabilities as well as communications of which primarily concentrated upon influencing networks and forging novel connections within and between them. Significantly, traditional sovereignty (whether in the form of authoritarian governance or demagogic leaders) as well as essentialist identities are at one and the same time a reaction against this viral hegemony and ironically a tool for its spread.

Critically, these efforts represent a contemporary update of the abiding significance social 'influencers' have had in spreading historically important ideas in the past. Leerssen (2011), writes of the existence of 'viral nationalism' in the 19th century, highlighting the role that a global network of romantic 'intellectuals' had in promoting discourses of national identity and the nation state. Likewise, while managers and managerialism are often viewed as inherent parts of capitalism and its development, the growth of 'managerial capitalism' as a concept and set of practices was in fact uneven and very much a historical phenomenon. According to Chandler in his landmark article 'The Emergence of Managerial Capitalism': 'Managerial hierarchies of this kind are entirely modern. As late as the 1840s, with very few exceptions, owners managed and managers owned' (Chandler, 1984, p 473). Historically, he observes, 'in the late nineteenth and early twentieth century, a new type of capitalism emerged. ... It differed from traditional personal capitalism in that basic decisions concerning the production and distribution of goods or services were made by teams, or hierarchies, of salaried managers who had little or no equity ownership in the enterprises they operated' (Chandler, 1984, p 473). The appearance of managers was moreover an outgrowth not of industrialization per se but of the revolutionary technological developments in communication and information sharing that accompanied it. Chandler (Chandler, 1984, p 474) writes that while the second industrial revolution of the 19th century was defined by 'the railroad, telegraph, steamship, and cable', ultimately 'these new high-volume technologies could not be effectively exploited unless the massive flows of material were guided through the process of both production and distribution by teams of salaried managers' (Chandler, 1984, p 474). To this end, the use of managers for regulating workers and ensuring organizational success was itself a viral concept that was manifested differently across international contexts and whose strength, in part, was found in its capacity to adapt and spread locally and globally in a nonetheless homogenizing ('mass') way.

Such historical antecedents help to clarify the current change in power and hegemony. Specifically, they speak to concepts related to the 'political event' espoused – though in different ways – by critical theorists such as Alain Badiou and Jacques Rancière. These writers envision revolutionary change as connected to 'events' which disrupt the 'sensible' of the present and open up the possibility for new 'truths' to appear in the world (See Bassett, 2016). For Badiou, 'a truth is sparked by an event and spreads like a flame fanned by the breath of a subjective effort that remains forever incomplete' (Bensaïd, 2004, p 97). Consequently, there is a virality to truth at all times, 'for truth is not a matter of theory but is a "practical question" first and foremost: it is something that occurs, a point of excess', and as such 'it is an entirely materialist concept ... there can be no transcendental truth, only truths in situation and in relation, situations and relations of truth, oriented toward an atemporal eternity' (Bensaïd, 2004, p 98).

The import of such thinking (acknowledging that this is only a mere skimming of the surface of the depth of its profundity) is that it reveals the mobility of truth and its always-present viral dimensions. According to Badiou, 'The relation between Truth and truths is not one of domination, subsumption, foundation or guarantee. It is a relation of sampling: philosophy is a tasting of truths' (quoted in Bensaïd, 2004, p 98). Just as notable is that a dominant rationality, a prevailing and possible truth, can and must exist in a number of different ways. There is not just one scientific truth but rather scientific truths – depending on the context. Their flourishing depends on their mutability and virality, their capacity to both adapt and spread. Somewhat paradoxically, in the contemporary epoch, this virality of 'truth' is being performed in the service of promoting and entrenching a more viral form of hegemony. The event of neoliberalism is in actuality a continual process of discursive growth, change and expansion of mobility and virality. It taps into the fundamentally mobile and viral aspects of power and hegemony, respectively, in order to construct a viable rationality for its constant innovation and spread to interlapping host bodies.

Yet it also produces the very viral rationality for new revolutionary truths to emerge that directly challenge and seek to replace patriarchy, classism and sexism. In this respect, 'digital platforms offer great potential for broadly disseminating feminist ideas, shaping new modes of discourse about gender and sexism, connecting to different constituencies, and allowing creative modes of protest to emerge' (Baer, 2016, p 17). In particular, it reveals the connective aspect of viral hegemony, as 'the example of hashtag feminism makes clear how the increased use of digital media has altered, influenced, and shaped feminism in the twenty-first century by giving rise to changed modes of communication, different kinds of conversations, and new configurations of activism across the globe, both online and offline' (Baer, 2016, p 17). Tellingly, this 'redoing of feminism' is not centred on simply replacing older definitions with newer ones (or supplanting one wave with another). Rather it is focused on opening up the possibility – via a networked and often covert form of feminist 'infrapolitics' (Vachhani & Pullen, 2019) – for new networks to emerge for challenging the diverse manifestations of patriarchy and sexism as they presently exist. Thus 'by working through, making visible, and re-signifying central tensions in contemporary feminism, as well as the precarity of feminism itself in neoliberalism', Baer (2014, p 201) contends, 'these protests have begun to re-establish the grounds for a collective feminist politics beyond the realm of the self-styled individual.' Here, the digital nature of these viral communications help catalyze, in turn, novel power relations and radical 'objective capacities' for bringing about radical political transformation. Indeed, digital platforms are crucial to this redoing of feminism as they represent 'the transnational mediascape of the internet, a space encompassing and highlighting difference, in which discussions play out in a disembodied and sometimes anonymous forum' which combines with 'local protests that draw attention to the female body as a site of contention in the politics of gender, sexuality, race, religion, and culture today' (Baer, 2016, p 19).

Such radical viral interventions allow for the diverse and quite mobile spread of novel truths. They reveal the possibilities of conventionally anti-capitalist values and methods for reorganizing society and the economy. The fostering of 'open workshops' is a case in point. These spaces, marked by collaboration and common information sharing, exist as 'sites of innovative socio-economic practices' which also represent the possibility of 'approaching urban post-growth' frameworks which see beyond the capitalist logic of constant GDP growth, extraction and exploitation (Lange & Burnker, 2018). Required for realizing this vision are the objective capacities forged in the making of new political connections which can 'adequately capture the variety and complexity of these "labs", their heterogeneous causation, their contingent proceedings, their surplus of latency, their peculiar power relations and their local embeddings' (Lange & Burnker, 2018, p 680). This insight resonates with Foucault's tripartite conception of power and the subject presented previously – in that power relations rooted in capitalist growth are concretely broken down through the communication of new ideas such as post-growth and the diverse and context-specific construction of new skills for practically manifesting these alternative values.

The use of new mobile technologies for producing a radical viral politics reflects, in turn, their profound present-day counter-hegemonic potential. While the concepts of mobility and virality, as put forward thus far in this analysis, may seem to emphasize the flexibility of dominant and dominating discourses to change in accordance with context, they are also key forces for the broader transformation of these contexts. The use of new mobile technologies, moreover, exposes the ability of alternatives to escalate within and between people and places, acting as contagions that a prevailing hegemony cannot fully contain or extinguish. Viral politics is accordingly concerned with the 'making of worlds'– a performance in creating something new from the old, experimenting with what may be in one area in the hope that it may spread to others based on their own particular conditions. Importantly, it is precisely this paradox, in that change is both immanent to an existing system and seeks to transcend it, that makes it so dangerous. On the one hand, its rootedness in relation to the status quo can render it easily co-optable – as will be shown in the next chapter in regards to innovations for updating and therefore strengthening contemporary power relations – and on the other hand, its rootedness in relation to the status quo is exactly the space and opportunity for its fundamental subversion and reimagination.

Conclusion

This chapter introduced the significance of virality for deepening our understanding of social ordering and hegemony, both fundamentally and as specific to the contemporary period. It highlighted the existence of 'viral logics' as representative of the capacity of a dominant discourse to spread across contexts. To a certain extent, virality is a foundational dimension to any and all social orders and forms of hegemonic domination. However, it has become especially salient in this time of greater mobile organization, when the emphasis is less on controlling territories or conforming populations and more on shaping and forming hegemonic networks and connections.

In our viral times it is, hence, not a question of whether or not different and new worlds will be created. The very mobility of power and the virality of modern life make this not only inevitable but a defining feature of our existence. The real question, rather, is what type of mobile and viral worlds will emerge. More precisely, will we be exposed to the infection of more contagious capitalism or can we build our resistances to this viral discourse in the name of spreading a new revolutionary contagion?

4

Infectious Domination, Contagious Revolutions

The memory of the Vietnam struggle for liberation continues to loom large even into the new millennium. For many, it was the war that gave birth to the US counterculture, the catalyst for a radical energy spurred on by their conviction that their own freedom should not be won by the blood of a repressed people halfway across the world. For others, it remains a testament to the possibility of a heavily outgunned and out-resourced force defeating a colonial oppressor. At the time though, driving this deadly military conflict was the fear, above all else, of contagious revolutions. It was the threat of one country after another falling like dominoes to Communism. In his now famous introduction of the 'domino theory', which helped give birth to this war a decade later, then US president Dwight D. Eisenhower proclaimed the danger of the 'falling domino principle', whereby, similar to dominoes in a row but with countries, 'you knock over the first one, and what will happen to the last one is the certainty that it will go over very quickly'.

Indeed, in retrospect, scholars have critically described this perspective as 'the notion of a contagious epidemic process in the incidence of political violence' (O'Sullivan, 1996, p 106). Even after its genocidal consequences in the 20th century, it retains its relevance into the present – now rebooted to explain, for instance, the Arab Spring (see Fregonese, 2011). While the symbol of dominoes falling may be at this point bordering on the laughable, the spectre of viral social change is as potent as ever. The popularity of social media has made information, and hence politics, one of competing viral ideologies vying for dominance and power. It is fundamentally altering politics in ways previously almost unimaginable. One study drawing on data from the 2014 Hungarian general election campaign 'showed that citizens are highly reactive to negative emotion-filled, text-using, personal, and activity-demanding posts. Virality is especially facilitated by memes, videos, negative contents and mobilizing posts, and posts containing a call for sharing' (Bene, 2017, p 513).

From infectious domination to contagious reconnections

This book has thus far introduced the ideas of mobile power and viral hegemony to describe the eternally and increasingly dynamic character of social order and political transformation. In this chapter, we turn our attention to the contemporary rise of host networks, the reconfiguration of individual and collective relations as a set of interlocking digital and in-real-life social and political connections. It is notable here that what distinguishes a social and political network is not its capacity for change or ability to spread. Rather, it is the degree to which it adapts an existent status quo (with all its associated dominant discourses and dominating power relations) for its survival within diverse contexts or its radically introducing alternative ways of being in the world. In other words, does it effectively innovate hegemonic networks or disrupt them?

To explore this mounting present-day challenge, it offers the concepts of infectious domination and contagious revolutions. More precisely, it explores how hegemony and counter-hegemony both exist in epidemic sociopolitical conditions. Hegemony as a type of infection, one that enters into a network and begins to alter and ultimately transform it. Thus these connected populations must work to build resistances to these networks, ones which are network specific and share common antidotes. Counter-hegemony is also contagious, a type of experimentation and novel social order that can allow for fresh forms of existence and relations to emerge and spread. Hegemony, in turn, must constantly inoculate itself in ever more diverse ways against these contagious revolutionary possibilities.

At stake is the challenging of infectious domination through the forging of contagious reconnections. Domination may be subjugating, but it is also supple and customizable. A colonizing discourse at once changes the culture of a host context and adapts to it. This process of constant contextual mutation is progressively significant in light of how quickly and forensically people's data and therefore preferences can be collected, analyzed and exploited. These mutations also forge hegemonic networks which reproduce us as viral subjects exploited by user-friendly ideologies in support of materially exploitative (and often invisible) sets of relation. To counter these dominant and dominating connections, it is necessary to interrupt them and discover the possibility of new networks for directly challenging such injustices and collaboratively as well as concretely producing new social realities. More precisely, it involves and demands a form of political reconnection which allows new people to connect with one another in radically new ways.

Networking society

It is progressively proclaimed that we have entered into the age of networks. No longer are populations and communities primarily defined by human interaction or even 'imagined' relations. Now they are marked by digital communications and shared predictive preferences. Human belonging is found in the present time as much on Facebook and Instagram as it is in-real-life contact. For sure, there is much to despair over and fear from this historical turn of events. It can ironically lead to profound feelings of disconnection and alienation. Yet it can also allow people from different backgrounds to connect and experience a sense of kinship even if only virtually. Equally significant, though perhaps too often overlooked, is that it has bred a particular way of viewing and engaging with politics, as evidence reveals that those who are more active on social media sites like Twitter tend to be more politically engaged and simultaneously more distrustful of elites (see Bode & Dalrymple, 2016).

Revealed are serious questions with respect to what it actually means to now live in a 'networked society'? The first real profound engagement with this idea came from Castells' groundbreaking work. He contends that

> the definition, if you wish, in concrete terms of a network society is a society where the key social structures and activities are organized around electronically processed information networks. So it's not just about networks or social networks, because social networks have been very old forms of social organisation. It's about social networks which process and manage information and are using micro-electronic based technologies. (Castells, 1996, p 34)

These theoretical ideas are borne out by the increasingly 'networked' character of communities. These further speak to broader issues of networks and power.

Significantly, networks create their own types of social and political agency, ones that rely heavily on the mobility of power and the virality of order. They demand and catalyze the fostering of new capabilities which provide fresh opportunities for hegemony and counter-hegemony. Castells speaks of 'networks of outrage and hope'– exploring the relation of networked societies and social movements. He highlights the emergence of autonomous user-led networks, declaring: 'By sharing their sorrow and their hope in the free public space of the Internet, by connecting to each other, and by envisioning projects from multiple sources of being individuals formed networks regardless of their personal views or organisational attachments' (Castells, 1996, pp 1– 2). Tellingly, while these networks represent a fresh form of sociality between individuals and groups, they also emerged within established social relations. He proclaims that 'it began on the Internet Social Networks, as these are spaces of autonomy, largely beyond the control of governments and corporations that had monopolised the channels of communication as the foundation of their power across history' (p 21).

The wider hope of social media networks is the creation of more engaged and participatory forms of social production, a hope that seems more tinged with ambivalence than it might have been when Castells was writing, prior to the more complete commercialization of social networks. The internet, under a hopeful scenario, could be a force for the democratization of communication and political participation (see Benkler, 2006). It could also reframe civic culture around the formation of and struggle between hegemonic 'publics' and resistant 'counterpublics' (Warner, 2002). Whereas there appears to be a quite pervasive and far-reaching discussion of digital disconnect, erosion of attention and the tendency towards superficiality, there is less awareness of how digital connection also creates feelings and experiences of belonging. Networks provide a sense of personalization, ironically through their opportunities for digital collectivity. Indeed 'Net Geners', who are often excluded from the public sphere, can use social networking sites to better make their voices and views heard (Bennett, 2012). Social networking sites can, moreover, produce new democratic networks, often serving to link previously excluded voices into a powerful political movement (Loader & Mercea, 2011). Similarly, they can be the basis for real-time movements of counter-hegemony across disparate populations and locations. To this effect, they can allow for the fostering of an 'active online counterpublic' that challenges a dominant 'common sense' and hegemonic relations both virtually and IRL (Leung & Lee, 2014).

These new forms of politics and resistance are perhaps most evident in the rise of platform activism. This represents, in turn, a nascent type of network-based political logic (Klinger & Svensson, 2015). It also gives rise to the emergence of 'cyber-movements'. (Palczewski, 2001). Significantly, these movements are to a certain extent simply building on the narrativization of politics connected to the importance of film and propaganda. Cody recently made this connection in relation to the contemporary politics of the Tamil nation, arguing that 'networked publicity of satellite television and new media have layered themselves over existing infrastructures of mass-mediated populism' (Cody, 2020, p 392). Here, what appeared radically new was an updating and speeding up of old forms of political propaganda and mobilization, as 'many of the political challenges to existing structures fuelled by newer media forms appear as shorter-term events, consisting of tighter, sometimes explosive temporal loops intersecting with longer-term formations' (Cody, 2020, p 392). Ultimately, in Cody's view, such 'new media' has exploited the 'affective and narrative potentials within cinematic populism, all the while reflexively marking themselves as "new" in relation to the forms they have become parasitic upon' (Cody, 2020, p 392).

This further gestures towards the construction of new forms of viral exclusion, inclusion and elitism, rooted in 'the importance of Internet-mediated social networks in providing a "media filter", functioning as a kind of collective gatekeeper to spread news and information perceived as important, in contrast to the image of the single individual media consumer faced with an insurmountable mass of information' (Gustafsson, 2010, p 1). Such gatekeeping through social media platforms can re-perform elite social structures and inequalities. Revealed, consequently, is the dual rise of the hegemony of networks and networks of hegemony. The former refers to the dominant ways in which social relations are being articulated and operationalized via discourses of networks. There are primarily rooted in the digital sphere but extending to physical encounters. We are now less part of coherent communities and discrete ethno-national populations, than we are linked up to diverse interconnecting networks of shared preferences and common platforms. The latter describes how different networks combine to promote a hegemonic discourse. Both of these combine to reflect a more mobile and viral form of hegemony. New big data methods, such as sentiment analysis of social text, for instance, are being used to 'nowcast' elections – thus producing rapidly changing, real-time 'common sense' that can equally spread rapidly across different networks and adapt to their culture as well as permit alternative ideas to enter into the mainstream and spread in similar ways. These developments speak to the rise of 'platform power', which according to Culpepper and Thelen (2019) primarily relies not on traditional political lobbying but rather on 'the tacit allegiance of consumers, who can prove a formidable source of opposition to regulations that threaten these platforms' (Culpepper & Thelen, 2019, p 288).

Yet platform power can permit new actors and ideas to deconstruct, disrupt and challenge this alliance for the creation of less-consumer-based and more political identities. Therefore, for example, despite the immersion of Facebook within norms of neoliberal hegemony and its, at best, neutral stance in relation to authoritarian right-wing political regimes, left projects and organizations are still able to use its infrastructure to grow and spread messages and affects. Facebook remained the most effective communications platform for the left-wing political group Momentum during the UK's 2017 general election, for example, who managed to reach a third of the country's Facebook accounts with its content during the campaign (Hughes, 2017), usually through organic outreach/reach (that is, not paid-for) What is increasingly clear, thus, is that whether dystopian or utopian, the present and future of society and politics will be much more networked.

Infection vs contagion

The key question, then, is not whether or not we live in a network society but which networks will gain the upper hand. More precisely, whose voice is digitally 'heard' and whose interests are being concretely promoted? The concept of hegemony is important, in this respect, as it shifts the discussion away (for the moment) from existential questions regarding the emancipatory potential of digitalization and online culture and towards who it is actually benefiting. Thus, while it is commonly assumed by scholars and pundits alike that 'online politics is a democratizer', a recent study based on the 2010 US senate elections found that 'some nontraditional voices do get heard on YouTube, but most of these voices have difficulty breaking through when it comes to media coverage' (Ridout et al, 2015, p 238). Hence the problem of digital media 'bubbles', the phenomenon of like-minded people closing themselves off from outside influence, and learning from and following people and groups with similar views to theirs. Such bubbling of subjectivity can lead to an inflation of the assumed traction of one's views, which cannot be tested until the bubble is burst.

The current period is composed of a hybrid media culture characterized by a mix of media-ized approaches for shaping networks

(Chadwick et al, 2016). Mobile power during this time, accordingly, involves the ability of a dominant discourse to adapt its message to the various information sources of diverse networks. Older generations, thus, may mix Cable TV, newspapers and Facebook, while younger ones move rather seamlessly from TikTok to Snapchat to Instagram. The goal is not to prioritize one over the other but to recognize and accommodate these differences in messaging. Yet it is also critical to recognize the power imbalances created by these hybrid configurations when it comes to infecting diverse but connected populations with a dominant discourse. Hence, it is important to remember that 'participation does not equate to power' and just as significantly that 'disruptive power is not equally distributed'). Rather, 'those who have the resources and expertise to intervene in the hybrid flows of political information are more able to be powerful', notes Chadwick and his colleagues. They continue: 'As the process of hybridisation develops and adapts in unpredictable ways, the agency of elites and non elites remains in flux. There is a need to focus on the specific conditions under which hybridity empowers or disempowers' (Chadwick et al, 2016, p 24).

The growing cultural prevalence of 'life hacks' and 'hack-a-thons' is a concrete illustration of this increasingly innovative 'hybrid' society. While hacking was traditionally viewed as a subversive and even revolutionary activity (and as will be shown later in this chapter, still very much can be), breaking into digital systems and manipulating their information and compromising their security, recently this perception has shifted onto the positive ability of individuals to find innovative ways, various digital and IRL tricks, to increase personal well-being and professional success. These personal efforts have expanded to encompass collective hack-a-thons to creatively solve chronic and arising organizational and societal problems. These are usually defined by short but intensive collaborations between technologists and others for producing new products and solutions. These are commonly jointly organized and promoted by governments and private firms, existing thus as a hybrid initiative that must balance public good with private profit (see Briscoe, 2015). This emerging mainstream hacking culture reveals the problem-solving ethos so crucial to our progressively mobile and viral times. It also points to how dynamic and 'reformable' these supposedly entrenched status quos must be if they are to survive and thrive. Indeed, rather ironically, it is precisely this ability of people to creatively customize the system to their local conditions (whether in their personal life or within their communities) that allows these hegemonies to remain so infectious.

It is worth returning to the previous distinction we have made between innovative and disruptive technologies to better theoretically understand this phenomenon and its practical implications. Disruptive technologies are those that interrupt networks, identifying their infectious qualities and revealing the ways communities can build resistance against them. A case in point is the recent use of digital technologies by youth in Kenya for radical purposes. As Nyabola notes, 'Young Africans especially are embracing technology and digital platforms as spaces to have their opinions articulated and amplified, as well as to speak directly to power in their respective societies', (Nyabola, 2018, p 3) Critically, they are doing so in a way that goes beyond mere representation in established forms of political participation and influence. It is, instead, serving as a space and set of concrete networks for expanding the polis and the category of people whose voices matter. In doing so, it is forging novel connections for subverting the traditional public sphere, where they have been historically ignored, and reconfiguring it in ways that allow such conventionally marginalized populations to have their voices diversely heard.

The example of recent protests in Hong Kong can illustrate how these dynamics can spread from offline to online and vice versa. The introduction of a new bill that would allow the government in Hong Kong to extradite suspects to mainland China was met with fierce opposition. Technology played an important role in mobilizing and organizing these protests. Protestors discussed action on the secure messaging app Telegram – both in large groups and in smaller more localized ones – as well as voting on LIHKG – a Hong Kong–based internet forum like Reddit (Tufekci, 2019). Smartphones helped protestors to develop new tactics and strategies for the movement, allowing them to become highly mobile. As one protestor explained: 'Our aim is not to let the police arrest us. We need to be like water' (quoted in Hale, 2019). This call to 'be like water' became a rallying cry for the movement, riffing off Bruce Lee's quote about being 'formless, shapeless, like water.' After months of protests, the demands of the demonstrators had grown, with new targets being added to their growing list of grievances. Surveillance was one aspect of this, focusing on the use of CCTV cameras. While umbrellas provided one way to avoid surveillance, an increasing number of 'smart' lampposts were being installed in the city. While the government claimed these would not be used to collect facial-recognition data, the use of surveillance against the Uyghurs in mainland China had clearly shown the power of these technologies. In response, protestors organized using digital technology, combined with more 'basic technologies ... a handheld saw and a rope', to bring down smart lampposts (Tufekci, 2019).

However, there is a risk in focusing only on online communication. The obvious challenge is how 'power pushes back' and 'the extent we can say that what is being developed online is a real reflection of the state of affairs offline' (Tufekci, 2019) – the bubble problematic highlighted previously. In light of these very real and concrete concerns, though, there lie even more revolutionary (though also quite dangerous) possibilities for drawing on such virtual networks for fostering a more 'speculative politics' (see Rojecki & Meraz, 2016). This is rooted in allowing differing networks to explore, even if only online, alternative versions of the present and conventional accounts of what the future may bring. Its promise is in encouraging a radical break from the prevailing 'common sense', producing imaginative networks for retelling their given objective realities, while its threat is in its mobilization of these networks to embrace misinformation and its viral spread.

Nevertheless, this evolution of a network society reveals the important role of these technologies for transforming social relations and perhaps more fundamentally mobile power. In terms of technology, it is progressively claimed that we are in the 'smartphone age' (Bene, 2017). Political participation, further, is becoming defined by mobility – specifically, the ability to effectively engage in various social networks (Yamamoto et al, 2015). Exposed is how contemporary power regimes must navigate and keep pace with such diverse networks. Networks, in this respect, become 'living hosts' for infection and resistance, as well as the counter-hegemonic movements of contagion and inoculation.

This provides, in turn, new ways of understanding hegemony linked to mobile power and virality. Hegemony is more and more a matter of continually and successfully infecting networks. This breaks with traditional 'geographies' of hegemony, which assume explicitly and implicitly the presence of a 'centre'. It is more accurate to understand hegemony as diffuse and dynamic, moving flexibly between networks. As such, hegemony is akin to an infectious, discursive disease. This diffuse epidemic is witnessed, for instance, in the spread of neoliberalism. Specifically in the ways it makes its power and control diffuse by relegating it to a set of instrumental goals to be individually and collectively achieved – often with a relatively high degree of autonomy and perceived indirect regulation (Leitner et al, 2006, pp 3–4). However, this diffuse character should not be confused with a sense of either weakness or a lack of hegemonic *power*. By contrast, neoliberal 'institutions, agencies, and individual citizens are expected to make their activities visible to centers of calculation, but these centers are less often required (much less enticed or persuaded) to make their activities transparent to neoliberal subjects' (Leitner et al, 2006, pp 3–4).

The attempt to challenge and struggle against such infectious domination without an obvious centre can be equally reframed as building up local and shared resistances to these hegemonic epidemics. The establishment of 'orders', then, is the continual mobile attempt to negotiate such resistances and allow hegemony's infection to go viral. This dynamic between infection and resistance in the play of hegemony is again seen in the efforts to contest neoliberalism – especially within urban contexts where 'cities are bound to experience relatively frequent crises or disruptions', but where, nonetheless, 'these same mechanisms also tend to reinforce precisely the sorts of dynamics – corporate flexibility, policy decentralisation, interlocal competition – that localize crisis, isolate opposition, and punish would-be progressive innovations' (Sites, 2007, pp 133–4).

If hegemony is rooted primarily in the struggle between infection and resistances, then counter-hegemony is marked by the relation of contagion and inoculation. Alternative discourses not only threaten the rationality and power of a dominant discourse locally but also potentially regionally and globally, spreading across and disrupting different hegemonic networks. Hence, new discourses are contagious – able to emerge within a given context and spread to others. It represents an ethos not of simple resistance to infection but of experimentation that can be contagious (Papadopoulos, 2018). Yet hegemony is again never static, and can always engage in reactionary forms of inoculation to such contagions (Manacorda & Tesei, 2018), as capital has always responded to and adapted to resistances from labour. That is why there is a need for contagious networks to continually articulate and resist these inoculating efforts on the part of the powerful.

Change is then found in the continual ordering and reordering within and across networks linked to processes of infection/resistance and contagion/inoculation. This involves making disruptions everyday and mobile, especially as hegemonic innovations will also be continual, widespread and ongoing. This relation between infection and contagion can be glimpsed in current transhumanist imaginaries linked to the use of AI in daily life, studying explicitly the growing desire of individuals, companies and governments to exploit home-based brainwave monitors. According to Gardner and Wray, 'At stake is our agility in undertaking politically astute interventions as consumers, artists, and scientists with and through biometric devices that capture our personal data, frame it as information, and transform it into knowledge' (Gardner & Wray, 2013, p 7). Here the self is composed of a range of different and quite changeable identities one has linked to real-time information gathering and the updating of current trends. Values such as efficiency can thus traverse these various selves as an everyday process of informing people of tips for 'gardening better' or 'cooking while you work' while giving them access to examples of how others are doing the same (and often presumably better). The introduction of the 'internet of things' thus prospectively bombards people with an environment that is continually monitoring and informing them of their 'progress' in embodying these social values. It can be considered infectious, hence, on two accounts: firstly as a suddenly spreading virus that infects one's very constitution and performance of selfhood; and secondly as an infectious set of data and information for continually improving and expanding one's self based on these hegemonic discourses.

It is vital then to critically illuminate both theoretically and contextually the evolving relation between the hegemonic forces of infection/resistance and the counter-hegemonic forces of contagion/inoculation. Doing so provides a clearer view of how populations can disrupt and recreate networks. This disruptive ethos is evident, for example, in the emergence of radical 'do-it-yourself' communities. According to Delgado and Callen (2017), these hacks have a viral effect in that they empower people to do and accomplish tasks usually reserved for experts, thus allowing them to share the fact 'that things can be done otherwise and that "you" can also do it'. Further, these radical hacking practices and incipient networked cultures grow out of the speed at which new technological products are produced and how rapidly such otherwise still functional products are deemed obsolete. They reflect more than just a set of resistance practices in this regard. They also offer a counter-hegemonic network for transforming the social in a way that is both attuned to local conditions and potentially universally contagious. This is witnessed in E-waste hacking, which saw a mass effort to repair and reuse previously discarded electronic devices (many of which were abandoned not due to their lack of operability but due to consumers being incentivized to buy expensive new upgrades). Significantly, these hacking cultures transcend established counter-hegemonic efforts focused on either challenging prevailing values or existent power relations. Conversely, they gesture towards the attempt to create an alternative ordering that can evolve and spread for remobilizing and reconnecting the social. This process of material repurposing as a form of radical praxis is crucial to our understandings of guerrilla democracy and 'radical (im)materialism' explored respectively in the next two chapters. What is particularly relevant, though, for our current discussion of discursive infection and contagion is the ways the social produces the very material for communities to inoculate themselves against its hegemonic values and desires and moreover forge alternative principles and practices which themselves can be spread.

While the case of E-waste hacking may appear rather technologically straightforward, it also applies to more supposedly hi-tech instances of resistances such as DIY bio-hacking. Here, the increase in underemployed but technologically literate people – most of whom were primarily young – combined with the drop in price of once rarefied techniques like gene sequencing and synthesizing. This has given rise to DIY biolabs based on an open exchange of information and the ability of individuals to come together and collaboratively research and produce new bio products that can have profound social impacts. These include the sustainable creation of 'real vegan cheese', the production of 'open insulin', and a project for openly sharing 'brain data' information so as to prevent its manipulation by government and private elites.

What this also reveals is how opportunistic these counter-hegemonic contagions can be, relying upon the dynamism of hegemony for their emergence and reproduction. The economies, then, of our current viral hegemony, which entail the fostering of a range of mobile capabilities and new networks, lend themselves simultaneously to an infectious social logic of neoliberalism and a contagious political logic challenging this rebooted capitalist order. Crucial, then, is how resistant these networks can become to this hegemonic infection (such as those associated with the free market) and how well these diffuse hegemonic orders can inoculate themselves against contagious alternatives.

Viral agency and epidemic capacities

The critical importance of infectious and contagious discourses reveals the fundamental and contemporary significance of mobility for understanding power and virality for analyzing hegemony. These point to the rise of epidemic networks – imagined and material communities that help to spread, resist and transform ideologies and diverse social orderings. Here the articulation of a society as a living host is reinforced by a further idea of its being composed of intersecting virtual and IRL networks. The notion of global assemblages discussed by Collier (2006, p 399) helps to clarify this relation, describing them as 'the actual configurations through which global forms of techno-science, economic rationalism, and other expert systems gain significance' (Collier, 2006, p 399). These global assemblages, in turn, represent emergent and adaptable epidemic communities. They are the criss-crossing networks which permit the spread of viral infection and radical contagions. In the present context, this is most often associated with online interactions and 'tribes', as 'geographical borders lose significance, and political content is shared and considered relevant by a community of users that is not necessarily identical to the national community of citizens' (Barisione & Michailidou, 2017, p 56). This is as much an actual virtual reality as it is a digital 'participatory promise' of social connections which transcend conventional geographic borders and foster, instead, global networks.

It also reflects the growth of what can be termed 'epidemic social knowledge', whereby users are aware to some extent of both the content of the information they are engaging with and its potential for virality. The growth of such epidemic knowledge is perhaps ironically witnessed in the various ways that individuals and communities are constructed through awareness of real diseases. Writing on Hepatitis C, Fraser and Seear (2016) note that such pathological knowledge and the discourses underpinning it create a heightened awareness of infection and its consequences, producing 'new subjects and new relations' even for those who have not contracted the disease. Here it is not just the disease that is significant but its social framing and the way it structures knowledge sharing. In 'neoliberal societies the making of disease is also necessarily the making of subjects, of rights and of responsibilities', as well as creating 'new spaces of subjectivity' (Fraser & Seear, 2016, p 1). This pathological modern subject is centred, in part, around the need to manage infection – a subjectivity that resonates with the ongoing demands to manage, contain and shape the seemingly infectious and borderless qualities of modern digital social relations and information sharing.

Domination can thus be recast as an epidemic that can become a global pandemic. Crucial to the virality of hegemony is then the ability to make host conditions right for discourses to deepen their hold within their borders and effectively spread beyond them. As such, the difference between a prevailing ideology and a hegemonic discourse is that, while the former constitutes a coherent vision of the social based on its ideals, the latter is the concrete and uneven implementation of this vision within and across host contexts. It is the mixture, in this respect, of the imaginative and the connective – the abstract and the concrete. Consequently, if ideology is the disease (to return to the example of the epidemic) then discourse is the family of symptoms that uniquely infects a host context. This distinction is captured, for instance, in the common distinction between neoliberalism and neoliberalization, which Heeg (2019) describes 'as a process rather than as a condition ... a logic of governing that migrates and is selectively taken up in diverse political contexts and urban settings'. Consequently, while neoliberalism can be studied as an ideology, neoliberalization must be regarded 'as a place-sensitive and process-oriented analysis' (Heeg, 2019, p 19).

In this sense, neoliberalism is the ideology while neoliberalization is the hegemonic discourse – one which Heeg traces from its intellectual beginnings in the Global North to regions including the Middle East and North Africa. Just as importantly, as it spreads, these dominant discourses become both more diverse and more refined. Hence, discursive epidemics and pandemics reflect the transition from philosophical ideology to applied science. For this reason, Ylönen (2016) has referred to neoliberalism increasingly as a 'technoscience'– a set of standardized practices and processes for deepening and expanding infections within and to ever-newer host contexts. It also creates the very social space for power relations to emerge, as it sets the ideological coordinates and discursive conditions for actors to negotiate with and empower themselves through these infectious realities. They do so through infiltrating, manipulating and seeking to control the diverse informational networks. Consequently, the discursive infection of hegemony is translated over time into the unequal contest between would-be hegemons – in this case over who will get to control and most profit from the context-specific processes of marketization.

These insights do much to help illuminate the critical import of viral agency. More precisely, this refers to the socially produced resources and skills available within a given space and time for the spread of infectious discourses. It is worth returning again to the tripartite characterization of power introduced earlier by Foucault (1982) – one that is composed of power relations, produced capabilities and shared communication. While the exact relation of these elements is never made entirely clear, nor is how they relate to Foucault's broader project of interrogating power/knowledge, they nonetheless hold important hints about the relation of hegemony and agency – particularly as it theoretically and contextually applies to hegemony's virality. The philosopher Ian

Hacking has taken just such an approach in his own discussions of Foucault and ontology – acknowledging that his interpretation is less a strict reflection of the source inspiration's own views and more a gesturing towards its possible implications. Similarly, the development of capabilities points to the creation (often unpredictably so) of diverse methods, technologies and abilities associated with the viral spread of dominant discourse. Specific to themes of power and hegemony, it is worth exploring how dominant logics (such as those associated with virality) ultimately produce and rely upon associated capabilities, representing forms of socialized agency that can both reinforce and challenge hegemony.

Returning to the present epoch of virality and networks – over time and across host contexts – these develop further into capacities which infected populations either have or can cultivate. Accordingly, the move from capabilities to capacities is one of viral disciplining. At the most basic level, they can be used to shape the 'conduct of conduct' of these populations while also serving as a set of standards upon which to evaluate, judge and if necessary punish them. Infusing these thoughts, though, with the broader theory of mobile power introduced in this work, they are also a means for disciplining individuals and communities to themselves discover and improve upon these new capabilities for enhancing the capacity of host contexts to receive and adapt to these infectious discourses. Thus, capacity is at once a disciplining set of entrenched capabilities and an imperative for the disciplined invention and refinement of new context-specific capabilities. In this sense, viral capacities both serve as the means and ends of an infectious hegemonic local epidemic and global pandemic.

Again, it is telling that these epidemic capacities are evident in the play of hegemony associated with actual medical diseases and conditions. Rajan recently introduced the notion of 'pharmacology' to refer to the hegemonic role of Western pharmaceutical companies in shaping global governance to reflect their economic interests. For this reason, 'the global harmonisation of clinical trials and intellectual property regimes must be understood in terms of this expansion of multinational corporate hegemony' (Rajan, 2017, p 6). Indeed, Rajan (2017) claims that the spread of pharmacological solutions – antidepressants, primarily – is a way of treating and making subjects responsible for sociopolitical-economic problems, or more specifically of ameliorating the diseases wrought by the insensitivity and hyper speed of the contemporary capitalism of multiple signs. Yet the growth of pharmacology is a supple form of power, one that must be remobilized so that Third World contexts can meet the needs of First World corporate interests. In practice, this requires a set of viral capabilities and agency, so that 'state policy, industrial competitiveness, and public health' can 'materialize in specific ways in different national contexts' (Rajan, 2017, p 6). In particular, the spread of pharmacology in the ongoing creation of new capabilities and in real-time viral capacities associated with these health-based regimes of power. Accordingly, health is discursively linked to 'experimentation and therapy', so that it is 'no longer just an embodied, subjective, experiential state of well-being or disease; it can be abstracted and grown, made valuable to capitalist interests' (Rajan, 2017, p 7). It is critical to remember, though, that such medicalized 'logics of capital are not seamless. They materialize differently in different places and times through different forms of capitalism and often consequent to deep contestation' (Rajan, 2017, p 8). Hence, this marketized culture of corporate health is obstensbily concerned with arresting the spread of diseases while being engaged in a mobile and quite viral project of expanding the social infection of neoliberalism.

Interestingly, at the heart of these emergent capabilities and entrenched capacities is an ethos and praxis of continual innovation. In an analogous way to pharmacology, the current attempts to foster greater digital consumption can be viewed as disciplinary forms of viral agency which must be crafted to reflect the particular cultures and histories of local networks and IRL contexts. They reflect not just a culture of capitalist innovation but one that relies upon the manufacturing of what can be termed experimental subjects – the disciplining of populations to accept such constant product testing, and indeed to welcome it. However, there is a significant distinction between the marketized subject of actual diseases and the infectious subject of digital capitalism: notably, the latter is concerned with using such constant experimentation to strengthen the 'infection rates' of their products. The constant use of real-time online product testing turns people at once into incubators of this neoliberal virus and its intended infected victims. Yet this social logic of capitalist experimentation and consumption also provides the very cultural resources for inoculating ourselves against these infectious discourses and building up concrete everyday resistances to this neoliberal epidemic. The DIY hacking communities covered earlier reflect the possibilities of potential experimentation. They are also witnessed in the rise of experimental cultures for enhancing political participation and civic engagement (see for instance Lezaun et al, 2016). These can range from rather conventional E-government programmes to sophisticated community data-mapping initiatives. The risk, of course, is that this turns populations into socialized objects for political experimentation and manipulation (Chilvers & Kearns, 2020). Yet there is the political potential to reverse this relationship, to disruptively transform existing power relations and social environments into objects for radical experimentation and transformation. To turn the status quo into a 'living experiment' for testing emancipatory alternatives, and if successful, sharing them with others to test and adapt to their own infected contexts.

These demands for constant innovation can cultivate, in turn, socially infectious and politically contagious cultures of 'good practice' across existing and emergent networks. While locally instituted, they foster a broader 'common sense'— mediating a shared knowledge that can allow successful experimentations to go viral. Represented again is the transition from capabilities to capacities – as a set of knowledge about empowerment, one that is both disciplining and expansive, on the one hand, and disruptive and liberating, on the other. Take the case of the use and exploitation of big data, about which Caplan and Boyd (2018) presciently observed that actors must have some knowledge of inscriptive systems, such as bureaucracy, if they are going to effectively operate within them. Turning their attention to the contemporary period, they note that 'algorithmic bureaucracies' can often obfuscate their deeper power relations and the interests they serve through their presented technological complexity. Nevertheless, individuals can still challenge, subvert and even reshape these regimes without being experts as users. They do not, metaphorically, need to fully comprehend the architectural design of these systems to find novel and quite disruptive ways to live with them. What is crucial in this insight is that people do not have to know the inner workings of digital networks in order to engage with and enhance their digital networking capabilities and viral sense of agency.

Nevertheless, this agency is always socially constructed and to a certain extent hegemonically limited. It reflects both dominant values as well as the elites who are most responsible for materially and culturally creating and controlling the tools through which this agency is expressed. Hence it must be remembered that while platforms such as Facebook offer individuals new ways to connect with one another, they also 'show that power rests not in an algorithm's capacity to induce a new logic into an industry, but in its function as an administrative mechanism that is embedded with the values and cultural and economic environment of [its[creators' (Caplan & Boyd, p 9). The globalization of infectious discourses then involves their relative sychronization through the convergence of evolving individual capabilities into disciplined shared capacities. An obvious but still instructive historical example would be the creation of the 'hegemonic metronome' representing the international acceptance of Western Standard Time (see Hom, 2010). In the present day, this is revealed in the developing standardization of formal and informal regulations for shaping individuals' online behaviour. Additionally, it is evident in the ubiquitous data mining of users' personal preferences while logged on to these digital platforms which allows corporations and governments to profit off people's activities and connections regardless of their substantive ideological content. The E-business entrepreneur and the radical anarchist Facebook groups are equally ripe for such profitable data extraction in this respect.

These social epidemics are also characterized by the divergence of knowledge. It is the translation of global knowledge into localized solutions. This is aided and abetted by the use of social media to create localized viral networks of hegemony. Yet it can also be used to foster stronger resistances to such hegemonic knowledge and create contagious insurgencies. This can be seen in the Umbrella Movement in Hong Kong, where protestors used social media to create an 'insurgent public sphere' (IPS) (Lee et al, 2015). These online sources directly counteracted traditional media, as data revealed that they directly increased support for this insurrection and decreased satisfaction with and trust in existing authorities including the Hong Kong Special Administrative Region Government, the Hong Kong Police and the Chinese Central Government. Significantly, this radicalization of public opinion was incubated in the construction of networks of online knowledge sharing and digital socializing prior to the crisis. For this reason, 'it is difficult for the state to distinguish insurgencies from socializing activities. Surveillance of social media incurs heavy economic and political costs' (Lee et al, 2015, p 371).

Revealed, in turn, are the diverse aspects of epidemic knowledge and counter-knowledge. They map onto contemporary ideas of convergence and divergence linked to globalization. Both processes represent the move from ideology to science. Beniger (2009) aptly refers to this as the 'control revolution', tracing from the 19th century onward how social regulation and discipline were maintained through evolving and increasingly sophisticated regimes and techniques for collecting, collating and deploying population information. These practices of informational control, while hi-tech, are bio-political in their underlying logics. The very basis of existence becomes a matter of gaining greater knowledge about and management of individual and collective data. As Beniger observes, 'Life itself implies control, after all, in individual cells and organisms no less than in national economies or any other purposive system' (Beniger, 2009, p vi). The need for information and its ever-expanding deployment for population control is then naturalized as essential and technoligized for preserving our personal and shared existence. It is not surprising, then, that the control revolution has so seamlessly spread to the data tracking of our physical and mental health as well as the disciplining of our behaviours for this purpose, such information gathering and use presented as critical to our biological survival and psychic well-being.

However, these are fundamentally social processes of power and hegemony. Infectious discourses combine global and local capacities to assure their hegemony. In the present age of mobile technologies, social media makes individuals and groups complicit in their own ideological indoctrination and hegemonic infection by turning them from passive users into active participants who both consume and spread (create and distribute) viral campaign messages. Crucially, these are not confined, so to speak, to borderless online communities but can play out in actual physical ones as well, as evidenced in the employment of social media campaigns as part of place-based marketing strategies (see Ketter & Avraham, 2012). Here, ideas and products are consumed and spread by local residents through electronic word of mouth and localized online networks, making them appear to be community generated and promoted rather than externally conceived and introduced. This points once more to the quite strategic way this informational power and control is made to look and feel organic. Moreover, it illuminates how viral hegemony is socially naturalized through the concrete and strategic processes through which it is actively spread.

Contagious forms of counter-hegemony also rely, though, on making localized alternatives go global and turning global counter-knowledge into localized revolutions. Postill (2014, p 51) highlights this exact phenomenon in the recent Indignados movement in Spain, where Twitter and other viral platforms were key to its success. Crucially, it repurposed digital techniques developed by political professionals for its own radical purposes, deploying online campaigns and communications for 'setting the tone and agenda of the protests, spreading slogans and organisational practices, and offering alternative accounts of the movement.' Of equal import, though, was that these efforts were not meant to be a force for social naturalization, making seem organic a proscribed 'viral reality', but were instead a space of digital and physical political intervention and invention, where this 'reality' and the practices being used to subvert were continually questioned and transformed as evolving spaces of disruptive experimentation and creation.

Tracking infections

Knowledge has arguably never been so viral, and equally important, the knowledge of virality, paradoxically, has never been so great. There is a growing recognition of how all the information we are exposed to has spread across networks that span and transcend geographic boundaries and traditional IRL communities. The desire to quantify such everyday infections is, thus, understandable – an effort to make visible that which is often invisible. For this reason, we 'should take numbers and statistics seriously not because they are "nature's own language", which was their justification in the quantitative revolution, but because they are a crucial component in the construction of social reality' (Barnes & Hannah, 2001, p 379). Hence our arguably inherent sociality is always formed within the production of power and is linked to hegemonic ordering. In the contemporary age, our capacity to adaptably form networks and diversely consume information is critical to the cultural construction of our realities and a primary factor in crafting and implementing processes of domination and control. For this purpose, 'the inscription of figures, and later their joining to probability calculations within a burgeoning set of both commercial and statist networks, produced worlds to be organised, controlled, manipulated, studied, and known' (Barnes & Hannah, 2001, p 379). Likewise, the capacity to make knowledge go viral and to mobilize it within and across a wide range of social networks is a key component for understanding how people exist and act within the present period.

It also reflects deeply shared desires to make sense of and know more about these infectious discourses on the part both of elites and non-elites alike. As network society grows, so too does the need to quantify and track the viral spread of knowledges, and by association the mobility of power. Yet in tracking these infections, measuring network capital and the role of capital in shaping networks, so too does the possibility for using these tools for disciplinary purposes. As Porter (1996) reminds us, the proliferation of the desire and demand for 'quantitative objectivity' goes beyond the creation of a new class of information experts but reconfigures the very basis of social authority generally.

In the current era, perhaps more than ever before, we are faced with a complex form of subjection that exists at two levels. The first is in relation to invading discursive infections and the second to the host context in which one is socially included. More precisely, an individual is a subject of both the living and unique context in which they reside as well as of the hegemonic discourses interacting with, adapting to and dynamically transforming these contexts. There is thus a continual need to negotiate both of these forms of subjection – of being a cell in a host body exposed to ongoing viral infections. This simultaneously requires flexibility and the ability to continually 'adapt to adaptations'. Speaking of neoliberalism in Dubai, for instance, Kanna contends that a rich empirical analysis of its neoliberalization reveals how customizable and localized this presumed global spread of neoliberalism is as an 'actually existing' hegemonic epidemic. Indeed, contrary perhaps to expectations, 'unlike other national contexts such as Singapore, local inflections of neoliberalism in Dubai are governed more by notions of ethically "valuable" citizenship and authentic identity than by economically "valuable" citizenship' (Kanna, 2010, p 100). As such, it is critical to stress and continually remember that virality is always 'glocal' in its scope, global in its intentions and local in its implementation. Its capitalist insatiability is translated, then, into discovering and infecting ever-newer contexts, customizing its ideological values and practical techniques into novel profitable opportunities whose local lessons can be shared and utilized by others to aid its global spread.

There is, accordingly, a constant need and longing to better understand this virality, to prepare and fortify oneself against infection and also take advantage of its incoming opportunities. A danger lies, however, in the fact that, while viral information can be easy to access, the means by which this information goes viral is often subtle and hidden. This is evident, for example, in new studies that found that people tend to ignore online posts that are explicitly and obviously political – especially among those who do not identify themselves as particularly politically oriented or interested (Bode et al, 2017, p 1). Also revealing is that this was evidenced using sophisticated monitoring and data-collecting techniques such as corneal eye-tracking software. Once again revealed is how populations are becoming objects of study and experimentation for understanding and then activating what makes knowledge viral and, consequently, what makes a valuable viral subject.

Nevertheless, subjection occurs, albeit not usually under directly 'political' discourses but via work and lifestyle content. Subjection to these infections contributes to our broader subjectification as quantified, networked subjects. Scholars have increasingly spoken, in this regard, of the prevalence of the 'quantified self' (See especially Moore, 2017). It also reflects an attempt to identify with and create a sense of self around increased quantification, especially as hegemony becomes progressively more viral in line with advances in mobile and digital technologies. Catlaw and Sandberg (2018) observe this trend in the realm of public administrations where emerging 'info-liberal governments' reflect and to a certain extent rely upon a malleable and rather ambiguous set of normative expectations whose purpose is to cultivate cultures of 'personal responsibility' and community resiliency in the face of greater marketization. Nevertheless, this quantification also breeds its own social antibodies as it creates 'opportunities for enriched self-subjectification and self-care that allow for a reconfiguration of one's relationship to one's self such that [they] offer a modicum of distance, counter-practice, and autonomy from the demands of neoliberalisation' (Catlaw & Sandberg, 2018, p 19).

Similarly, such quantifications allow for the creation of a networked subject. This is one that not only allows subjects to track data about themselves but also the various networks they are part of and the different ways they are exposed to infectious discourses. In this respect, the quantified self and the activities that surround it have a distinct and profound qualitative aspect linked to the subjective experience of how people take in such information and personally perceive its effect on them and others (See Swan, 2013). Already individuals are having their emotional states and moods tracked and quantified as a means for utilizing feedback loops to incentivize and induce behavioural change. Looking ahead, though, to the not-so-distant future, these same technologies and methods can be deployed to expand one's sense capabilities and therefore sensibilities beyond their current physical limitations. Consequently, it is important to highlight that such quantification and tracking is not a bloodless affair, the mere cold administration and domination of the modern mobile subject. Rather, they are interwoven with a deep sense of affect and attachment, which find much of their appeal and ultimate force in just how personalized this data-derived sense of self can be. As such, the very quantification presently used to construct social realities and discipline people within them produces an 'intimate relationship with data' for potentially mediating alternative realities (Swan, 2013).

In being better able to quantify these discursive infections, individuals and communities gain a greater ability to both become more deeply infected and potentially build up resistances to these infections. It creates a basis for subjects to 'care' for themselves in relation to these continual infections. Online activity is, thus, reframed not as mere idle entertainment or virtualized spectacle but as a set of 'curatorial practices as acts of self-exploration, self-cultivation, and self-care, which nourish offline identity and which ultimately work to shape the offline, corporeal self' (Weisgerber & Butler, 2016, p 1340). This is witnessed in the South African example of using alternative technology to replace conventional toilets. As Redfield and Robins (2016) observe, these innovative solutions are often rejected by populations who feel they are 'second solutions for second-class citizens', especially in a historical context of apartheid where access to state infrastructure denoted one's ability to live a 'dignified' life. Yet the development and spread of alternative technologies in this context remains quite prevalent, driven both by the demands of meeting basic social development needs and the profitable opportunities for social enterprises. Moreover, despite their success and effectiveness often being challenged due to these popular resistances, they remain 'living labs' in which for foreign donors and social entrepreneurs to better learn how to market these products. What is revealing about this example is not so much the question of whether or not vulnerable South African citizens should embrace these efforts to 'reinvent the toilet' but the ways that they are seeking to reverse their subjectification, from being subjects who are experimented upon to ones who can themselves have the knowledge, resources and agency to materially transform their own social context. Foundational to these radical gestures is the remobilization of power to reflect local histories and conditions and the political reconnection of individuals for this socially subversive and transformative purpose.

Consequently, it is imperative to track these social epidemics across networks. Counter-hegemony, thus, is in large part a matter of tracing out how one is being secretly and not-so-secretly counted as an infected host subject. More precisely, it is articulating how one is being quantified and qualified and then finding novel ways to resist and reconfigure such tracking. Infection then becomes a social and political game, a way of playing with data either in support or subversion of an existent status quo. The danger, of course, is that it is precisely this ongoing play of control and hegemony (whether over oneself or populations) that can be so disciplining and dominating, especially as one easily can become entangled within this dialectic, unable to envisage alternative modes of living. Hence, it is a control regime that continually draws people into its web of data tracking and informational manipulation, most often through 'incentivisation and pleasure rather than risk and fear to shape desired behaviours' and by 'injecting a spirit of play into otherwise monotonous activities' (Whitson, 2013, p 173). As such, it can be hard to discern where this line is between infection and resistance, inscription and freedom, particularly as the mobile tracking apps often provide individuals with a profound sense of agency by transforming self-improvement into a daily game that they can voluntarily choose to play or ignore. What is perhaps especially revealing, though, is how this bounded experience of viral freedom, made possible through quantification, tracking and networking, leads individuals to ignore (or renders invisible) the powerful interests and regimes profiting most from these mobile social relations. However, it also provides individuals with a sense of personalized control, as they feel they have relative independence to only use the quantifying tools that they find most helpful. To this extent, subjects have the ability to somewhat freely navigate the play of viral hegemony while having a relative ability to alter its underlying rules or the game itself. It also reflects how the increasingly viral character of hegemony is strengthened, ironically, by dominant views of control which see it as based in coercion and conformity rather than mobility and diversity.

A crucial way, thus, to discern infection from resistance is to uncover and articulate not just 'what is being counted' in this data collection and tracking but, more fundamentally, 'what counts'. In other words, it is imperative to consider what values are driving this quantification and what this reveals about the broader character of existent infections and the power relations sustaining them. For instance, in the contemporary period of hyper-capitalism, quantification within workplaces and beyond is developed as an updated form of 'scientific management' for maximizing individual efficiency whether at work or home (Moore & Robinson, 2016). Even when presented as just an enjoyable exercise in everyday personal development, its aim and the ultimate agency it provides is to help people – especially an increasingly precarious workforce –'keep up with the cut-throat competition' of the contemporary neoliberal labour market. It also puts to the test the myth that such hegemonic infections are merely a matter of choice – rather, they are viewed as potentially crucial resources for sustaining one's competitive advantage and as such material survival. They may be making this exploitation and process of self-commodification more enjoyable (or at the very least offering people a literal and figurative sense of quantifiable control in the face of an unpredictable and unequal economic market), but they are doing little to change it or actually improve the very conditions which are largely responsible for physical and mental unwellness.

Nonetheless, this opens up physical and digital space for tracking infections and, in doing so, building up a better critical understanding of their mobility and virality. It permits a deeper and rigorous personal understanding of how one is being targeted by economic and political elites via big data (see Fuchs, 2019); in doing so, helping to articulate and foster a constituent 'outside' to these seemingly all-pervasive regimes of tracking and control. Equally significant is that such tracking of hegemonic infections entails a process of critical and politicized discursive articulation. In labelling a discourse as infectious and tracking it, its ability to go viral is better understood and resisted. It turns what is naturalized within a given context into a colonizing force that must be challenged and treated. It also helps to foster viral resistances. A contemporary example of this phenomenon would be the growing linking of different resistance politics, such as those from feminist movements, what Ferreday and Harris (2017) call 'fame-inism', the ability to draw on celebrity culture and social media communication to spread messages subversive to patriarchal hegemony. It tracks how otherwise vapid celebrity cultures spread corporate and sexist values, and uses these same networks and viral capabilities to expose these practices and promote alternatives. Such an ethos can additionally serve as an everyday opportunity to subvert and build up resistances to these infections. Writing on the contemporary context of democracy and politics in 'digital India', Punathambekar observes that satirical videos can go viral so as to directly address 'long-standing political issues and debates around caste, class, gender and sexuality, and religious nationalism' (Punathambekar, 2015, p 394). It is precisely from this greater ability to name and track infections that revolutionary alternatives can emerge and become contagious.

Contagious reconnections

Tracking infections also reveals the importance of moving from resistance to more revolutionary forms of contagion; in other words, going beyond simply shielding yourself and others from infection and actually creating counter-hegemonic pandemics. The underlying dynamic of hegemony, in this respect, is one of mutations and preservations. This is readily apparent in the actualities of elite power under neoliberalism, wherein, according to Davies (2017, p 230), rests the capacity to translate and the overall authority of their translations. This power is strengthened by not attributing any such authorship to theses social realities, framing them as complex but nonetheless trackable phenomena. This has the effect of not only granting these elites the primary legitimacy for establishing a 'common sense' but also acquitting them (or those who support them) of any responsibility for this status quo. They thus serve as the brokers of these complex social formations, the meteorologists of a fickle market economy, for a public that wants to feel ever more informed and knowledgeable. Critically, this ongoing process and performance of elite translation is itself incredibly mobile – able to adapt to a wide range of cultural contexts and digital networks. Corporations and their PR machines are as seemingly comfortable justifying their wealth and influence through preaching the virtues of libertarianism as in a right-wing message board or through 'philanthrocapitalism' to professional liberals. There is no longer the 'masses', per se, that need to indoctrinated but diverse demographics that must be convinced in accordance with their own perceived values and vocabularies.

Viral hegemony is, hence, boundaryless in terms of its insatiability and bounded in terms of the multiple networks and host contexts it must infect and traverse. This complex but complementary character of being both boundaryless and bounded is reflected in the emergent 'anytime, anywhere' employee subject, for whom mobile technologies and 'flexible' working arrangements have made their professional experience an inescapable or all-encompassing part of their existence, trailing them and enveloping them whether they are at home, in a cafe, on holidays or in the office. For Fleming and Spicer (2004) it is a capitalist reality akin to the nightmarish Hotel California where 'you can checkout anytime, but you can never leave'. Yet this boundaryless culture also creates hardened hegemonic networks – where hegemony is ironically maintained through the building up of resistances and counter-resistances. Here, the once bright promise of social media to democratize and invigorate contemporary politics is replaced by a troubling world of closed digital networks where viral misinformation is amplified in their online echo chambers and can be used to mobilize communities IRL for various causes, which may or may not be in their ultimate interests. Törnberg (2018, p 2) describes these networks as fundamentally defined by their culture of 'polarization', marked by the amplification of their 'favourite narratives' and rejection of all countervailing knowledge. Equally troubling but also potentially dangerous to the status quo is the potential for these communities to be quickly rallied and mobilized in support of a preferred product, figure or political cause.

Foundationally, this points to how such viral connections are simultaneously an opening and closing of knowledge – as they at once disclose possible new connections for infection and contagions and close others. This represents a fundamental and unavoidable part of hegemony *tout court* – in so much as any social ordering allows for new social formations while eclipsing others – and one that may have particular resonance in this more mobile and viral age, as the apparently infinite openness of social media to all ideas and new networks masks its influence in closing off certain ways of thinking and being in favour of others. This critical contradiction is again evident in the actual impact of technologies like big data on disease prevention. Here, digital health information has principally revolved around disease treatment while detracting from the radical use of big data for addressing disease prevention through focusing on preventable and often socially produced risk factors (Barrett et al, 2013). While the quantified health subject has thus far been exploited for neoliberal purposes of profiting from an individual's and community's physical and mental well-being (or more precisely, their lack thereof), it can also be applied to delivering community-based approaches that transparently measure and analyze data that would improve their collective health.

The idea, then, of complete openness or closure is impossible given the mobility of power and the virality of hegemony. Rather, transformations occur in the shift from social to political counting – the creation of new ways to imagine social relations and fresh networks for the realization of this radical vision. Taking again the example of big data, while it certainly can contribute, and has contributed, to the suppression of democratic forces and further power inequalities, it also has the potential to be far more radical and disruptive in the name of justice. Arora (2019) depicts, to this effect, the growth of 'benign dataveillance' in India and China, observing that standard Orwellian visions of data surveillance exist in parallel with constructive and not necessarily unwelcome data-driven approaches to public governance. A more critical approach would, by contrast, 'situate these techno-developments in the long and complex socio-cultural legacies in both regions'. Doing so not only provides a deeper understanding of these mobile and infectious discourses but could also highlight their potential for locally and even globally radically transforming 'what constitutes as social inclusion, free market participation and citizen rights in this digital and global age' (Arora, 2019).

It would be absurd, of course, to ignore the ways that such data collection and analysis are being used for more insidious purposes by the authoritarian and illiberal status quos in these contexts. Nonetheless, these help uncover uses of big data that, within these infectious contexts, could breed contagions of serious change. The example of the biometric registration, which began as part of the Unique Identity Project created by the Indian government to collect a range of personalized biometric and demographic data about citizens, is a case in point. While the programme has been rightly criticized for reducing civic society to a set of marketized relations for monitoring and promoting values of capitalist growth and state security (see Sarkar, 2014), it has served as a means for ensuring that those who have traditionally been socially marginalized are now officially counted and recognized and can have their needs better met and served by authorities (Arora, 2019). Though originally voluntary, once it became compulsory in 2012 the perhaps obvious fear was that it would be used as a force for disciplining populations to reflect dominant values. Yet it has also been viewed as a 'welcome intervention' for strengthening elite accountability. Indeed, in principle if not always in practice, the system served as a basis for supposedly investing resources where they were most needed and as a point on which to politically question elites when this failed to occur. The continued problems experienced by the system are certainly attributable, in part, to elites, but are also due to more prosaic issues of 'weak computational facilities, chronic power shortages, inconsistent connectivity and [there being] no legal recourse to reclaim hijacked identities that end up excluding genuine beneficiaries' (Arora, 2019). This is particularly interesting as it reveals the potential for individuals and groups to move beyond sovereign paradigms of power and authority and instead begin focusing on how they could systemically and practically repurpose and improve data collection resources and techniques to more empowering ends.

Represented, in turn, is the imperative and ongoing need to not simply open up knowledge but to pluralize its sources, movements and possibilities. This pluralization of knowledge exceeds the bounds of conventional liberal perspectives, which focus increasingly merely on its diversity. Yet, as the focus in this analysis on mobility and virality exposes, a key aspect of the knowledge/power dynamic is precisely the encouragement of dominant discourses to embrace variation and difference. Lupton critically exposes this hegemonic reliance on diversity in his pioneering work on the quantified self, claiming that, far from being monolithic, it actually exists in an ever-expanding set of 'diverse domains' composed of a 'range of actors and agencies in diverse contexts' (Lupton, 2016, p 101). Paradoxically, it is exactly in the diversification of such quantified knowledge that it becomes universal and almost compulsory, able and now expected to proliferate sets of social fields 'including the workplace, education, medicine and public health, insurance, marketing and commerce, energy sustainability initiatives, the military, citizen science and urban planning and management" (Lupton, 2016, p 103).

Instead of simply demanding more information or greater diversity in available knowledge, it is crucial to create sustainable contagious networks for the incubation and spread of alternative social imaginaries and counterpublics. This can mean allowing for and fostering what can be called 'dormant contagions'– the production of alternative networks that, while relatively benign to the status quo in the present, have the capacity to be disruptive in the future. This radical dormancy is seen, for instance, in how the perceived ultimate failures of the Occupy Movement gave birth to the 'viral growth of a connective action network ... [which] still exists and is not entirely quiescent' (Hemsley, 2016). Like the 'insurgent public spheres' discussed previously, these have the capacity to be remobilized for supporting new struggles and forging novel radical connections.

These insights open up the potential for creating contagious knowledges. These are imagined and lived alternatives that draw upon the multiplicity of networks to foster challenges to an existent status quo and encourage novel interpersonal and social relations. Such contagions are both ideologically imaginative and radically connective. These can, and often do, start as localized forms of contagion with incipient global ambitions. A present-day instance of such a possible contagious knowledge would be the collaborative production of a 'post-capitalist collaborative commons'. In particular, this entails allowing people to upscale their 'momentary alternative impulses' into a global vision for how to topple and supplant the international capitalist order (Gerhardt, 2020, p 681). These potentially contagious glimpses of an emancipatory future can be found in the establishment of 'autonomous zones' within cities (often at what is otherwise the epicentre of these capitalist systems), which apply revolutionary values to addressing and radically solving local injustices – ranging from anarchist mutual aid services in support of the homeless (Heynen, 2010) to the use of squatter principles for creating affordable housing (Chatterton, 2002) to interactive spaces for experimenting with DIY sustainability practices (Carlsson and Manning, 2010; see also Gerhardt, 2020, p 684). Yet, to be effective, these 'site-specific' disruptions must be conjoined with an internationally oriented reimagination and reordering of the global order itself. Doing so will necessarily involve a profound political reconnection with one another. Such efforts are already witnessed in the rise of the 'collaborative commons network' which relies upon a range of non-capitalist methods including open-source knowledge exchange, crowdfunding and peer-to-peer production such as 3D printing to create transnational supply chains and voluntary economic relationships between local anarchist and socialist groups across the world (Gerhardt, 2020. This reflects the broader recognition that 'realizing a successful transition to a post-capitalist, commons-based political economy will not only depend on the capacity for new technologies and social relations to alter the balance of political and economic power; it will also depend on developing social practices that underlie a broader cultural shift" (Day, 2017, p 1). Here the local dismantling of existent power relations provides the impetus for discovering radical capabilities and capacities for concretely transforming the social.

These are also catalyzed by ongoing sparks of contagion, continual flickers that it may be possible to live otherwise than we are currently. This speaks to the need to develop resistance networks such as 'insurgent public spheres' or 'connective action networks' into sustainable movements to disruptively create novel types of economies and societies. The discovery of local capabilities evolves into contagious capacities for diverse actors and communities to disrupt and radically recreate their own environments. This is not to be naïve, of course, or to assume that the mere knowledge that others are doing so will suddenly alleviate all localized power structures and barriers. But what it does accomplish is to shift the question from innovation to disruption, from how to best improve and reform a mobile status quo to why it exists in the first place and how is it preventing people from existing otherwise in more egalitarian and freer ways.

Critically, this reflects the progressive import of open-sourced forms of resistance and contagion. In the mobile age of viral information, openness has shifted from simply a more inclusive and less censored public space to the cultivation of new, more equitable and transparent ways to produce, share and use information and potentially our concrete existence. Thus, just as mobile technologies have been used to highlight mobile power, so too have open-source technologies been used to help foster contagious knowledge. The creation of open data can therefore put into question not only who counts but fundamentally how we should be counted. At the very least, open-source models of participation rooted in digitally aided, real-time knowledge exchange and problem-solving can help reinvigorate conventional representative democracy. Perhaps more importantly, they serve as an incipient political framework and culture for collectively enacting contagious revolutionary change. Indeed, instead of either embracing or challenging traditional liberalism or deliberative variants of democracy, these activists stress how these democratic practices should be 'flexible' so that 'the inclusion and coordination of citizens' voluntary, "self selective participation" should be adapted to the issue at hand and to the local context' (Baack, 2015, p 5).

This is not to assume that technology is merely a tool. Rather it is to highlight that, just as it creates new forms of viral agency for spreading infectious discourse, it can also enhance the potential to foment, experiment with and promote contagious counter-knowledges. Through cultivating novel proficiencies in using such civic data and technologies, these actors are able to repurpose them for pursuing their radical agenda. This contagious agency can encompass the use of these mobile applications in rather traditional ways as resources for lobbying or reappropriating existing digital platforms for crowdfunding ideas, resources and projects. Crucially, the cultivation of these resistance capabilities ultimately provides the inspiration and confidence for these communities to develop novel capacities that seek not merely to reform the existing system but to reinvent it. This bears witness to emergent cultures of 'political hacking' that foreshadow the rise of guerrilla democracy to be introduced in the next chapter. In this respect, it is notable that 'to datafy a phenomenon is to re-materialize it into a highly modifiable form: in its essence, data is structured information that can be analysed, edited, and combined with other data' (Baack, 2015, p 8).

Equally significant is how these contagious gestures can serve to reverse the boundaryless/bounded dynamic characteristic of hegemonic epidemics, especially in the contemporary period of mobile neoliberalism. Viral infections, in this regard, bind people in specific ideological limits, while expanding the scope of how these delimited values and principles can diversely shape and discipline their existence. By contrast, revolutionary contagions inject an ethos of boundarylessness, both in terms of our ideologies and connections. They open the potential for going beyond these discursive limits while forging new networks for their radical realization. Hence, they provide the foundation for the creation of contagious counterpublics that combine imagination and connection (Dahlberg, 2011). These counterpublics deprioritize individual actions, instead emphasizing how digital media forges novel political networks for fostering diverse struggles and points of contestation. The democratic subject then is 'constituted through engagement in such group formation, activism, and contestation' (Dahlberg, 2011, p 860). At stake, again, is not to see technology as neutral but to assess its various possibilities within contexts and via virtual and IRL networks to build up resistances and spread disruptive contagions. In terms of resistance and revolution,

> digital media is seen as enabling voices excluded from dominant discourses to do three interrelated things with respect to democratic politics: to form counter-publics and counter-discourses; to link up with other excluded voices in developing representative, strategically effective counter-discourses; and

subsequently to contest the discursive boundaries of the mainstream public sphere. (Dahlberg, 2011, p 861)

Activism, in turn, becomes transformed and rechannelled into constructing new 'publics' whose commonality is not race, ethnicity or even consumer preference but a commitment to halting hegemonic epidemics and opening the way for alternative relations to emerge and spread. The figure of the civic hacker is in some ways emblematic of this shift. Their power is not necessarily in their proficiency as coders (as it is often portrayed in popular media programmes like *Mr. Robot*) but in their capacity 'to ease societal suffering by bringing the hidden workings of abstract systems to light and improv[ing] their functioning' (Shrock, 2016, p 594). In doing so, they are also able to expose 'contagious openings' for discovering fundamentally different ways of living and relating with one another.

This constructive form of political deconstruction of the social is perhaps especially important as domination itself becomes seemingly ever more decentred. This may be a precursor to reactionary desires for individuals to 'recentre' themselves, linked to essentialized identities of race, ethnicity, religion and nationalism. By contrast, it could also be an opportunity to embrace this fragmentation, to view it as the very welcome force necessary for allowing a reimagining of the social and reconnecting it across diverse political spaces. It may just also be the grounding for a new and more radical practice of democracy aimed at building up resistances to infectious strains of domination and proliferating contagious revolutions.

Conclusion

This chapter has introduced into this analysis the concepts of viral innovations and disruptive contagions. Building on the insights which have preceded it, it eschews conventional conceptions of the social as 'stable' and the political as 'dynamic'. Fundamentally, it takes seriously the fact that power is always necessarily mobile and that therefore any and all social orderings will be in a constant state of flux and reconstitution. Moreover, it understands hegemony as a viral discursive that is marked primarily by its contextual adaptability as opposed to ideological uniformity or 'actually existing homogeneity'. To be clear, these postulations are a far cry from asserting the total randomness of the social or its complete variability. On the contrary, they show how a relatively coherent set of logics can be flexibly customized and 'infect' otherwise contrasting host contexts. Its strength, hence, is found in its infectious qualities, not necessarily or even primarily in its orthodoxy. Practically, this mobility of power and virality of hegemony translate into dominant cultures of constant innovation rooted in the social production of 'cultural environments' which must be creatively and continuously improved upon by their populace (and if necessary by outside actors). These innovative cultural environments extend from physical spaces, digital networks, to internal subjectivities. They proliferate into epidemics precisely in how they begin to constitute hegemonic networks of innovation and knowledge sharing; 'global assemblages', as Aihwa Ong so aptly describes them.

The purpose and character of resistance must then be to disrupt these innovative and adaptive systems of hegemony. These movements and events act to fundamentally put into question the 'problems' we are meant to be solving, why we been tasked to solve them, whose interests it serves, and what alternative problems could we collectively pose and practically address that would allow us to think, live and relate radically differently. If domination is infectious, then revolution is contagious. More precisely, while viral hegemony is, at its core, marked by the infectious and flexible mutation of global ideologies to reflect localized conditions, viral forms of counter-hegemony are characterized by local disruptions that can spread across the world – not merely as isolated paradigms of 'existing otherwise' but as interconnected networks for its mass but diversified achievement. Doing so involves seeking out 'contagious openings' and cultivating novel skills for the sake of incubating these revolutionary 'glocal contagions'.

Tellingly, counter-hegemony is not completely distinct from hegemony or its broader dynamics of social ordering. Both revolve around the discursive production of contexts for experimentation, adaptation and growth. At stake, though, is whether these contexts will simply reproduce culturally essentialist identities which incubate inequalities and foster racialized, colonized, and marketized subjects and subjectivities or if they can be repurposed, reopened and reinvented for forging novel connections between actors and 'things' to inoculate populations against such dominant infections and develop revolutionary capabilities for transforming their world. It also opens up, theoretically and practically, the possibilities for reconceiving and rebooting democracy – shifting away from its traditional focus on sovereign elections, popular representation, power-sharing or even fostering radical disagreement and instead focusing on its opportunities and capacities for reimagining and rematerializing the world.

5

Guerrilla Democracy

As part of a campaign at Picturehouse Cinemas in the UK, workers experimented with a new form of digital activism. As Kelly Rogers, one of the organizers, explained, "We are going to start pushing cyber-pickets ... where supportive members of the public who can't come down to a picket line spend their day block booking seats and keeping them in the online basket, so they can't be sold on tills or online." She argued that this "makes the strike much more effective when they keep cinemas open on strike days – and Hackney had managed to keep their cinema pretty much empty this way!" (quoted in Caramazza, 2019). In response, the Picturehouse sacked Rogers. She fought this later and was found to have been unfairly dismissed.

In a particularly amusing blog post from an employment law solicitor, Toby Porchon (2019), who provides legal advice to businesses, he warns of the risks of 'cyber picketing'. He argues that it 'ha[s] the potential to be vastly more detrimental than simply calling for a boycott. Or even standing in front of their premises so members of the public [can] make their own decisions about which business they choose to support.' He observes that 'this practice would have prevented unaware customers from being able to make bookings without ever knowing why.' Equally, in the case of Picturehouse, it meant the cinema could have been open and operating with full staff but without customers 'coming through the door'. To this end, he notes that 'the cyber picket could have happened at any time without anyone really knowing when. Such is the nature of a remote or diffuse style of disruption.' However, he also points to some advantages this type of digital activism may hold for workers. As Porchon explains: 'At least with a strike the employer has the ability to not pay staff who aren't providing services. And they'd have been forewarned their operations were going to be undermined on a set day, for a set purpose.'

Although he pitches this as advice to businesses, it could also serve as useful advice for workers to adopt new forms of struggle: 'Such tactics would be similar to disruption that could be caused to a lot of online retailers or web-based businesses ... The judgement in this case [against Picturehouse] did not go so far as to rule on whether cyber picketing is actually lawful or not. It focused on why Ms Rogers was dismissed and found that this was the sending of the email only.' For this reason, he predicts that 'cyber picketing may become more prevalent for those employers with a unionised workforce. The issue being that it is inherently subversive.'

From infectious democracy to radical democratic 'resituating'

These struggles may seem, on first glance, to be rather small instances of digital subversion. Yet they represent profound and dramatic possibilities for reimagining and reconnecting 21st-century democracy. This chapter will present the growing infusion of mobile activism with a transformative guerilla ethos. It signals how democracy can expand from the ballot boxes to build up localized resistances to hegemonic viral infections and foster contagious virtual networks of 'glocal' revolutionary change. For this purpose, it seeks to 'repoliticize' and, as such, 'reradicalize' democracy. If democracy is to be more than just a force for hegemonic innovation it must take seriously the possibility of transforming present social relations. It is, if you will, highlighting the often ignored existential aspects of democracy (both theoretically and in practice), revealing its power to collectively alter the very basis of our shared existence while continually unveiling its fundamental contingency and alterability.

Crucial for such a completely democratic rethinking is to consider the type of practical ethics and skills required for individuals to engage in these types of disruptive experiments. Contemporary perspectives on 'aversive democracy' proposed by Aletta Norval do much to help in this regard, as they are premised not on simply defending existing democratic institutions or merely allowing for new views and voices to be heard but rather on the possibility for people to actively engage in seeing themselves and society fundamentally differently. Again as with the processes of political reimagining highlighted in Chapter 1, this is not a matter of mere speculation but also of praxis. A historical example may be the now-famous rise of skating culture in the US among kids in California (part of the Dogtown crew), repurposing empty swimming pools and abandoned concrete urban spaces as organic skate parks.

What would make this transformation not a simple guerrilla act but a democratic one is how it could open up novel collective rethinkings and policies around who 'owns' the city and how private property could be evolved into vibrant 'shared spaces'. To this end, these ideas resonate with Alain Badiou's notion of 'the situation'— how a given society is structured around certain 'truths' and how new truths can lead to a 're-situating' of these orders.

Absolutely critical, then, is to explore the theories and praxis that encourages such 'democratic resituating'. It is a question of the ways in which certain events and guerrilla interventions can permit us to think about how we could be politically 'counted' differently, and as such can allow us to create radically different social situations. Just as Badiou highlights how a given situation repeatedly counts us as a subject of a certain 'historical truth' in ever-newer (though fundamentally similar) ways, so too does power remobilize us as innovative actors, constantly discovering new contexts in which it can spread and evolve. Guerrilla acts that interrupt such remobilizing not only hold out the possibility of reordering and reconnection but allow us to make a decision about what type of existential situation and according to which structuring 'truths' we would like to live within.

The threat of infectious democracy

This book has emphasized the implications of the fundamental mobility of power and the virality of social ordering in practice. It has shown how these foundational aspects have taken on special import due to the prevalence of mobile technologies. The question of democracy, thus, holds a rather paradoxical place in such an analysis. By its very nature, it speaks to the changeability of the social. Conversely, the very instantiation of democracy represents the standardization through which such popular transformations may or may not happen. Accordingly, democracy is at once infectious and contagious – hegemonic and counter-hegemonic.

Its potential for domination, in this respect, exists at two distinct but interconnected levels. Firstly, its own internal values and processes can be hegemonic, its own 'common sense' for regulating popular participation and decision-making coming at the expense of other democratic values and practices. More precisely, the defining of what constitutes a 'legitimate democracy' necessarily renders 'illegitimate' or invisible alternative democratic ideas and practices. Equally significantly, it can provide ideological and procedural legitimacy to quite dominating economic and social discourses in support of an existent status quo, through a form of 'managed democracy', whereby the levers of state, media and civil society are mobilized to restrict the available choices within a narrow ideological window. Democracy can be said to be an epidemic when its presence is used for spreading this 'deeper' hegemony throughout a host context and to others.

Neoliberalism is perhaps a perfect example of an infectious democracy. Its introduction was linked to the ending of formal political authoritarianism in a range of contexts, notably Latin America, the former Soviet states and the non-aligned but previously socialist Yugoslavia. Yet these processes of democratization were contained within the extraordinarily narrow ideological boundaries of the free market. Writing in the mid-1990s, Conaghan and Malloy note that this political opening was ironically coupled with an economic 'narrowing' as 'political arrangements were to be restructured around principles of competition, participation, and representation' (Conaghan & Malloy, 1995, p 4). The events of the proceeding decades have only made starker the need to build up political resistances to this neoliberal democratic epidemic, where a separation of people from control over their economies and everyday lives has gone hand in hand with a formal, if managed, 'democracy'. This requires reinvigorating democracy as a force for existential, ideological and material change. The 'start of a political future beyond neoliberalism' requires, according to Holloway, prioritizing 'destituent' over 'constituent' forms of power. 'Whereas constituent power attempts to reform one's government through demonstrations in public space' declares Holloway, "destituent power abandons the project of reforming one's government momentarily or even completely in order to experience another form of life entirely' (Holloway, 2018, p 627).

Critically, democracy has always been both a hegemonic infection and a revolutionary contagion. The modern roots of liberal democracy from the Enlightenment onward reveal this contentious and commonly contradictory past. Israel (2009) distinguishes the Enlightenment from the 'Radical Enlightenment' for this reason, contending that the former represents 'the system of ideas that, historically, has principally shaped the Western World's most basic social and cultural values', including 'democracy; racial and sexual equality; individual liberty of lifestyle; full freedom of thought, expression, and the press; eradication of religious authority from the legislative process and education; and full separation of church and state' (Israel, 2009, p viii). Yet the radical implications of these Enlightenment values are continually subverted by other Enlightenment principles ranging from elitism masked as meritocracy to the use of science to justify social hierarchies.

Fast-forward to the late 20th century and these opposing forces were still on display, though with an added twist of profound historical irony. The more reactionary elements tapped into the revolutionary spirit of the age in order to recast their own conservative programme as a revolution in its own right. Duggan laments this turn of events, describing the liberation movements of the 1960s as ones that inspired hope but which were ultimately hijacked, proclaiming that struggles for civil rights, women's liberation, gay liberation and anti-imperialism 'were producing innovative critiques on a widening variety of constraints on human possibility' (Duggan, 2012, p ix). She notes that 'despite all the internal tensions and conflicts, it also seemed possible that cross-fertilisations would excite exponential growth in the scope and impact of our shared or overlapping visions of social change' (Duggan, 2012, p ix). Present was a moment of contingency, whereby a hegemonic articulation could have gone in several different directions, and the dual attempt to both politically reimagine and reconnect the social should not therefore be so lightly dismissed. However, much of this revolutionary ethos is now found in the movements of the far right with the promise to rescue those 'left behind' by globalization and completely transform the present status quo.

An important component of the paradoxically hegemonic dimension of democracy is the role of technologies promising to expand political participation and civic engagement for critically reinforcing dominant ideologies and power relations such as those linked to neoliberalism. New 'civic tech', for instance, extols the value of ICTs for reinvigorating civic debate and community-public consultations. Yet, in practice, this is often also a space for spreading infectious hegemonic values via these rebooted democratic technologies. Indeed, their novelty is commonly underpinned by rather conventional and conservative appeals to centrist values, with any change restricted to ameliorating, at best, the harsher edges of neoliberal governance. Crucially, this is driven by consultants who largely consider their work as 'enabling healthy democratic participation to build strong communities and uplift individual voices' while also promoting 'a moderate, centrist stance perceived as frequently absent from many public engagement programs' (Brabham & Guth, 2017, p 462). Hence, their idealism is mixed with the deployment of these technologies and democratic techniques to reinforce dominant norms and principles associated with the free market and a notion of civic engagement modelled on consumer feedback. Consequently, 'through their civic technologies, designers of the consultative layer discipline communication in support of some democratic ideals more than others in and on behalf of society' (Brabham & Guth, 2017, p 462).

This critique, of course, is not meant to dismiss the potential importance of civic tech wholesale. Rather, it is meant to highlight the need to understand how such innovations can be used to restrict the overall capacity of democracy to effect wider social, economic and political change; in particular, to include it as part of a broader forensic analysis of how certain democratic norms contribute to the viral spread of hegemonic values and regimes. The need for this type of viral analysis of the infectiousness of democracy (and its contagious possibilities) is evident in ongoing discussions concerning deliberative democracy. Neoliberalism, by definition, stands opposed to meaningful deliberative democracy, drawing us away from forums and processes that require collectives to make sense of their shared norms and demands for a communal good, instead favouring individual units of shareholding and home-owning citizens to express preferences through markets. Yet deliberative forums can be employed piecemeal and superficially and used to manipulate or restrict democratic choice – the kind of mixing of 'strategic' norms (those of personal or instrumental gain) with communicative norms (those that represent moral claims) that Habermas (1996) warns us is anathema to a healthily functioning deliberative practice. Such practice should be constituted by communicative action that established the moral direction of a community. As Fishkin and Mansbridge presciently observe, 'The ideal of democracy as the rule of "the people" is deeply undermined when the will of the people is in large part manufactured' (Fishkin & Mansbridge, 2017, p 7). For this reason, they maintain that 'if current democracies cannot produce meaningful processes of public will formation, the legitimacy claims of meritocratic autocracies or even more fully autocratic systems become comparatively stronger' (Fishkin & Mansbridge, 2017, p 7). Search as one might for superficial and conspiratorial reasons for the UK's Brexit vote, such as Russian manipulation or shadowy internet psy-ops, a simultaneously more straightforward and complex answer is that a large swathe of people had been starved of meaningful deliberative forums, and as such their political or economic education left them ill-equipped to judge the 'validity claims' (Habermas, 1984) of either side, preferring in the end the hard-right nationalist neoliberals to the faceless neoliberal bureaucrats of the political 'centre'.

If not part of the systemic fabric of a nation state or organization, deliberative forms of democracy soon transition from disruptive discourses to an epidemic 'strategic' science, creating an increasingly refined framework for providing the status quo with formal popular legitimacy (though with often rather unpredictable results – for example, populist backlashes such as Brexit). Nevertheless, in theory, deliberation can also have much more radical effects, ones which mix a popular mandate with the use of empirical evidence that can challenge the status quo's assumptions. For Fishkin and Mansbridge, this democratic renewal is rooted in and primarily revolves around traditional forms of public deliberation which in principle produce policies which they theorize will be not only more inclusive but evidence based. However idealistic and perhaps unrealistic this may appear, it does point to the contagious potentialities of even conventional democratic engagements, as here these discussions can become – again in theory more than in practice – not just explorations of the best policy solutions but also cultures of shared discovery for reimagining what is politically possible and fostering new social connections to concretely realize these expanded possibilities. The fact that we can name these outcomes as possible indicates the contingency of the social, which is grounds enough to redouble our conceptual and practical efforts.

Required, therefore, is the reframing of democratic history and, as such, theory – exploring the transitions from epidemic infections to revolutionary contagions (and back again). Doing so acts, at the very least, to situate our present democratic situation as a contingent historical phenomenon that is premised on formal equality, human rights and a market economy. Here, according to Ayers and Saad-Filho, 'Political community is understood in terms of nation-states, constituted by three domains – the neoliberal "minimal" and "neutral" state, the neoliberal public sphere ("civil society"), and the neoliberal individual ("self")' (Ayers and Saad-Filho, 2015, p 598). Yet this democratic infection associated with the spread of neoliberalism also serves to catalyze new democratic resistances within infected populations, as witnessed by the large-scale rejection of elections and political elites in 'advanced' Western democracies. To this end, it is the very instantiation of an infectious democracy, and the threat of it becoming a hegemonic epidemic, that fuels the need and desire for building up counter-hegemonic resistances and contagious alternatives. Through showing the limits of 'freedom' and 'agency', the boundaries of our social imagination and connections, their potential for being transcended becomes both more longed for and tangible.

This history of democracy is, of course, rich and varied. In the present age, it is progressively derided as unable to fully address the myriad of problems associated with contemporary capitalism. Yet our analysis hopes to show that there remain glimmers of possibility for democracy even within our severely managed neoliberal forms. The promotion of democracy and its expansion can be both infectious and contagious. New theoretical insights and understanding are therefore imperative for ensuring its contagiousness and to stave off its infections.

(Re)radicalizing democracy

In many ways, the 20th century can be considered the apogee of global democracy. It saw the spread of liberal values and elections across the world, coming in various waves to all continents. Yet it also revealed the precise limitations of this dominant democratic order – showing how it was not an antidote to chronic problems of inequality, poverty and political repression (see Bloom, 2016). In support of this statement we can offer the authoritarian managed democracies of Hungary, Turkey, Russia, the former Soviet states and most of the former Yugoslavia, in addition to the militarized coups removing democratically elected socialist regimes in Latin America. The parallel failures of 20th-century, notionally Marxist but in truth brutish regimes are hardly case studies in vibrant democracy, and have spurred efforts to reimagine the form and purposes of 'actually existing' democracy.

Perhaps one of the most celebrated of these attempts is Chantal Mouffe's notion of radical democracy. She offers a new framework that builds on liberal democratic traditions and signifiers in order to propose an ethos of what we refer to in this work as 'creative deconstruction'. In particular, this aims to infuse established democratic processes and liberal rights with a renewed emphasis on contestation and the fundamental questioning of existent identities, one that views political identities such as 'citizenship' as 'something to be constructed, not empirically given' (Mouffe, 1992, p 231). In a certain sense, it is possible to view Mouffe's project (and the desire to radicalize democracy generally) as the evolution from democratic innovation to democratic disruption. Indeed, Mouffe envisions her ideas as a means for reinvigorating and redirecting the emancipatory promises of the Enlightenment and modernity. For her, the fundamental challenge to existent social and political relations is, in fact, an attempt to revive 'the Enlightenment project of self-foundation' and its ultimate goals of achieving 'freedom and equality for all' (Mouffe, 1989, p 34). In this respect, she desires to plant the theoretical seeds for a new type of democratic politics that does not simply improve on what has come before it but fundamentally transforms it via concrete social struggles that coalesce into a viable 'democratic alternative' (Mouffe, 1995, p 316).

Yet there remain serious questions about just how 'radical' radical democracy in fact is – both in concept and practice. For thinkers such as Martin (2013, p 2), the real contribution of this approach is its renewed emphasis on disagreement over traditional liberal democratic desires for consensus, whereby disagreement and conflict rather than consensus are seen as 'the fundamental source of its virtues'. Nonetheless, its retention of core liberal principles and procedures, albeit as contingent signifiers inviting dissensus, puts into question whether radical democracy is building up resistances to its less desirable qualities or if it is genuinely aiming to expand existing democratic imaginaries. Rather than being merely an either/or proposition, it is perhaps better to approach this as a critical and productive tension within any radical struggle – one which includes and incorporates both resistance and revolutionary energies and aspirations. This tension is captured, for instance, in current global struggles against neoliberalism. Ishkanian and Glasius (2018) find that protest movements ranging from places as far afield as Cairo, Athens and London have a similar complex dynamic of commonality and difference in terms of their critiques and demands. Looking in particular at the so-called Squares Movement, they assert that what made these protests radically democratic was not necessarily the radicality of their positions or even their ideology (which in fact was not monolithic by any means) but rather how they translated differences into incipient cultures of solidarity and mutual aid. As such, they stress these 'attempts to construct alternative economic and societal models, rather than just practices of resistance to neoliberalism' (Ishkanian and Glasius, 2018, p 528).

The deeper democratic struggle is how to transition from building up resistances to hegemonic infections into devising contagious forms of revolutionary reimagination and reconnection. The articulation and expansion of a 'radical democratic imaginary' must take as one of its founding principles that 'political struggles do not merely realign already fully constituted subjects. Every struggle entails the far more profound process of working with partially formed popular identities and reconstructing them according to the values of the warring forces' (Smith, 2012, p 151). Yet it also reveals how deeply sedimented the liberal ethos of reformism and innovation remains – rooted in the dominant and ultimately dominating conception of politics as one perpetually defined by managed conflict between erstwhile 'enemies'. Thus, Mouffe is prescient in her diagnosis of the affliction of liberal democracy while also offering an opportunity for considering a radically new type of political engagement. According to Roskamm, it is a direct and potent challenge to a prevailing democratic 'politics of consensus and cessation' in which 'the dominant ideology is to claim that there is no alternative – no alternative to the primacy of the economic (managerialism, profit-maximisation, over-expansion, growth orientation, etc.), and no alternative to the existing world of inequality' (Roskamm, 2015, p 385).

The danger, though, is the temptation to concentrate more on resistance than on revolution, the inoculation as opposed to the new contagion, if you will. Returning to Roskamm, he points to this issue in his characterization of how Mouffe differentiates 'politics' from 'the political', maintaining that ' "Politics" is the realm of planning, of data, of society; "the political" is a modus of being, a paradox foundation consisting of contingency and antagonism'. Ultimately, he is doubtful of Mouffe's fundamental project 'to bring both categories together: to import antagonism theory from the sphere of the political into the realm of politics' (Roskamm, 2015, p 397). However, such criticisms are somewhat unfair, as ultimately any political moment or act, if it is to engender change, must eventually work through some form of politics, even if only to revolutionize this politics. Such is the emphasis in Mouffe's more recent work, where she emphasizes the importance of left-populist movements to transform politics (Mouffe, 2019). Of course, such a porousness between the more radical and democratic political activities of movements holding the potential to revolutionize politics seems like a fragile project, one that in recent years offered moments of possibility in European countries, only to be extinguished and smothered by the politics of the status quo (Sinha et al, 2019). Yet even in their failure there remains a hopeful question – in their temporary setbacks it is suddenly asked once again, even more forcefully: How else can radical democratic change ever be instituted?

Nevertheless, the main thrust of radical democracy, at present, is towards treating the viral infection of democracy, not so much returning the patient to some pre-existing state (for example, pre-1980s social democracy) but building itself a new, transformed patient. While we do not accept the critiques of Mouffe's work as a capitulation to extant liberal democracy, we do recognize that its key foundations require further development so that we can recast democracy to better reflect its viral origins and contagious possibilities. Required for doing so is a reconsideration of the concept and practice of 'antagonisms' in light of notions of mobile power, viral ordering and the infectious/contagious character of hegemony and counter-hegemony, respectively.

'Glocal' antagonisms

The role of antagonisms has been central to contemporary critical understandings of hegemony. Mouffe, for her part, distinguishes between antagonism and agonism, with the former associated with (sometimes violent) conflict aimed at destroying an 'enemy', whereas the latter refers to conflictual engagement that (loosely) abides by the liberal democratic values of liberty and equality and treats others as adversaries to be respected and defeated (Mouffe, 2013). Distinctions between agonism and antagonism are not so straightforward in practice, however, and there is always the possibility of the political spilling into antagonism or reverting to agonism (Smolović Jones et al, 2020). Furthermore, we cannot dismiss the fact that institutions of liberal democracy may be unresponsive or not even recognize legitimate agonistic engagements. Oftentimes, agonism between equals is impossible without a preceding antagonism operating outside what could be strictly considered the 'proper' channels of liberal democracy or even the law. Forceful insistence upon equality – such as the illegal occupation of public spaces or the tumbling of statues of slavers, often labelled as 'vandalism' or 'lawlessness' by critics – is antagonistic precisely because agonistic engagement has proven time and again to be useless. For this reason, we maintain and defend the phraseology of antagonism, albeit from a position of advocating non-violent (when possible), if highly assertive and often dissensual, democratic practice.

The emergence of digital communities has provided new opportunities for virtual antagonisms – the use of social media to counter 'mainstream' knowledge, even if often in quite troubling and reactionary ways. The popular condemnation of 'fake news' is indicative of this broader virtual politics that eschews consensus and is built on mistrust of established institutions and elites. According to Farkas and Schou, it 'has become a deeply political concept used to delegitimise political opponents and construct hegemony' (Farkas & Schou, 2018, p 300). Significantly, the appeal of these discourses is not exclusive to one ideology but rather feeds into a general distrust and dissatisfaction with the status quo that spans the ideological spectrum. While understandably the dominant focus of most commentators has been on the considerable damage caused by such a 'post-truth' society, it also gestures towards a more fundamental threat to conventional liberal democracies. It puts to the test the very credibility of claims that society is or can be fundamentally improved within the current system. It undermines the daily ways that the status quo tries to imbue its continued existence with a sense of hope.

A crucial, though at times underexplored, aspect of capitalism, for instance, is the way in which, despite being *a priori* structurally exploitative, its everyday experience cannot be one of total oppression. Even the most hyper-marketized order must incorporate within itself spaces and times for feelings of success and enjoyment. This can range from the thrill of finding a new, 'better' job, to the sense of accomplishment in getting a 'well-deserved' promotion, to the continual hope one has for a peaceful and fulfilling retirement. It is these personal and collective achievable milestones that sustain the vision of capitalist progress and thus allow for its continual social and material reproduction. In the timely words of Eagleton-Pierce, 'The spirit of capitalism cannot exist as a fantasy which is never concretely realised: the system must, at least partially, follow through on its promises' (Eagleton-Pierce, 2016, p 49). Consequently, 'it is this potential to hold up tangible illustrations of "success", along with cultivating the hope that others may enhance themselves in ways that achieve similar success, which enables a refreshing of confidence in the melioristic disposition' (Eagleton-Pierce, 2016, p 49). This critique can also easily apply to contemporary democracies. The introduction of regular elections represents not merely the orderly transfer of power but an opportunity to feel as if the democratic process is 'working' and that progress is being made. It permits a sense of regulated change and the chance to remake society. Crucially, it reflects an insatiable desire for reform, highlighting a system that is still unfinished and can always be improved upon. The presence of the guerrilla and an ethos of insurgency, as is evident in the rise of a 'fake news' society, represents, by contrast, the widespread rejection of such 'progressive' beliefs. It is a testament to an acceptance that, in fact, the present system cannot be 'fixed' and that economic justice and political rights can no longer be obtained through normal means.

Theoretically, this speaks to the productive tension between agonism and antagonism. At first glance, this would seem to be a struggle between progressive engagement and destructive resistances. More precisely, agonism is a form of constructive deconstruction while antagonism is an instance of radical destruction. While it is tempting to oppose these concepts – and there are definitely points where Mouffe certainly does so in her own work – they are better understood as productive complements to one another (for example, it is unlikely that any authorities would pay heed to Black Lives Matter were it not for assertive, sometimes antagonistic and not strictly 'legal' street gatherings during a pandemic). In particular, it is precisely in the efforts to establish an agonistic politics globally, one built on contestation, consensus and inclusion, that the potential and necessity of antagonisms reveal themselves locally. Mouffe, in this respect, contends that 'political practice in a democratic society does not consist in defending the rights of preconstituted identities, but rather in constituting those identities themselves in a precarious and always vulnerable terrain' (Mouffe, 1995, p 261). The move from agonism to antagonism is a shift towards making people and identities vulnerable to forces from the social order itself: Breaking up with your identity is hard to do.

It is, therefore, worth reframing democracy as a form of disorientation and 're-engagement' rather than of disagreement and consensus. To this end, it concerns more than just the establishment of new 'friends' and 'enemies' or 'problems to be solved'. Instead, it is the political capacity to reimagine an existent order and in doing so find new ways to connect. Woodford (2016) refers explicitly to the emancipatory possibilities of such a 'disorienting democracy', describing the ability of people to adopt alternative social relations acts to break down the police order and introduce a radical rupture with existing knowledge. An emphasis on mobile power, furthermore, reveals the dangers of relying solely on agonism, as power is inherently multiple and pluralistic – thus revealing the remaining theoretical need for antagonisms not simply to disrupt a status quo (which can be achieved internally via agonism itself) but to reveal previously discarded and marginalized bodies and accounts of how we could exist otherwise. The mere assertion of difference in a given order, then, and a focus on disagreement within it, ignores the multiple realities that could emerge through the disruption of the present order and the commitment to discovering present and future alternatives.

The focus on agonism without the threat and potential for antagonism reflects the underlying dangers of viral infections in practice. The domination of hegemonic epidemics flows precisely from their transforming of ideologies into discourses that fuel multiple modes of existence within their narrow limits. The universalization of hegemony, in turn, is found exactly in its ability to be universally applicable and therefore seemingly infinitely pluralized and variable, or in capitalism's case, 'a near global level of shared norms, driven by the market logic of commodity and service production for profit and consumption' (Jones & O'Donnell, 2017, p 5).

Antagonisms, significantly, can help to articulate geographically dispersed and socially diverse discourses as a common infection whose logic must be multiply challenged. They serve as the reversal of hegemony, literally its countering, where the potential for discursive disruption is what drives the possibility of ideological replacement – the creation of a new imaginary horizon within which to conceive and reorganize the social. Consequently, antagonism is a spark of contagion, the promise of deconstruction and reconstruction – not merely the pluralization of the sensible but the 'redistribution of the sensible' proposed by Rancière (2013). The ethos of agonism is then supplemented by one of dissensus, allowing for a challenging and reordering of the sensible both ideologically and materially. Democracy exists, thus, in 'a space we use to order our perception of our world and how we connect our sensible experience to intelligible modes of interpretation' (Huault et al, 2014, p 33). In this way, 'creating a dissensus ... interrupts the order of the sensible' (Huault et al, 2014, p 23).

Antagonisms represent, then, a restlessness with the current system, a recognition that it is limited and, just as critically, can be transcended, expanded and transformed. It is at once a creative ideological disruption of hegemony, an inoculation against its infection and a disruptive creation of new social connections and relations. Arditi bears witness to this simultaneous dynamic of creative disruption and disruptive creation within present-day radical movements. He observes that while 'many faulted these revolts for their lack of plans and proposals', nonetheless, 'this criticism misses the point by confusing the disruption of the given with the task of reconfiguring it.' To this end, 'insurgencies are about saying "enough!", refusing to go on as before and opening up possibilities that may or may not prosper', he contends. 'They are the plan in the sense that they make a difference by moving the conversation, they are political performatives – participants start to experience what they strive to become – and vanishing mediators or passageways to something other to come', he adds (Arditi, 2014, p 113). Antagonism is less, in this regard, a programme of inscriptive change – though this can occur – and more an 'interruption' of the sensible – both in terms of that which is considered reasonable and knowable and how we experience the world as sensuous beings – and as such gestures towards the chance for its collective recreation. Such insurgencies thrive on an ethos of 'inventiveness' for 'tactics and practices devised by activists become part of a collective political know-how, a political jurisprudence that functions as a toolbox available for anyone to use' (Arditi, 2014, p 113). This collective know-how reflects the importance of developing contagious capabilities – ones that can concretely contribute to 'glocal' revolutions.

Crucially, these reflect an almost organic relationship between democracy and a commons-based economy, as these disruptive tactics and political skills become themselves mobile – continually being adapted to given situations and contexts. It would be a mistake, though, to exalt the insurgency, to assume that the movement itself and the radical creativity it unleashes is the entirety of what a revolutionary democratic gesture and order can and should be. At stake, instead, is the move from a viral epidemic to a contagious pandemic. Specifically, it is the geographic reversal of hegemony, which moves from the global to the local, to counter-hegemony, which spreads from the local to the global as alluded to in Chapter 4. Imperative to this purpose is our adopting a politics around what Hennessy calls 'local-izing', seeking to uncover global relationships of power and exploitation through establishing 'a way of seeing or knowing the world that imagines any social entity – for example, a collectively shared identity or social practice – to be simply a temporary occurrence or a provisional point of departure for defining the goals of emancipation' (Hennessy, 2017).

An interesting and important contemporary example of commons-based democracies is the Digital Democracy and Data Commons, which is a Barcelona-based pilot project 'that aims to construct legal, technological, and socioeconomic tools that allow citizens to take back control over their data and generate more common benefits out of them' (Anon, 2019). It draws its inspiration from the new participatory democracy platform Decidim, which allows for organizations and communities to collaboratively consult on initiatives and make collective decisions about them in real time through such hybrid techniques as digitally arranging face-to-face meetings, creating surveys, new proposals and interactive feedback mechanisms.

These efforts speak to a range of new 'digital-democracy' initiatives that can allow people to collaboratively share their expertise to directly propose and inform how resources should be spent in their area. A contemporary example of such digital democratization is the LabHacker/e-Democracia platform created by the Brazilian government in 2009. This 'political portal' is meant to allow citizens to directly engage with policies via public 'hack-a-thons' and wiki-like additions to draft bills. It also reconfigures, to a degree, traditional liberal democratic representation, as it has introduced legislative consultants who are meant to be 'technical translators' of online and IRL communities needs based on such digital participation – a role which also demands that they provide feedback to the communities themselves about how influential their input has been. Another, more direct, use of digital democracy is the 'Madam Mayor, I Have an Idea' programme instituted by the Parisian mayor Anne Hidalgo. The programme has allowed citizens to directly propose and vote upon how to invest up to €500 million in city-wide projects between 2014 and 2020. These have included the building of 40 vertical gardens, recycling centres and shared spaces for students and entrepreneurs.

Democracy then, at its most radical and counter-hegemonic, can be seen as a local intervention with global implications. Antagonisms reveal the limits of an infectious democracy and its ongoing 'glocal' impact. 'At a time when modern democracy and its institutions are coming under increasing scrutiny and challenge from citizens who feel disaffected and disconnected', according to an influential NESTA report on digital democracy (Simon et al, 2017, p 96), 'it is all the more important that tools which can help to alleviate those tensions are adopted and ways of working adapted to bridge the gap between citizens and those in power'. Yet this does return us to the danger of reifying 'site-specific' projects of emancipation – which was highlighted in Chapter 4 drawing on Gerhardt's (2020) insights regarding the need to overcome the isolation of local 'autonomous zones' through the creation of a transnational 'collaborative commons'. Similarly, how can these localized democratic interventions go global through fostering international peer-to-peer networks of participation, knowledge sharing and liberation? Indeed, the examples of Brazil and France discussed previously reveal the limits of focusing only on democracy as a form of inclusive 'high-quality' decision-making. Both countries, despite their democratic innovations, remain plagued by deeper structural problems related to capitalism, racism and patriarchy. The widening of participation did not ultimately dismantle these fundamental issues – as witnessed in the populist far-right victory in Brazil and the continual unrest against the centrist leadership of Macron in France – and indeed, if anything, revealed the need for a type of politics that can go beyond the mere 'hacking' of the system.

These types of democratic innovations, even ones that are viral and arguably, on first glance, ineffectual, nonetheless provide the space for reimagination and reconnection rather than simply deconstruction or destruction. They also spatialize and temporalize radical democracy. This resonates with earlier efforts by Massey (1995) to theorize 'radical democracy spatially' where 'social space can be conceptualised as constituted out of social relations, social interactions, and for that reason always and everywhere an expression and a medium of power' (p 284). For this reason, any and all spaces become politically negotiable, available to alteration, and sites for alternative social relations to be incubated in. Any radical democracy worthy of its name, or in fact any democracy period, in this regard, must always be willing to exceed itself. To put into question its hegemonic implications and its potential for creative disruptions.

Required, though, is a reframing of 'place' and 'geography', not in terms of socially constructed power relations but as living hosts evolving in relation to viral epidemics and the incipient threat of contagious pandemics. Sovereignty here, then, is the subjugation, the making of individuals into viral subjects, adaptable to hegemonic discourses and, when necessary, adapting them in turn. They must adapt to its principles, mutating their context to conform to its prerogatives. These infections then take on an almost mystical form in their transformation from mobile ideology to viral epidemic. In the case of neoliberalism, for example, the market was transformed from a set of knowable economic relations into 'a new supernatural entity that overwhelmed human comprehension, and to which man must bow' (Söderberg, 2018, np). Infectious democracies are similarly deified, granted an almost divine status as the sole way for ordering a just society. They are, therefore, exploitative rather than emancipatory – always seeking out innovative ways to embed themselves and take advantage of a given host context for the benefit of an existent status quo. Contagious democracy, by contrast, is necessarily unfinished, an antidote to the 'diseased' belief that our current mode of existence is permanent. Radical democracy must not, then, be simply inscriptive or interruptive but revelatory. Rather than merely building up resistances to these divine revelations, we can see antagonisms as exposing the limits of the social, the possibilities of the political.

'Glocal' antagonisms, accordingly, act to reorient, redistribute and ultimately resituate meaning. They articulate the concrete intersections of mobile power and the virality of a dominating discourse. As such, they forensically trace out infections, uncovering how they spread. An infectious democracy, then, is one where change is bounded within certain ideological limits, in which possibility is confined to particular social spaces. Kelty (2017) speaks about this in highlighting the danger of ironically having 'too much democracy in all the wrong cases', encompassing the workplace, public administration and international development. He notes that 'in all three places it is possible to see how the grammar of participation works: the normative enthusiasm for it, the anxiety about co-optation, and an array of other "grammatical" features that are used to make sense of participation' (Kelty, 2017, S78). Critically, new technologies have done little to change this grammar, for 'if anything, there is continuity between these past cases and contemporary "new media and new publics" that itself structures the grammatical case of participation today' (S78). Revealed, in turn, is that simply introducing more consultative processes or supposedly new participative technologies is neither sufficient nor always conducive for genuine democratization or radical change.

Democracy requires more than difference, it demands the possibility of transformation. Agonism, hence, can become, absent an antagonism or the threat of one, a type of epidemic situation, the expansion of a given hegemony both in terms of how it is included in its negotiation of power as well as in how far and deep it can spread within and across host contexts. By contrast, antagonisms reflect the process of contagious political 'desituating' and 'resituating' of the potential for reimagining and reconnecting of the social.

Guerrilla democracy

A central aim of this work is to promote the importance of a new democratic ethos focused on reimagination and reconnection. 'Glocal' antagonisms are imperative for such a project, in that they reveal the limits of existent democratic imaginaries and their supportive innovative networks. They also provide the impetus for the spreading of contagious possibilities. These insights echo, to a certain extent, the critical notion of truth and 'event' proposed by the French philosopher Alain Badiou, discussed in Chapter 3. He highlights a seemingly defining contradiction at the heart of Being, noting that, despite in fact inhabiting multiple ways of existing in the world, actual beings still insist on Being's singularity (Badiou, 2007). Using alternative language, while it is philosophically and even at points socially accepted that things could be otherwise, individuals largely accept their given historical circumstances as either inevitable or permanent. Accordingly, people are confined to a repetitive 'situation' of Being, one which repeats in ever-newer configurations a singular interpretation of and foundation for reality. The appearance of truth, by contrast, is an event for transcending this repetition towards a revolutionary new shared existence. Badiou declares that 'for the process of a truth to begin, something must happen. What there already is – the situation of knowledge as such – generates nothing other than repetition. ... A truth thus appears, in its newness, because an evental supplement interrupts repetition' (Badiou, 2007, p 62).

This philosophical intervention speaks to the political promise of contagious democracy. Hegemony is akin to a ceaselessly innovative situation, while counter-hegemony is the disruption of this infectious reality for ideologically and materially expanding existence. At stake, then, is not how dynamic a given social context is or could be. Indeed, the very mobility of power and virality of hegemony mean that domination is always in flux and is indeed paradoxically stronger for it. Ironically, it is only when a situation appears to be unreformable or completely unalterable that it becomes fully vulnerable to total systemic transformation. These insights provide, in turn, a more complicated picture of the 'realism' of hegemony – one captured in the brilliant analysis of the critical theorist Mark Fisher in his theories of 'capitalist realism'. His view, in this respect, is that people, ultimately, in the early 21st century have come to assume that capitalism cannot be fundamentally changed, that the only pragmatic thing to do is to accept it as a type of 'end of history', whether or not they morally or ethically support it. Yet this realism is not one of stagnation, as perhaps Fisher and his interpreters may have unduly highlighted. Instead it is a pragmatism rooted in the supposed capacity of people to personally negotiate and collectively improve on this otherwise permanent social reality. It is not surprising, therefore, that entrepreneurship would take on such importance – not only as an economic value but as a cultural life – as it represents a profound sense of individual and collective agency for innovating and improving a quite fixed ideological system of capitalism.

Viral logics represent at once the active denunciation of truth (that existence is multiple and could be otherwise) and its fervent embrace. More precisely, they reveal that things could be different – and in fact must be, given cultural specificities – while also channeling such multiplicity into rather narrow hegemonic boundaries based on dominant values and practices. An antagonism, then, is a truthful democratic gesture whereby that which was previously ignored, rejected or undiscovered becomes recognized as a new condition for possibility. Significantly, it is not merely the outlining of possibility, the presentation of an alternative, but a revelation of radical difference that can allow for the flowering of new possibilities. Hence, the occasion of truth is one of systemic disruption and contagious resituating.

Yet what makes it a democratic revolutionary event, rather than being merely counter-hegemonic, is that it does not simply reimagine the social but reconnects it in ways that perpetuate rather than close down these truthful possibilities. For Badiou, 'Being is power because it is strictly coextensive to the actualisation of the virtual and the virtualisation of the actual' (Badiou, 2007, p 193). Significantly, antagonism, if it is to be democratic, must, therefore, be more than the introduction of a disruptive truth. The fundamental character of social order is that it is at once mobile and viral; its adaptability and diverse spread is underpinned by underlying ideology. New truths will always emerge and replace older ones. While the toppling of one hegemony for another is certainly emancipatory in its own right, it is not necessarily liberating or democratic. By contrast, a democratic contagion is an event that resituates the social, which does not simply exchange one hegemon for another but alters the very contours, the underlying power relations, capabilities and communication, of the construction of order itself. Just as significantly, it is one that invests itself in a problemization of who is being counted and in what way. Thus the emergence of a new democratic truth is one that revolves around not only a reordering or a process of replacement but alternative and expanded forms of legitimization and valuation. It echoes, in this sense, Badiou's ultimate notion of Being as a 'moving gap ... which is neither virtualisation nor actualisation, but rather the indiscernible middle between them, the movement of two movements, the mobile eternity that links two divergent times (Badiou, 2007, p 193). Democracy, at its most radical and politically potent, resides in this 'indiscernible middle', between the virtual and actual.

The contagious investment in truth and the exploration of its multiple possibilities for revealment represent an underlying foundation for a democracy based on reimagination and reconnection. In praxis, this can echo recent work on ideas of 'guerrilla employees' and the notion of internal antagonism or of undermining and re-envisaging a system from within. This modern guerrilla recognizes the incompatibility of 'legal' or conventional action for making change within existing licit pathways. They therefore must find new institutional capabilities. These institutional insurgencies become the basis for exploring 'guerrilla capacities'– what opportunities a given context or network provides for building up resistances to prevailing discourses and spreading contagious truths. Practically speaking, they combine a sense of institutional 'credibility', based on their knowledge, with a willingness to creatively deconstruct this system in order to realize what they see as important moral ends which the present status quo cannot or will not achieve. O'Leary notes that, for this reason, despite often being 'on the inside', they 'tend to be independent, multipolar, and sometimes radical. ... They are not afraid to reach into new territory and often seek to drag the rest of the system with them to explore new possibilities' (Badiou, 2007, p 9).

This guerrilla spirit is captured politically in a range of new radical initiatives happening across the world. These efforts deploy digital technologies and mobile communication for understanding and promoting the 'wisdom of the crowd'. The Better Reykjavik project in Iceland collaborated directly with the Occupy movement and utilized the Your Priorities platform to help citizens directly influence policies. What makes this somewhat different than the digital democracy examples discussed in the previous section is that it is explicitly aimed at simultaneously working with authorities to craft better policies while expanding democracy beyond its liberal democratic limits to become ultimately more collective and bottom-up in its power-sharing and decision-making. "Changing your world takes time and persistence", to quote the two founders of the project, Gunnar Grímsson and Róbert Bjarnason: "Crowd-source the highest priorities, organize through ideas and speak with one voice. Get media attention and work with it instead of being frustrated about it. Also, use social media to promote eDemocracy and organize open meetings offline" (quoted in Rushton, 2013). The Your Priorities platform has proven such a success in Iceland that it has spread throughout Eastern Europe and the Balkans, including, notably, Estonia.

These insights point to the potential of infusing democracy both in theory and practice with a profound guerrilla ethos. It concerns the mobile and potentially viral ways contextually embedded actors can experiment with virtually reimagining the social and forging new connections for its actualization. It is an ongoing creative subversion of present truths for the concrete exploration of fresh ones and, in the process, the 'glocal' resituating of existence. Hence, a guerrilla ethos serves to (re)radicalize democracy, while democratic commitments to questions of what is and isn't valued ensure that such guerrilla cultures are not rebellious but liberating.

This has perhaps special resonance under neoliberalism, where marketization is considered unquestionable but nonetheless requires constant innovation. It is the movement from infectious neoliberalism to contagious guerrilla networks and thus radical reconnections. Returning to O'Leary (2019, p 12), it is a call to 'obey your superiors in public, but disobey them in private; Ghost-write letters, testimony, and studies for supportive interest groups ... Build public–private partnerships; Build partnerships among entities at all levels of government; Forge links with outside groups: other professionals, nongovernmental organisations, concerned citizens', among other seemingly duplicitous acts. Such guerrilla actions may appear to be a mere instance of subterfuge and diversion. However, they represent the transition from an innovative social context (an ;infected host') to a disruptive and potentially democratic political space. Alex Honneth's notion of radical democracy highlights this shift, whereby the continual struggle for recognition expands the category of who is included within a *demos* and as such its ideological possibilities and discursive connections. Democracy is reframed as a continual struggle for recognition combining deliberation, culture and conflict (see Lysaker, 2017).

Radical democracy, though, must reflect the mobile and viral aspects of power and order by adopting an agile guerrilla ethos. Emerging theories of 'protean power' serve as a good model for such a radically democratic guerrilla mentality. According to Katzenstein and Seybert, protean power is the result 'of actions by agile actors who are coping with uncertainty that bedevils and frustrates a multitude of Leviathans exercising control under assumed conditions of risk' (Katzenstein & Seybert, 2018, p xii). Tellingly, it gains its strength directly from attacking the central paradox of mobility at the heart of mobile power: namely, the need for all dominant ideologies and regimes to be adaptable while also attempting to assert their singular rule. In contrast to relatively predictable control power, protean power stems from processes that are 'versatile' or 'tending and able to change frequently and easily', Katzenstein and Seybert observe. 'Protean power emerges in uncertain contexts often experienced as such, when previous performance does not provide a reliable foundation for future moves. ... Rather than emerging as a competing force, protean power is often closely related to and co-evolves with control power' (Katzenstein & Seybert, 2018, p xii).

However, it would be a mistake to assume that such power is not dangerous. Indeed, its ability to tap into the mobile and viral aspects of power and hegemony can render it a valuable tool for a status quo as ' "viral" manifestations of protean power invite attentive actors to adopt and normalize emergent innovations, converting what was once a novelty into best practice, and eventually an attribute of control power' (Katzenstein & Seybert, 2018, p xii). Nevertheless, they can also help build up creative forms of resistance through the production of guerrilla subjects. An example of such viral resistance is witnessed in the LGBT rights revolution. Ayoub highlights 'the innovative practices and little surprises that come along the way, which taken together explains the big transformations' (Ayoub, 2018, p 80). Perhaps more significantly, these emerged out of ostensibly progressive policies of top-down rights promotion, a form of control power that in practice commonly resulted in increased on-the-ground repression of LGBT individuals.

In the face of this 'uncertainty', actors can adopt guerrilla methods for shaping these new norms in quite radical directions as 'local advocates, embedded in transnational networks, navigate these uncertain and complex terrains with practices of improvisation and innovation that are inherent to the concept of protean power'. Just as importantly, these activists do not operate based only on survival but out of a desire for creative reinvention, for a 'glocal' effort to foundationally resituate the social. Crucially, 'these actors are attentive to the realities that remain invisible to the top – realities that render control power ineffective on their own – and help generate transformative change in world politics' (Katzenstein & Seybert, 2018, p 80).

As such, the adoption of a radically democratic guerrilla ethos can also provide the foundations for more revolutionary pandemics, making such guerrilla insurgencies 'glocal' acts of not only constructive deconstruction but also contagious recreations. Udayagiri and Walton (2003) describe 'the prospects for democracy under neoliberalism' as ones of countering 'global transformations' with widespread and connected 'local counter movements'. To this effect, they note that the end of the 20th century did spawn an apparent unalterable commitment to the free market: 'By extending the market economy to new terrain, each regime introduced contradictions revolving around social protection and currency. ... [T]hese "disruptive strains" fostered "countermovements" or defensive reactions intent on saving society from the destructive effects of unfettered market competition' (p 310). This is the domain of 'infrapolitics' theorized by Vachhani and Pullen (2019) in their study of the Everyday Sexism Project, wherein women would digitally share experiences, strategize and develop new forms of agency under the radar of a domineering patriarchy.

This points to the importance of recapturing guerrilla ideas and actions for reinvigorating democracy and making it a flexible and potent force for revolutionary contagions at a 'glocal' scale. They are continual 'events' for the spreading of contagious pandemic-truths that disrupt. Crucially, such events are forms of praxis that politically open us to fresh horizons for social ordering, enabling us to make novel connections for a diverse actualization that is at once always contextually specific and universally applicable.

Contagious aversions

This analysis gestures towards the creation of a new form of guerrilla democracy. It is based on a recognition that liberal democracy and its 'radical' attempts at democratic reforms are insufficient for adequately challenging neoliberalism, fully addressing the mobility of power and channelling the potential of the virality of order into revolutionary and fundamentally more egalitarian and freer directions. By contrast, a radical democracy based on a guerrilla ethos emphasizes the possibilities of using creative disruptions for reinventing the social through continual 'glocal' attempts at reimagination and reconnection. Such guerrilla strategies are especially urgent given the 'extreme' character of contemporary politics – as those with the most polarized views tend to most easily go viral. A recent study based on the 2014 Swedish elections revealed, for instance, how more provocative, 'extreme' parties (such as those from the far right) appear to attract the most attention (Larsson, 2017). Their power lies not simply in their salaciousness or anti-elitism but in their providing dangerous instances of reimagination and reconnection. They point to the growing appeal of guerrilla mentalities and their mounting threat when not combined with democratizing desires and values.

It is absolutely imperative, in this respect, to revitalize the existential component of democracy – to transcend its currently limiting, infectious liberal horizons. On the one hand this entails moving beyond 'realism', the turning of a hegemonic discourse into an experimental science of continual innovation and hegemonic reproduction. Here everything is changeable and improvable but nothing is fundamentally alterable. Returning to the landmark work of Mark Fisher, he captured this sentiment in the title of his now classic book *Capitalist Realism: Is There No Alternative?* This feeling of existential alienation has spurred, in turn, renewed attempts to dramatically reimagine the future beyond such capitalist realism. This includes, perhaps most notably, exploring and extolling the post-capitalist possibilities of a 'world without work'. 'The technological infrastructure of the twenty-first century is producing the resources by which a very different political and economic system could be achieved', Srnicek and Williams proclaim: 'The internet and social media are giving voice to billions who previously went unheard, bringing global participative democracy closer than ever to existence. Open-source designs, copyleft creativity, and 3D printing all portend a world where the scarcity of many products might be overcome' (Srnicek & Williams, 2015, p 1; see also Bastani, 2019 for similar sentiments). They highlight further developments paving the way for such an emancipatory socialist future, such as 'new forms of computer simulation [that] could rejuvenate economic planning and give us the ability to direct economies in unprecedented ways. The newest wave of automation is creating the possibility for huge swathes of boring and demeaning work to be permanently eliminated'. Ironically, they note, 'many of the classic demands of the left – for less work, for an end to scarcity, for economic democracy, for the production of socially useful goods, and for the liberation of humanity – are materially more achievable than at any other point in history' (Srnicek & Williams,

2015, p 1), even if in practice we seem further away that ever from achieving socialism.

Their goal, then, is to in a sense recapture the optimistic spirit of the 20th century, asking presciently, 'Where did the future go? For much of the twentieth century, the future held sway over our dreams. On the horizons of the political left a vast assortment of emancipatory visions gathered, often springing from the conjunction of popular political power and the liberating potential of technology' (Srnicek & Williams, 2015, p 1). Yet they are not mere dreamers, nor are they divorced from the contemporary reality wherein such potentially liberating technologies are most often used for deepening capitalist exploitation and control. Moreover, they are wary of what they term 'folk politics', whereby politics is confined to the creation of localized resistance. Hence: 'Under the sway of folk political thinking, the most recent cycle of struggle – from anti-globalisation to anti-war to Occupy Wall Street – has involved the fetishisation of local spaces, immediate actions, transient gestures, and particularism of all kinds' (Srnicek & Williams, 2015, p 1). While these localized resistances (however supposedly global in scale) have much to offer and have been inspiring, they have also failed to foster sustainable forms of reconnection necessary for spreading these alternative social visions. Or, to offer a slightly different interpretation, the affects and people energized by these moments and movements have yet to potentiate, congeal and connect, but this may yet transpire. Srnicek and Williams contend ultimately that 'rather than undertake the difficult labour of expanding and consolidating gains, this form of politics has focused on building bunkers to resist the encroachments of global neoliberalism. In doing so, it has become a politics of defense, incapable of articulating or building a new world' (Srnicek & Williams, 2015, p 3). Moments take root and are unrooted. Spaces remain confined as islands of resistance and fail to go viral or fundamentally disrupt and transform the broader world in which they exist.

This return of a folk politics, moreover, exhibits the danger of populism to democracy. Positively, populism helps to build up resistances to infectious democracies, such as its current liberal variant, through directly and passionately challenging a status quo. More than merely condemning elites it can also help articulate and expand the very notion of who counts as 'the people'. In doing so, it provides a nascent impetus for a type of politics that centres on reimagining power relations through the reinforcing of old social connections in new ways and new social connections in old ways. It also plays on a guerrilla ethos of subversion, whereby institutions, processes and norms go from being rather unalterable parts of one's social reality to political tools for undermining and potentially replacing existing regimes of power. 'Populist practices emerge out of the failure of existing social and political institutions to confine and regulate political subjects into a relatively stable social order', Panizza (2005, p 8) critically argues. 'It is a political appeal that seeks to change the terms of political discourse, articulate new social relations, redefine political frontiers and constitute new identities', they continue. Yet its appeal and lifespan is often temporary, 'characteristic of times of unsettlement and dealignment, involving the radical redrawing of social borders along lines other than those that had previously structured society'. As such, this resurgence of populism commonly devolves into what we have termed forms of repressive deconstruction rather than a creative disruption. Indeed, populism can be a resistance and then become its own reactive infection. This move from resistance to reaction instead of disruption and transformation is evident in current populist movements – especially from the right. While they rail against elites, they put their faith in corrupt businessmen who speak of 'defending the people' while in practice strengthening the oligarchy.

The goal then must be transitioning from popular resistance to contagious democracy – from a populist to a democratic guerrilla politics. This is similar to the account of a more left populism extolled by Laclau (2018) and Mouffe (2019). The strength of their respective theorizations of a left populism is the emphasis on chains of equivalence between previously disparate, even 'folk', causes and discourses, brought together by a common antipathy to the status quo. For example, trade unionists agitating against precarious working conditions alongside environmental activists seeking green futures that necessarily entail non-exploitative work. What differentiates left populism, of course, is the institution of radical forms of democratic practice that offer not only a set of governing norms but also the horizon of possibility for the movement itself, where radical democracy becomes the means and end of struggle. We are reluctant to discard the possibilities of a left populism entirely, as its inclusive yet confrontational energy connotes working within and sometimes against local cultural forms, but we need to reflect more on how the scaling up of diverse and previously folk connections can be achieved – a shared hostility to an antagonistic outside may not be sufficient.

If regular populism is an attempt to redefine and remobilize 'the people' against a status quo, the guerrilla-democracy near relative seeks to politically uncover the limits of the social and reimagine its possibilities. This distinction is implicitly captured in democratic theorist Aletta Norval's ongoing work on aversive democracy – especially in her treatment of the relation between hegemony and deconstruction. At stake is the decision of politics and the multitude of possibilities – the eternal and tension-filled relation between closure and openness. 'If, however, one of the characteristics of the terrain of the undecidable is that it resists closure', Norval writes, 'it is also that which inaugurates the need for certain "decision", for it marks an irreducibly plural terrain, a terrain in which identity is still at stake waiting to be inscribed' (Norval, 2004, p 17).

Aversive democracy represents the ability of democracy to politically expand the limits of the socially possible. Notably, Norval depicts this as a process of ongoing revelation which she presciently links to Wittgenstein's earlier notion of 'aspect dawning'. Here, new dimensions or 'aspects' of an object or context are revealed through one's seeking to look at it from a new perspective. Significantly, this process of democratic reimagination is not wholly novel but rather finds its transcendent qualities, ironically, in a politics of immanence. Put differently, the ability to conceive and concretely realize new social relations beyond what is hegemonically given requires deconstructing the underlying grammars and everyday norms of hegemony so that they may be seen anew. The shift, then, from aspect dawning to what she terms 'aspect change' is a move from reimagining to reconnection. Further, it is a radical development aided and abetted by the adoption of a guerrilla ethos fostering these cultures of constructive deconstruction. Hence, 'if aspect dawning connotes the new, that element of initial surprise, when a novel set of connections or articulations offers us a picture that allows us to make sense of disruptive experience'. Norval declares, 'aspect change may be utilised to capture the sense in which the initial moment of dawning could be reactivated at a later stage' (Norval, 2004, p 134). Folk moments need not all be lost, wasted and failed moments but ones pregnant for reactivation, reimagination and reconnection.

These insights also serve to redefine domination as 'deprivation of voice'– not merely in terms of inclusion or recognition but of the possibility of giving voice to alternatives and the ongoing 'decisions' to make singular the multiple possibilities of any given context. Norval thus 'foregrounds the need to engage with emerging identities, demands, and claims that fall outside the parameters of dominant discursive order' (Norval, 2009, p 297). Crucially, it is necessary to avoid traditional binaries whereby domination and, as such, closure somehow signify a dearth of possibilities. Rather, it is a question of how the inherent dynamism of a social order is channeled and manifested. Norval thus takes seriously emerging identities and political demands 'that fall outside the parameters of dominant discursive order'. Consequently, for Norval there needs to be at all times 'an analytical engagement with the emergence and articulation of new struggles and voices ... the processes through which inchoate demands are given political expression so as to counter the ongoing possibilities of domination, understood here as a "deprivation of voice"' (Norval, 2009, p 297). Aversive democracy, then, is the evolution from the innovative social potential of domination to the contagious political possibilities of revolution.

A guerrilla ethos shows, in turn, how such a radical project of aversion can allow for viral forms of reimagination and reconnection. It permits aspects of reality to emerge and spread. It speaks to how a reorienting of the social, the opportunity to see and know it from a radically different perspective – as simply one potential actualization of a range of virtual possibilities – can lead to new contagious truths and (re)situations. The forward looking insights of Frase (2016) in his attempts to envision 'life after capitalism' highlight the relation of aversive democracy and a guerilla ethos for reimagining and reconnecting the social. At stake, he contends, is 'the political question that we have faced ever since the industrial revolution: Will new technologies of production lead to greater free time for all, or will we remain locked into a cycle where productivity gains only benefit the few, while the rest of us work longer than ever?' (p 1).

This political 'question' can lead to a range of contagious solutions which can 'redistribute the sensible' and spark diverse 'glocal' antagonisms. A guerrilla ethos highlights the viral aspects of an aversive radical democratic project – one that is about both ideological and material expansion in a highly mobile and infectious social order. Democracy, in this sense, can be considered in continual flux between infection and contagion. These are not mutually exclusive, and each democratic gesture contains the potential for both simultaneously. Such gestures are not about plurality or inclusion but are a decision concerning innovation or disruption, global resignation or 'glocal' aversion. Quoting the incomparable critical theorist Judith Butler (2001, p 19): 'At stake here is the relation between the limits of ontology and epistemology, the link between the limits of what I might become and the limits of what I might risk knowing'. It is this existential risk that inspires a revolutionary guerrilla strategy for aversive change.

Democratic resituating

The figure of the guerrilla is not usually associated with democracy or necessarily with being overly concerned with democracy. Instead, the emphasis is on revolution and subversion. Yet it also represents the ability to go beyond resistance – to recognize the limits of a given politics and its established contestations and engage in revolutionary political acts. Democracy here is radically recalibrated, highlighting the ability for social change and popular decision-making. It is a promise – as Derrida (1993) suggests – in two ways: existential and representative; reimagination and reconnection.

This dual promise is once again evident in Fishkin and Mansbridge's (2017) critical reflections on deliberative democracy, positioned as practice which can persist and subsist within larger systems, including 'competitive democracies, authoritarian regimes, and developed and developing countries' (p 12). Radical values of deliberation put into question how effective and actually democratic current practices of deliberation are within existing governing institutions and civic life. They may be an antidote to the failures of social media and our contemporary mobile culture to foster such empowering and transformational deliberative engagements, as they warn against 'the increasing pressures of narrow-casting in the commercial media, self-sorting into information bubbles on social media, and geographic sorting by ideology as people move to more politically homogeneous communities' (p 12). In this respect, they transcend conventional processes of deliberation and ask fundamental and context-specific questions concerning the political agency of people to collectively shape their social conditions, representing 'a vibrant area of democratic experimentation at a time when many have lost confidence in the processes of electoral representative democracy' (Fishkin & Mansbridge, 2017, p 12).

Ironically, it shows the ongoing importance of 'repoliticizing' democracy. In the present era this means identifying liberal democracy as a hegemonic infection that is mobilizing populations in quite ideologically narrow but socially dynamic ways. As Vázquez-Arroyo (2008, p 127) observes: 'The historical trajectory of liberal democracy, as a theory and as a practice of power, betrays an anti-democratic tendency that leads to depoliticisation and has quelled the democratic politics that once gave credence to it, thus paving the way for the rise of neoliberalism'. Guerrilla democracy is about developing capabilities through building resistance that will allow for such radical democratic capacities to emerge. This can be seen in current efforts to create what

Banks (2016, p 1) refers to as 'sense-making tools for post-capitalism'. He argues that there are three in particular, respectively stressing: 1) that capitalism is always emergent and never static; 2) that we can exchange the instrumentalism characteristic of the free market for an emphasis on 'recursivity' that 'prioritizes organized complexity over rationalised efficiency'; and 3) that the term 'online' can be retranslated away from capitalist social media platforms into a general ethos 'describing and understanding humans' relationships to networks of communication and economic exchange' (p viii).

Depicted, in turn, is the move from creative destruction to disruptive creations. This type of radical guerrilla democratic politics is witnessed, for instance, in the rise of the open innovation economic system (OIES), which is 'a macroscopic economic system wherein a sub-economic system based on open innovation' can spread through a range of different economic sectors, fundamentally transforming them so as to become more collaborative and based on knowledge sharing rather than competition and exploitation. Significantly, it reveals not just how these different economic sectors and actors are 'interconnected, thereby affecting each other' but also their possible reconnections in the construction of new socioeconomic relations and practices. Yun notes thus that while 'OIES basically targets the economic system of one nation ... the concept of the same macroeconomic system could be applied to a global and regional economic system' (Yun, 2015). He tellingly refers to this as a type of rebooted Schumpeterian dynamic of creative destruction linked to open innovation. This speaks to the fundamental ways these 'open' networks can reconnect and resituate the economy and society locally and globally.

Guerrilla democracy is then a phenomenon of continuous 'glocal' reinvention. It is marked by efforts to transform resistance into revolutionary new transitional orders. Such an ethos is exhibited in the growing attempts to build 'transitions to post-capitalist urban commons'. As Chatterton (2016) relates: 'While this is quite a nebulous term, it points to a desire to reinvent and reinvigorate the revolutionary process away from older top-down, elite-led models of change' (p 405). These experiments may appear to be localized and overall doing very little to challenge the hegemony of neoliberalism globally. However, they reflect the desire to concretely reimagine the social, taking past revolutionary ideals and resituating them in light of present-day conditions. For this purpose, they can adopt a wide range of democratic values and practices, including principles of 'horizontalism, direct democracy and autonomy and the wider quest for self management' (p 405).

These represent thus the promise of guerrilla democracy – the ability to forge new connections for radically reimagining our shared existence. 'The idea of the urban commons points to a parallel set of social and spatial relations and values alongside traditional public and private ones to illustrate an emerging geography of post-capitalist transitions', Chatterton declares, 'critically exploring how daily post-capitalist practices get built and how they can embed an urban commons, especially those practices that go beyond the status quo of intense individualism, corrosive consumerism and financial austerity" (p 406). These are focused on fostering contagious networks of reimagination and reconnections – ones whose contingency is continually highlighted so as to engender the capacity to make radical decisions. Drawing on the radical UK housing cooperative Lilac, Chatterton further observes that, in practice, there existed a 'broad commitment to transformation. Daily activities in Lilac offer opportunities for behaviour change in broader ways beyond individualised and solely environmental responses'(p 408). Here, the often contentious binary between reformism and revolution begins to dissolve in the daily practices of creative disruption necessary for guerrilla democracy in practice. As such, Chatterton reports that 'members of the project express a commitment to "step change" in terms of their environmental impact, and also in regards to the kinds of relations they have with other people and the wider community'(p 409). For this reason, 'the communal context of the project is regarded as a catalyst to experiment with broader shifts in behaviour change entailing more structural rather than incremental changes in behavior'(p 409).

Significantly, this guerrilla ethos encompasses radical forms of experimental design aimed at encouraging novel and liberating forms of communal living. To this end, residents consciously inhabit a new identity of 'commoner' that sees them take an active part in 'moderating and laying down principles for interactions, sharing resources and negotiating boundaries and spaces between private homes, shared spaces and the external public realm'. Yet it also seeks to avoid the danger of simply reinforcing neoliberal demands for 'personal responsibility', taking seriously how to concretely subvert and reinvent traditional spaces for fostering these liberating commons-based relations. Central to these efforts is the need to provide residents with the ability to collectively manipulate these structures for this purpose, as 'the site has been designed to increase natural surveillance and neighbourly encounters, and therefore residents have to set their own boundaries and tactics for moderating levels of interaction with neighbours and visitors'(Chatterton, 2016, p 409). Consequently, they are charged with being democratic guerrillas, acting creatively and strategically to produce an alternative form of existence that must adapt itself to its local context while holding the potential to spread beyond its own borders. It is, then, the radicalization of mobile power and viral hegemony for revolutionary ends.

The danger, of course, is that these otherwise radical and exciting communities will be confined to their location, a place-based sanctuary for escaping from an oppressive and exploitative world. Required, thus, is the incorporation of these quite literally existential experiments into a broader revolutionary viral ethos – one evidenced, for instance, in the previous discussions of OIES. Reflected, in turn, is the need to cultivate contagious reproductions, not just localized emancipations. These begin with the growth of aversive capabilities, new skills flexibly formed as a means for reorienting a given social context. These develop over time and with diverse networked support into guerrilla capacities, a set of contingent but implementable principles to experiment with for transforming the social across diverse 'glocal' networks. The insights of De Angelis are especially relevant in this regard, in his discussion of the 'transformation to postcapitalism'. 'How can the social form shared by households, community gardens, neighbourhood associations, reclaimed factories, social centres, and commons ecologies in general', he asks, 'become a force of social revolution, of radical emancipatory change towards postcapitalism? What is emancipation?' (De Angelis, 2017, p 357) This is an admirable and indeed absolutely crucial ambition. Yet it remains to be seen how this can in fact be accomplished rather than just wished for. It is telling that while those against neoliberalism can progressively and rather easily spread 'good practices' for resistance, the hegemonic infection of neoliberalism is sustained through the sharing and adaption of constructive advice for its localized improvement and, if necessary, partial reform.

A 'glocal' antagonism, then, must do more than merely resist. If it is to be genuinely counter-hegemonic it must also be constructive in its virality. More precisely, it must seek to escalate not just the inoculation against these oppressive systems but the ideas and tools for their replacement. They serve, in this sense, as the means for locally reconnecting the social and then globally reimagining it. Returning to De Angelis, he notes that such transformation 'happens in waves, through social movements, unpredictable in timing and in form, but always bringing new energies inside the commons, rearranging resources and subjectivities, creating new common wealth together with new perspectives' (De Angelis, 2017, p 359). Through these guerrilla movements, the deprivation of voice, the call to do otherwise, of other possibilities, can emerge and flourish. Consequently, it initiates a shared 'emancipation journey' that bring individuals together 'within the emancipation climate of the commons, which in turn can rest on the emancipation climate of social movements' (De Angelis, 2017, p 364).

Yet it also allows for the transcendence of the liberal paradigm of power/resistance, which plagues even the most radical democratic theories. Guerrilla democracy is instead about existential insurgencies, ones which recognize the mobility of order and thus focus on continual reordering, on experimentation rather than simply inclusion or contestation. Perhaps one of the most exciting critical interventions for theorizing and enacting such a revolutionary guerrilla politics in the contemporary moment is what Papadopoulos (2010, p 134) has referred to as 'insurgent posthumanism'. He proclaims that 'an insurgent posthumanism would contribute to the everyday making of alternative ontologies: the exit of people into a common material world (not just a common humanity)'. Critically, he contends that this shifts the focus from questions of justice, such as 'political representation', onto a more existential 'processual and practical issue' revolving around 'moulding alternative forms of life'.

It is not, then, simply about reconnecting with an existing other or expanding marginalized individuals' (human or otherwise) access to established modes of connection but transforming, through these networked relations, the very ways in which we connect and expand our political and therefore existential horizons. Connolly, for example, proposes a 'politics of swarming' that is 'composed of multiple constituencies, regions, levels, and modes of action, each carrying some potential to augment and intensify the others with which it becomes associated' (Connolly, 2017, p 125). He links this in nature to 'honeybee democracy' whereby female bees scout different locations and bring back to the hive evidence of their potential attractiveness, which they let other scouts go and try, until there is a swarming effect.

Key here is the capacity of people and assemblages to fight infections through such radical reconnections. In order to do so, guerrilla democracy can manifest itself as a public performance for reorienting and resituating the social. This type of public guerrilla action can be viewed, for example, in the use of state-backed theatre to challenge existing perceptions of HIV and AIDS in order to create change in their social treatment (see Campbell & Gindt, 2018). Guerrilla democracy relies, then, upon a logic of radical connection rather than simply of collective action. 'Efforts to push these organisations into recognizable social movement categories diminish our capacity to understand one of the most interesting developments of our time', according to Bennett and Segerberg, which is 'how fragmented, individualised populations, that are hard to reach and even harder to induce to share personally transforming collective identities, somehow find ways to mobilize protest networks from Wall Street to Madrid to Cairo' (Bennett & Segerberg, 2012, p 751), thus, that 'when people who seek more personalised paths to concerted action are familiar with paths of social networking in everyday life, and when they have access to technologies from mobile phones to computers, they are already familiar with a different logic of organisation: the logic of connective action' (Bennett & Segerberg, 2012).

This 'logic of connective action', though, can transcend the realm of protest or traditional social struggles, and can become a powerful force for disruptive creation and for fostering 'glocal' contagions. These are ones that incorporate the latest advances in democratic technology for encouraging greater public participation in shaping public priorities and decision-making, with a commitment to transcending the mere innovation and reform of the contemporary status quo. It is an ongoing guerrilla ethos of repurposing these often ultimately social technologies for radical political ends – ones which concretely develop and help share the capabilities necessary for creating a 'glocal' commons. Guerrilla networks then take on a decidedly different character than those typifying conventional capitalist relations. The viral promise of guerrilla democracy is the capacity to transform the world, fighting off hegemonic infections and reimagining our existence through our ability to radically reconnect with each other and resituate our shared existence.

Conclusion

This chapter introduced the notion of guerrilla democracy. Theoretically, it is the culmination of the fundamental analysis of the mobility of power and virality of hegemony. These insights build on the last chapter, which focused on the infectious character of hegemonic networks and the possible contagions of counter-hegemonic networks. Specifically, guerrilla democracy is the ability to contagiously reimagine and reconnect the social. It is rooted in a guerrilla ethos of subversion for the purpose of disruptive creation – the effort to undermine and supplant an existent and seemingly more powerful status quo through alternative modes of existence that have the potential to become a viral political pandemic. Its strength lies in its capacity to harness the same dynamism and context-specific adaptability found in hegemonic epidemics.

Further, this guerrilla ethos is joined to a radically democratic politics. More precisely, it is concerned fundamentally with questions of who counts and, importantly, how they are counted. It is an often revolutionary demand to overcome the 'deprivation of voice', here expanded to take in the views of indidviduals and groups that are being marginalized, and those social connections that are being rendered invisible. If much of current politics is concerned with populist demands in the name of the 'people', guerrilla democracy asks directly and inventively: Who are these people? Who is defining them and for what purpose? And who could they be? The political is made manifest and cultivated as a 'glocal' antagonism, one which remobilizes power for reimagining and reconnecting the social.

This represents an expansion and significant advancement of contemporary perspectives on radical democracy. In particular, it takes seriously the insights about agonism most famously put forward by Chantal Mouffe, rooted in her theory of discursive hegemony formulated with Ernesto Laclau. However, whereas agonism focuses on disagreement, the emphasis here is on concrete forms of reimagination and reconnection. Hence, it shares much with Rancière's notion of democracy as a form of dissensus reflecting the 'redistribution of the sensible'. Yet, to our minds, this is still too steeped in sovereign models of power and politics; it portrays hegemony as an entrenched and repressive force that must be disrupted and its power relations redistributed. In a very strong sense, it shares with guerrilla democracy a concentration on the ability of public interventions to re-represent, and therefore point to, how the social can be reconfigured. Nevertheless, where we expand, we believe, beyond this approach is in giving greater emphasis to the ongoing ability of individuals and groups to foster dynamic resistances to hegemonic infections and build contagious radical alternatives.

Crucially, guerrilla democracy has perhaps the most clear historical and intellectual resonance with the concept of aversive democracy. Similarly, we consider democracy as a theory and praxis that transcends formal processes of either collective decision-making, elective representation or public deliberation. Rather, the 'promise' of democracy is precisely found in the eternal prospect of ideologically and concretely transforming a given social context. Moreover, it understands this politics of transcendence as one ironically made possible through a range of immanent democratic practices. Here, aversive change occurs through the emergent antagonisms catalyzed by and catalyzing new ways of organizing, relating and existing. Where we take this further is that, once again, we make paramount the importance of the mobility of power and the virality of hegemony. Hence, what is critical is the capacity to politically resituate the social, to interject a novel 'truth' within an existent situation that is in a constant process of innovation through disruption and reformulation. Consequently, these 'events' are made possible via the ongoing repurposing of available resources and materials, serving as a viral constructive deconstruction of prevailing norms and practices – a disruption that can be creatively adapted to the political and cultural conditions of other infected host contexts.

The political, in this regard, is a matter of continual reimagination, reconnection, and democratic resituation. What is imperative for such a radical resituating is to move beyond an account of discourse (and therefore counter-hegemony) as primarily linguistic or ideological. It is not merely, or often even primarily, a domination premised on the supremacy of certain ideas over others. Rather, it is premised in how diverse ideologies are successful in spreading across different contexts and within them. These significant reconsiderations of power and hegemony – ones in which mobility and virality are granted greater import than repression or production, on the one hand, or regulation and domination, on the other – gesture towards the need to also approach anew critical understandings of materialism: more precisely, to understand the social and the political as intimately bound up within ongoing processes of rematerialization.

6

Radical (Im)materialism

Are smartphones tools of oppression or resources for mobile resistance? This question is perhaps especially relevant for a rising new class of precarious workers who rely on 'smart' platforms for their employment and livelihood. Workers at Deliveroo, for instance, need to have access to smartphones in order to sign up to the platform. This means that all the workers have access to the means for mobile organizing. At first, some platforms, like Deliveroo, encouraged workers to join or start WhatsApp groups to keep in contact about shift patterns and changes to the platform. Where these were set up, it is very easy for workers to branch a new conversation out, excluding managers. In other cases, workers start WhatsApp groups to share knowledge about their work, routes, accidents, traffic and so on.

As Woodcock (2017) has found at Deliveroo, the 'action was organised primarily on WhatsApp, building on pre-existing networks, some of which were formed at the meeting points assigned in each area by Deliveroo. What followed was a lively campaign which was widely circulated on social media'. Furthermore, "on WhatsApp groups used by delivery riders in the UK, workers post jokes and memes to pass some of the idle time while waiting for work, but also share tips on how to increase earnings'. Likewise, when waitstaff at the restaurant chain TGI Fridays were told that the company was reducing the amount of money they took home from credit card tips, workers began to organize against the change through the very digital networks initiated and originally encouraged by the company. Such communication soon branched into mass and localized WhatsApp groups. This may sound inconsequential, yet it indicates how through such mobile-based social struggle, individuals can concretely challenge their alienation as capitalist workers. 'In all cases, what we are seeing is people refusing to accept the idea that they are atomized workers, and refusing to accept the idea that connectivity only runs vertically rather than horizontally',

Woodcock and Graham (2019, p 133) observe: 'Even if workers like drivers and domestic workers rarely if ever see each other, they can start to collectively challenge ways of structuring the work processes that they are enrolled in'. Ironically, workers in larger corporations with existing digital networks may find it easier to generate mass reach and traction digitally due to the number of potential worker allies on hand and the brand familiarity of the companies in question, enabling easier identification among potential allies and consumers, as was the case with the recent spate of industrial action among hospitality chain workers in both the UK and the US (notably McDonald's and the Fight for $15 campaign).

Such cases are obviously rich in potential insights and implications. Perhaps most important is how they point to the complex and dynamic relation of materialism and discourse in this age of increased virtuality and digitalization. They reveal the ways conventionally 'immaterial' processes and resources – such as mobile objects – have profound and commonly unpredictable social and political effects. Reflected, furthermore, is the critical need to make concrete the material forces and relations underpinning these digital objects and applications, as well as the ideological assumptions and fantasies which have given them birth and shaped their everyday use. In this respect, neither traditional theories of materialism nor discourse are sufficient to explain these mobile times. Required instead is a fresh perspective of 'democratic (im)materialism' that can best grapple with and critically illuminate the (im)materiality of present-day mobile power and viral ordering.

From new materialism to democratic rematerialization

Critically understanding the relationship between materiality and power has perhaps never been so theoretically necessary and politically urgent. This chapter seeks to draw on our combined insights regarding mobile power, viral hegemony and guerrilla democracy to better comprehend and practically engage with the political dimension of materialism. Put differently, while an exhaustive analysis of materiality, on the one hand, and of social materialism, on the other, is impossible for any one work, what is possible is to theoretically clarify and empirically illuminate how people and things (the assigned living and non-living, the organic and non-organic, the 'conscious' and 'non-conscious') share an existence as mobile resources which are in a constant process of social materialization and political rematerialization.

A hoped for key insight of this book is the introduction of the applicable concept of '(im)materialism'. We use this term in two distinct but interconnected senses. The first is that all 'material' is in a constant dialectic of 'virtualization' and 'actualization'. In other words, it is a matter of contingent (though often predictable) becoming – one which is both confined by existent material conditions and which, through processes of critical reimagining, expands such conditions. The second is that this continual process of materialization (making the virtual actual and the actual virtual) is conducted and made possible via creative 'immaterial labour'. To this effect, we combine Lazarrato's notions of the increasing digitalization and imaginative character of production with new materialist insights on the vitality and 'inter-action' of all existing things from the molecular on up. The core concern, in this regard, is how immaterial labour is utilized to continually materialize and rematerialize social realities. These questions are particularly relevant to the present period given the blurring of our physical and digital existences – creating 'hybrid' lives that must integrate and navigate between the traditionally virtual and concrete.

Significantly, this perspective entails moving beyond simple reductions of power to the stabilization of the material environment or discursive hegemony as the homogenous regulating of physical activities. Rather, it is critical to interrogate how a given regime of power and dominant ideology materializes itself continuously within given host contexts and diversely between them. It also involves examining the ways individuals and groups are tasked with investing and developing their creative immaterial labour into innovative materializations for the survival and reproduction of these infectious social orders. By contrast, an ethos and praxis of guerrilla democracy can lead to liberating forms of political rematerialization – whereby radically alternative values are experimented with for their local actualization and global spread.

Rethinking the material of hegemony?

Processes of digitalization are redefining and reconfiguring what counts as 'matter' and the processes of social ordering. They are rendering invisible the physical relations between digitally connected subjects, for whom communication and interaction occur almost as if by magic through easily transportable gadgets. They are also exposing the material implications of this increasingly immaterial society. These concerns are perhaps especially significant given that traditional theories of materialism have been almost fatally critiqued for the conceptual crime of essentialism. The focus on materials and physical relations has been altered and to a large extent replaced by an emphasis on social construction and the cultural production of the subject. This 'discursive' turn – one that thus far has been a key component of this work – raises fresh questions as to the actual materiality of power and hegemony.

It is, therefore, interesting that two of the supposedly biggest proponents of this prioritization of discourse does not ignore the continued relevance of the material world. Laclau and Mouffe's theory of discursive hegemony fundamentally, to an extent, revolves around the discursive defining of the material world and its role in shaping the daily physical regulation of individuals and communities. They are, in this respect, 'post-Marxist' without necessarily being 'post-materialist'. In their influential article 'Post-Marxist without apologies' (1987), they clarify their views on the concrete and dynamic intertwining of materiality and discourse in the play of hegemony. It is one captured in the ongoing effort to invest objects with meaning and mobilize them for sustaining an established set of social relations: 'Now turning to the term discourse itself, we use it to emphasize the fact that every social configuration is *meaningful*', they remark:

> If I kick a spherical object in the street or if I kick a ball in a football match, the physical fact is the same, but its meaning is different. The object is a football only to the extent that it establishes a system of relations with other objects, and these relations are not given by the mere referential materiality of these objects, but are rather socially constructed. (Laclau & Mouffe, 1987, p 82)

Hegemony, then, is at its heart as much a material struggle as it is a discursive or ideological one: or, better to say, the three are inseparable. What is central to their formation and perpetuation is the transforming of an independent material world into a dependent, socially constructed reality. Again quoting Laclau and Mouffe on the subject, they note that 'a stone exists independently of any system of social relations, but it is for instance, either a projectile or an object of aesthetic contemplation only within a specific discursive configuration'. Similarly, they argue that 'a diamond in the market or at the bottom of a mine is the same physical object; but again, it is only a commodity within a determinate set of relations'. Hence: 'For that same reason, it is the discourse which constitutes the subject position of the social agent, and not, therefore the social agent which is the origin of discourse – the same system of rules that makes the spherical object into a football, makes me a player" (Laclau & Mouffe, 1987, p 82).

Reflected, in turn, is the deeper material cycle of hegemony. Specifically, it involves the continuous investment of existent objects with meaning for the creation and maintenance of entrenched cultural interactions and, over time, enduring social relations. It may be more accurate, in this regard, to note that objects are invested with discursive potentials – representing material things that can be used in rather narrow legitimate social ways. In the moment, this results in formally coercive and informally prescribed (and proscribed) sets of social actions. Longer term, these catalyze sedimented social identities and dominant 'ways of being' in the world. Take the example of the football field used by Laclau and Mouffe – the material space of a grass field is transformed into a 'place' to play the game of football, which produces a range of socialized relations from 'sports culture' to 'the professional athlete' to being a 'fan'.

This admittedly brief, and somewhat crude, description of the material cycle of hegemony has a more formal relation to economic history. As Marx notes, the emergence of capitalism depended on the reification of private property and economic contracts for the justification and naturalization of wage labour and material exploitation, both of humans and of the natural environment. Critical, in this sense, was the rendering of all objects into potential 'things' for capital investment and profit. This process of reification relied upon the immaterial mediation of artificial social constructs such as, again, ideologies extolling the essential importance of private property rights and laws promoting the sacredness of contract. 'Before capitalism, power was visibly part of everyday life as it was directly experienced through explicit hierarchies, obligations and customs', according to Comor (2011, p 327). He continues: 'A core reason for this transparency was the very public nature of surplus extraction. Whether it was the tribute paid by the peasant, the tithe handed over by the serf, or the forced labor performed by the slave, workers were explicitly unfree.' Yet this changed dramatically with the ascendancy of capitalist relations and their basis in 'contractual relations "freely" entered into among seemingly equal participants.' Consequently, the basis of capitalist economies is founded less on coercion than on 'mystical "market forces" backed by a universally respected "rule of law"– a rule codified and enforced by state authorities' (p 316). While this analysis perhaps overlooks the forces of immaterial mediation key to feudal society, it nonetheless points to the historical role that that the material cycle of hegemony plays in perpetuating modes of economic exploitation. Notably, an object acts as the resource for the discursive investment that produces the exploitative social relation, which in turn reproduces the use of the object. Critically, the revealing of the contingency of these socio-material relations at any point of the process is key to the success of any counter-hegemonic movement.

This empirically rich but somewhat theoretically straightforward account of materialism and hegemony is is made more complex, however, by the increasing virtualization of the economy. Digitalization has made both objects more virtual and exploitative relations less visible. From the very beginning, the introduction of cyber-processes into the workplace led to more geographically dispersed and remote forms of interaction and control. (The first use, for example, of cyber-surveillance was in a Cambridge University laboratory by two computer scientists who deployed video to remotely surveil coffee drinking within their office.) This revealed, very early on, processes of virtualization by which technology serves to make the concrete virtual and therefore, ironically, collectively observable (see Hearn et al, 2014. In the ensuing decades, virtualization and digitalization have come to progressively define all aspects of human existence. Online 'life' shapes experiences of leisure and work alike, as 'social networking, as seen through Facebook, actively produces leisure spaces' which, in turn, 'produces new forms of often hidden labour from users, thereby further contributing to the biopolitical control over many of our everyday experiences" (Rose & Spencer, 2016, p 809).

This age of virtualization has led, in turn, to a rebooting of capitalist class conflict. It has seen the growth of the 'cyber-proletariat'. Dyer-Witheford (2015, p 8) declares, hence, that class remains very much real but is now entangled and reproduced through a range of digital processes and reproduced by 'simple, brutal algorithm'. Consequently, while the machinery of capitalism (both literally and figuratively) may have become less visible, its inequalities and deprivations remain clear for all to critically see. As he highlights, while the means of their exploitation has become considerably more hi-tech, the difference between 'financier super-yacht owners and immigrant *sans papiers*, [between] the social media billionaire and the minimum-wage fast-food worker' makes clear that class differences remain, arguably as strong as ever. Produced, thus, are different types of exploitative work and non-work subjects. As Dyer-Witheford further observes: "Now, as in Marx's era, proletariat denotes the incessant phasing in and out of work and worklessness, the inherent precarity, of the class that must live by labour, a condition raised to a new peak by global cybernetics' (Dyer-Witheford, 2015, p 13). This change in work has also witnessed the concurrent rise of the cyber-bourgeoisie taking advantage of and benefiting from this vast reserve of digital labour. 'This in effect creates a "live-in diaspora" of cyberworkers who are working abroad but living at home', observes Walberg, who continues: 'As with the industrial revolution which produced a proletariat and a lumpen-proletariat, this cyber-revolution has created a cyber-proletariat populating cyber-sweatshops and even a cyber-lumpen-proletariat, or a reserve pool of unemployed cyber-workers' (Walberg, 2007, p 29). The outsourcing of digital labour, evident in the 'huge volume of low-level computing (mostly updating of client databases for banks, insurance companies and health-care institutions)' (p 29) reflects the material basis for this seemingly immaterial economy.

Highlighted, thus, is the need for reconsidering the immaterial character of power and hegemony. The most obvious critique is that it is not immaterial at all – and in fact is very much a reproduction of capitalism's material relationships of exploitation. However, while this criticism has much value, it also misses a crucial aspect of the 'immaterial' in relation to this very material form of 21st-century oppression. Indeed, it can be said to be '(im)material' as it represents empirically a combination of the virtual and the physical. It is the ways in which digitalized processes and forms of consumption rely upon and serve to reproduce material social relations. Additionally, it is (im)material theoretically as it exposes the dynamic and dialectical relation of virtualization and actualization. Emerging, then, is the rapid transition politically from the hegemonic struggle for material rule to viral (im)materializations – or the ability to spread and make actual a 'way of life' across different contexts. This transformation requires first a deeper understanding of (im)material power.

Discovering the new (im)materialism

The 20th century appeared to signal not only the end of the Cold War but with it the philosophical death knell of materialism – or at the very least of a crude form of dialectical ('orthodox') materialism. However, the new millennium has witnessed the flourishing of vibrant new theories of materialism, emphasizing once more the importance of matter and the physical world for the production of the social. They are marked by their explicit resistance of essentialism and an often implicit commitment to move beyond anthropocentrism. Whereas poststructuralism and discursive perspectives consistently remain fixated on human perceptions and actions, these refocus attention on material potentialities and the novel social possibilities they give rise to.

These novel material theoretical interventions are often referred to under the common label of 'new materialism'. Coole and Frost presciently set the course for this perspective in the introduction to their now landmark collected edition *New Materialisms: Ontology, Agency, and Politics*, declaring: 'As human beings we inhabit an ineluctably material world. We live our everyday life surrounded by, immersed in, matter. ... At every turn we encounter physical objects fashioned by human design and endure natural forces whose imperatives structure our daily routines for survival.' Further, they note that at a more biological level, 'our existence depends one moment to the next on myriad micro-organisms and diverse higher species, on our own hazily understood bodily and cellular reactions'. For this reason they ask rather convincingly: 'In light of this massive materiality, how could we be anything other than materialists?' (Coole & Frost, 2010, p 1).

The full scope of the insights of new materialism obviously exceed any one work, yet what is perhaps particularly relevant to this analysis is its renewed concentration on the materiality of power and hegemony. The human, here, is reimagined as animated social materiality, which Braidotti memorably describes as 'a piece of meat activated by electric waves of desire, a text written by the unfolding of genetic encoding. ... A mobile entity, an enfleshed sort of memory that repeats and is capable of lasting through sets of discontinuous variations, while remaining faithful to itself" (Braidotti, 2000, p 159). To this end, Bennett (2004: 351) very early highlights the significance of 'thing-power' as a force that exerts an influence on material objects – living or otherwise. Thing-power crucially renders more complex the material cycle of hegemony – illuminating the power of things to concretely guide social relations in ways that are both unpredictable and challenging to dominant ideologies. Brandiotti discusses, for instance, how new materialism and feminism have combined to shed fresh light on conventional sexual and gender differences, and in doing so have subverted the very discursive constitution of the social generally in the midst of rapid technological change. She notes that as technologies have digitally connected the world, 'issues of embodiment and accountability, positionality and location have become both more relevant and more diverse" (Braidotti, 2011, p 128).

These insights allow for a deeper appreciation of the processes of material reimagining and reconnection we have spoken about throughout this study. Specifically, they starkly illuminate the need to more fully understand how material is used to create host contexts and the diverse, intersecting material networks from which they are composed. The increasing use of algorithms and big data, for instance, have allowed for a systemic and forensic investigation of how to materially 'individuate trajectories' (DeLanda, 2002, p 36) of different populations and places. Crucial, in this respect, is the standardization of social materials for creating a welcoming and customizable host context.

Again turning to DeLanda, he notes that 'if one rejects essentialism then ... all objective entities are products of a historical process, that is, their identity is synthesized or produced as part of cosmological, geological, biological, or social history' (DeLanda, 2002, p 39). Particularly relevant to this study is how this 'historical process' is captured and exploited through emerging digital methods.

It is worth taking a pause and unpacking the notion of 'material independence' before venturing further in our analysis. Such autonomy exists on two distinct but intertwined levels: that of the physical and that of the social. On the one hand, it is a recognition that the social is not exhausted by cultural understandings and discourses. There are a range of material forces, often unseen, unknown or misunderstood that exist beyond human knowledge and which can have effects that are either ignored or profoundly miscomprehended. Ironically, the independent status of the material is a prime driver of human speculation and virtualization, as it is an acknowledgement that there are forces of nature and power which transcend our current perceptions while nonetheless impacting us. On the other hand, such material independence has a significant social dimension – in that any and all social configurations must adapt to their material environment. Here we are in the realm of Marx's notion that labour exists within a holistic natural 'metabolism' and that humans must continuously labour in and with nature to survive: 'Labour, then, as the creator of use-values, as useful labour, is a condition of human existence which is independent of all forms of society; it is an eternal natural necessity which mediates the metabolism between man and nature, and therefore human life itself' (Marx, 1990, pp 171–2). Of course such a 'natural necessity' becomes obscured, commodified and fetishized, with nature itself absorbed into fantasies of anthropomorphic capitalist domination and infallibility. It is within this context of weaving and adapting between natural-cultural matrices of exploitation that the subject must persist. Further, this adaptative ethos carries over to the discursive articulation of the social more broadly as it relates to the subject. The context that one inhabits becomes a materialized environment bursting with observable and unobservable forces concretely regulating our existence, whose unpredictability we must continually navigate, adapt to and, if we are able, harness and exploit.

An obvious danger comes in dissociating this material-social explanation from themes of economic exploitation. This is arguably especially true as traditional manual labour has progressively given way to immaterial labour over the past several decades. Lazzarato famously defined this phenomenon "as the labour that produces the informational and cultural content of the commodity' (Lazzarato, 1996, p 133). In particular, this notion encompasses both the digitalization of labour and creative enterprises which impact cultural, economic and public opinions as well as norms. This transition reflects more than simply the virtualization of the economy and exploitation; it reveals the neoliberal process by which subjects become progressively, personally and collectively responsible for the material production of culture and society. In this respect, according to Lazzarato, 'manual labour is increasingly coming to involve procedures that could be defined as "intellectual" and the new communications technologies increasingly require subjectivities that are rich in knowledge' (Lazzarato, 1996, p 134). These represent the critical realities of what are popularly referred to as the 'knowledge economy' and the 'information age'. Here, material and immaterial labour are combined into a demand that subjects invest their creativity and agency into enhancing productivity and profitability.

Hence a crucial part of the shift from liberalism to neoliberalism, from modernity to postmodernity, is the creation of viral subjects who are tasked not just with inhabiting and adapting to their material social environments but also with the construction of these host contexts. Moreover, they are more and more made accountable for the material spread and maintenance of infectious discourses within these host contexts. The self-disciplining aspects of contemporary neoliberalism, whereby 'the worker is to be responsible for his or her own control and motivation' and 'the foreman's role is redefined into that of a facilitation' (Lazzarato, 1996, p 135), speak to the creative aspects of present-day capitalism, whereby individuals are made personally responsible for producing an environment conducive to value creation, whether that consists of their 'home office', their virtual meetings with workmates or their regulation of their personal life so as to best cope with the progressive demands of an increasingly competitive and precarious marketplace.

As such it relies upon immaterial labour in that it represents a new cycle of hegemony, spanning material labour, viral discourses and concrete social infection. More precisely, it is the ongoing investment of time and creative energies for innovatively using available virtual and material resources in order to flexibly materialize dominant values and norms. Once again drawing on the insights of Lazzarato, he notes that production has now transcended the 'four walls of a factory' and instead, it relies upon ongoing processes of mobile production, whereby 'small and sometimes very small "productive units" (often consisting of only one individual) are organized for specific ad hoc projects, and may exist only for the duration of those particular jobs' (Lazzarato, 1996, p 134). In this respect, contemporary capitalism is less a stable set of productive relations and more a set of viral and ever-adaptable networks that can be mobilized when deemed necessary and useful. Hence, Lazzarato concludes, 'the cycle of production comes into operation only when it is required by the capitalist; once the job has been done, the cycle dissolves back into the networks and flows that make possible the reproduction and enrichment of its productive capacities', and 'precariousness, hyperexploitation, mobility, and hierarchy are the most obvious characteristics of metropolitan immaterial labor' (Lazzarato, 1996, p 136).

Produced are viral but contextually specific immaterial realities that mix the virtual and the actual into integrated ways of physically and digitally existing in the world. Ideology itself is transformed into a product, a reflection of one's preferred 'reality' and world view. What these 'ideological products' reveal, thus, is the need for a better understanding of immaterial governance and disciplining. Contemporary forms of power and domination have largely moved beyond the search for essence and towards processes of materialization. Put differently, it is less about forcing people to 'think' in a certain way or even necessarily cultivating a mass conformity in beliefs. Rather, it is about forensically understanding the different cultural contexts and physical as well virtual networks that exist within them, so as to create products that meet their demographic preferences while supporting (explicitly or implicitly) the reproduction of existing exploitative material relations. Hence, Amazon can present itself as a 'boutique' online service by highlighting local businesses, be the largest provider of anti-capitalist literature, or tout its incredible global reach as a consumer platform. In each case, they are depending on a workforce subjected to difficult and at times brutal as well as quite precarious conditions, all along its supply and delivery chains. At stake, thus, is how ideology is becoming progressively more user-friendly.

Importantly, such new (im)materialism has become, ironically, a governing rationality – one that combines an emphasis on potential material capabilities and the virtual possibilities they may yield. These are premised not so much on 'programming' individuals but rather are 'geared towards unblocking and sustaining adaptive capacities of individuals and systems', Schmidt (2013, p 177) for ensuring the resiliency of a given status quo. Here the social becomes a range of differing immaterial host contexts for creating infectious solutions to shared 'problemizations'. Immaterial labour is translated into an affective investment into these host contexts and our perceived responsibility for producing and improving them. Reflected is a central paradox of contemporary corporate globalization. It is not, as perhaps is often assumed, a homogenous form of ideological or practical domination. Rather it is a call for integrating hyper-capitalist principles and power relations into a range of different and commonly dissimilar contexts. To this end, capitalist globalization relies upon 'subsuming different realities to the same logic and creating conditions for them to communicate with each other' (Dowling et al, 2007, p 6).

This new (im)material perspective offers fresh insights on contemporary power relations. In particular, it helps critically illuminate Foucault's previously discussed idea of the current 'government of things' whereby 'modern government treats human beings as "things" to achieve particular ends' (Lemke, 2014, p 10) As such, we become part of a broader viral ecology – an immaterial environment for testing and infecting its inhabitants with an infectious discourse. This process is aided by quantification methodologies such as big data which aggregate populations based on their perceived and behaved similarities and differences, thus making humans 'calculable and measurable' and conceiving of them ' as physical phenomena themselves' (p 10). Consequently, the human/non-human dissolves in the shared status of being viral material 'things'. It is not a form of governance that is 'restricted to humans and relations between humans' but rather 'refers to a more comprehensive reality that includes the material environments and the specific constellations and technical networks between humans and non-humans' (p 17). It would be a mistake, though, to think that such rendering of subjects into governable 'things' implies an emptying out of personal agency or reflexivity. By contrast, it 'initiates a reflexive perspective that takes into account the diverse ways in which the boundaries between the human and the non-human world are negotiated, enacted and stabilised' (p 17).

At stake is a new form of governance, representing the evolution from material subjection to virtual (im)materialization. It is one premised on a potent combination of mobile power and viral hegemony, whereby all 'things' must be made adaptable to capitalist expectations and demands. Further, to be human is to be a 'personally responsible thing', an innovator held accountable for ensuring that their own existence and contexts maximize their unique market potential. Fundamentally, it represents a foundational shift in the understanding and supposed purpose of power. As Senellart observes, we 'note a passage from the right of power to a physics of power' (Senellart, 1995, p 42, quoted in Lemke, 2014, p 10) where what is important is its effective use for achieving socially proscribed ends.

Yet this also puts into stark perspective the ultimate 'fragility of things'— our mobility and alterability as immaterial subjects within continuously materializing host contexts. 'From the perspective of the endurance and quality of life now available to the human estate in its cross-cultural entanglements', notes Connolly, 'in its exchanges with nonhuman force fields, and in the reverberations back and forth between several human and nonhuman processes, we once again inhabit a fragile world" (Connolly, 2013, p 410). Yet it is precisely this fragility, this increasing production of existence between the digital and physical spheres, that makes it so necessary and urgent to discipline people to continually, productively and socially materialize the world around them in ways that diversely and innovatively reflect the needs of capitalist society.

Mobile resources

Theories of mobile power and viral hegemony proposed and expounded upon in this work thus introduce a new lens for understanding materialism. Ironically, perhaps, given its preoccupation with matter, new materialism emphasizes the dynamism of the physical world. Quoting Deleuze and Guattari (1980, p 266): 'There are only relations of movement and rest, speed and slowness between unformed elements, or at least between elements that are relatively unformed, molecules, and particles of all kinds.' Yet it also contains a strong virtual element – the ability for it as a discourse to expand the 'sociological imagination' (Fox & Alldred, 2016). What are then prioritized are not static structures but evolving materializations of the social and the potential for more disruptive and transformative 'political rematerializations'.

Nonetheless, it would be misguided to assume that these materials are mere objects in flux. Mobilization is not simple fluidity. Rather, it is about how various physical and digital resources are continually materialized in accordance with dominant ideologies and practices. At stake, then, is a reconsideration of materiality and temporality, whereby duration is less about fixity and more about predictable mobility and virality. To this end, 'the focus on the materialisation of bodies and other so-called objects of investigation demonstrates how "duration" has in fact become "inserted into matter" … an object is no longer passive matter that has to be re-presented; meaning-making takes place along a two-way track' (Van der Tuin and Dolphijn, 2011, p 166). It is critical to take new materialism seriously as a novel means for understanding power and ordering in ways that reflect the simultaneous concreteness and malleability of social objects. Whereas the linguistic and discursive accounts often focus on stabilizing definitions, a materialist account of power concentrates on their mobility – on the controlling and harnessing of their diverse flows and possible materializations. Here, contemporary materialist perspectives are 'fascinated by affect, force and movement as it travels in all directions' and search 'not for the objectivity of things in themselves but for an objectivity of actualisation and realisation' (Van der Tuin and Dolphijn, 2011, p 169).

These insights return us to the concepts of capabilities and capacities. As new material capabilities are discovered, they become discursive capacities to be perfected. Coole observes that 'this is not about Being, but becoming: crucially, what is invoked is a process not a state, a process of materialisation in which matter literally matters itself' (Coole, 2013, p 453). Yet, just as significantly, it is always a matter then of adaptation and incorporation, the immaterial labour being involved in socially materializing a given host context in relation to infectious discourses. Material power, in turn, revolves around the allowance of new innovative or disruptive materializations to become immanent. Absolutely crucial, in this respect, is to reconsider the relation between materialism and domination. Conventional notions that attribute hegemony to the stabilization of the social – its homogeneity and regularity – fundamentally misapprehend what makes power ultimately strong and sustainable – as we have emphasized throughout this analysis. Paradoxically, the ideological and material naturalization of dominant ideas and practices is found in their continual availability to be modified to reflect the needs of a prevailing status quo and its underlying principles and interests. As such, 'new materialist ontology stresses immanence rather than transcendence, it has inspired references to matter as itself being vital or agential, and this, in turn, poses the intriguing question of the source and nature of this endogenous, lively immanence' (Coole, 2013, p 454). The 'source and nature' of this 'lively immanence' is mobile power, the innovative capacity of things (whether 'living' or 'inert') to be creatively adapted across a range of different contexts.

Hegemony – especially capitalist hegemony – thus is about immaterial reproduction, the creation of the new from the iteration and repeatability of the old. Freedom is made into a disciplining discourse of virality – the ability of people to be alive, to innovate and materially spread discourses. This (im)material domination is a process of continual mediation whereby the immaterial is made material or, again to use our terminology, constantly 'materialized' when necessary. Here, 'new materialism is already present in the way technical media transmits and processes "culture" and engages in its own version of the continuum of nature-culture ... or in this case, media natures' (Parikka, 2012, p 96). The appearance of new technologies – especially mobile ones – reinforces this process of materialization that is at once creative and disciplining. There is, then, a hegemonic process at work – deciding what is being materialized and materially empowered and what is not. The social, in this sense, is not the reduction of potentiality but its channelling so as to reinforce, often in wide-ranging ways, an existent status quo and its underlying ideology. We are all rendered into vital 'things' which must be innovatively governed so as to not only reflect hegemonic values but ensure their practical viability within a diverse set of host contexts.

A material ethics, therefore, involves critically understanding how we are involved in processes of material reproduction, specifically as linked to dominant forms of ongoing materialization. To do so is to highlight the mobility of any material configuration and the immaterial labour exploited for its creations and recreations. Materialism is dynamic in that it represents the continual process of materialization, the discovery of ever-newer capabilities and associated capacities for making virtual ideas of the social into actual empirical realities. It revolves around the materialization of an ideologically entrenched but always materially precarious social ordering. Yet it is precisely in this tension between imagination and realization that power is at its most creative and its 'grip' on us arguably most tight. It is in this eternal gap between virtualization and actualization that power and domination are forced to be opportunistic, constantly finding new ways to not just materially survive but thrive. Central to these efforts is its transformation of us from mere living 'things' into self-disciplined mobile resources for its constant materialization.

Political materials

The introduction and highlighting of materializing and mobile resources returns us to the so-called primacy of the political. Post-Marxists, in particular Laclau and Mouffe, challenge the historical materialism of orthodox Marxism precisely on the grounds that it ignores the contingency of the social and therefore the fundamental importance of politics rather than science in the development of events and history. Yet, as this analysis seeks to show, to take seriously materialism is to understand and prioritize the political constitution of the material and vice versa. A telling example is how indigenous Australians directly link their identity and sense of community to the land, declaring that they belong to it rather than any country or place belonging to them (see Martin, 2013). While this is an obvious but important instance of indigenous rationalities challenging Western models of ownership and imaginary communities, it also critically reveals a fundamental theoretical truth about our material relation to power. We are always implicated and shaped by various types of what we refer to as immaterial groundings, encompassing which materializations we are subjected to and what the material forces (seen and unseen) and immaterial labour are that contribute to their reproduction.

This reflects the existence of an active rather than a passive materialism. Materialization – whereby immaterial labour is combined with, and reshaped by, the exploitation of actually existing materials – is comprised of diverse 'ways of doing'. More precisely, 'if matters act, they never act alone. Relational materialism is in order' (Abrahamsson et al, 2015, pp 15–6). For this reason, 'in this context the general claim that "things have politics" has become too vague ... as "things" have widened from the category of technological artefacts and have come to include all possible materialities, it MAKES more sense to say that in political practices "things" figure variously' (Abrahamsson et al, 2015, 15–6). Again, however, in our view the process of socialization can transform an existing 'thing' into a 'mobile resource' whereby it becomes actively involved in dynamic and context-specific forms of innovative hegemonic materialization. It is this transition from 'thing' to resource that demands, and raises to new levels of import, immaterial labour. It is the creativity and effort involved in rematerializing dominant discourses within diverse host contexts that becomes so vital to social ordering and maintaining hegemony.

Returning to the example of the football and football field, the object neither defines the relation nor the discourse the object. Rather the object exists as a thing with discoverable capabilities for establishing and reproducing a socialized materialization. Hardt and Negri come perhaps closest to capturing this material dynamic of power. They note the historical shift within capitalism 'from the linear relationships of the assembly line to the innumerable and indeterminate relationships of distributed networks' and the critical reconfiguration of the city from an urban space for industrial production to the space for 'the inorganic body of the multitude' (Hardt & Negri, 2004, p 113). This helps to clarify the immaterial character of power fundamentally, and of this period specifically. It is about how any material and any existing materialization connects us in a concrete set of social relations that is at once mobile, in that it requires a dynamic and diverse set of capabilities, and viral, in that it is continually spreading and adapting and innovating within host contexts created by our material and immaterial labour.

Hegemony, then, is a matter of ongoing materialization and rematerialization. It requires forensically understanding the different material forces underpinning how a social order is materially constituted. It is the constant dialectic between virtualization/actualization – and the immaterial labour that this demands – that thus drives this political process of rematerialization.

This shift requires, in turn, going beyond conventional notions of inclusion or mere pluralization to critically interrogate emerging material differences, 'allowing for the virtual, for pure recollection, to be reflected in the actual, constantly exchanging the two into one another as it creates the circuit of duration' (Dolphijn & Van der Tuin, 2012, p 398). At stake, therefore, is not a return to meaning making but the articulation of material inscription and immaterial subjectification, how we are produced as things and then as active individualized mobile resources within a broader immaterial environment.

What then are the conditions of being a mobile resource – of thinking, perceiving and acting as and among 'political materials'? It is to be a host either for infection by or resistance to dominant materializations. It is to shift the condition of perception and thought to the ways knowledge is shaped around the construction of a viral subject who must continually reflect and concretely adapt to material infections, the discursive materializations of which they must immaterially labour to maintain and improve. To this effect, without this politicized perspective of viral materialism, one risks eliding just how mobile these things and relations are and must remain for their sustainability and spread. Importantly, each materialization has its own internal and constitutive relationship between the material and the discursive, its own immaterial intra-action between the two representing how the virtual and the actual interact and reproduce one another.

This speaks to and serves to critically expand Barad's notion of 'intra-activity'. She maintains that 'the relationship between the material and the discursive is one of mutual entailment. ... Neither has privileged status in determining the other. Neither is articulated or articulable in the absence of the other; matter and meaning are mutually articulated' (Barad, 2007, p 152). This reflects an infectious and more radically contagious type of 'bodily being in the world'. It gestures towards 'the inextricability of soma and techné, of bodily-being-in-the-world, and the dispositifs in and through which corporealities, identities and difference(s) are formed and transformed, come to matter, if you like', according to Sullivan (2012, p 302). 'Perception, then, is both the vehicle and effect of a particular situated somatechnics, an orientation to the world in which the I/eye is always-already co-implicated, co-indebted, co-responsible' (Sullivan, 2012, p 302).

Yet again, these are not static but mobile – as they are flexible to infectious discourses – so here materialization is the dynamic concretization and virtualization (representing new immanent possibilities) of a dominant discourse. Such a perspective 'foregrounds an appreciation of just what it means to exist as a material individual with biological needs yet inhabiting a world of natural and artificial objects ... well-honed micro-powers of governmentality, but no less compelling effects of international economic structures', Coole and Frost (2010, p 27) observe. Significantly, these discourses can never fully extract themselves from these infectious materializations – as knowledge is always bound up by the material conditions in which it is pursued. To us, the terminology introduced in this analysis signals the need for a critical investigation of the diverse mobile resources that have gone into materializing processes of knowledge production and transmission within specific contexts.

The analysis of discourse, then, shifts from one focused primarily on the emergence of dominant meanings and their constitution and regulation of concrete practices to one focused on the ways a social order is (im)materially manifested, linked to mobile power and viral hegemony. Discursive articulation, in this respect, is precisely that which allows for innovation, for materializations to be guided and directed, though always unevenly and never completely. It is never purely discursive or linguistic. It is always a material utterance, one bound up in the material means by which it is made and conveyed to others. Just as importantly, such articulations are an attempt to discursively circumscribe and express the material forces socially shaping our existence at any given time. 'What endures, what is fundamentally immersed in time is not what remains unchanging or the same over time, a Platonic essence', according to Grosz, 'but what diverges and transforms itself with the passage of time' (Grosz, 2005, p 110).

As such, our task is to paradoxically provide the material with an immaterial essence so that new materialities can be produced. The immaterial essence then is inexorably constituted through immaterial labour, in so much as it is mobile construction of the social eternally connected to a subject's relation with viral discursive materialization. The construction of the 'human', for instance, is a discursive attempt to essentialize us as a specific thing so that we can prescribe our materialities within certain ideological bounds and deepen the materializations that can occur within these narrow discursive limits. Posthumanism, thus, invokes the 'material heterogeneity that "the human" founds itself upon'. (Wolfe, 2007, p xii). It is a colonization – one that is discursively limited and materially expansive in terms of its potentialities. It echoes Foucault's previously discussed notions of the expansive economy matched by a delimiting politics, the cultivation of ever-newer capabilities for ever-narrower discursive ends. Here, these material capabilities are concrete manifestations of the immaterial labour that goes into producing ever-innovative materializations as part of a mobile host context.

The key then is not material or discursive, nor even essence or non-essence. Rather, it is whether a materialization is innovative or disruptive; the degree to which it is socially or politically creative. This involves going beyond values or even material 'interests'. Instead it is a renewed focus on materiality as a process of socialization, one that is enduring precisely in its mobility and which draws strength from its virality. A contemporary case in point would be the concrete effect of discourses of sustainability. In this sense, sustainability is 'largely a matter of material flows. The what, where, and when of those flows are intimately tied to culture', Scott et al argue, and as such, 'new materialism's attention to movements of matter can help create pathways for materials that make it easier, more convenient and more profitable to consume sustainably than to do otherwise' (Scott et al, 2014, p 288).

Importantly, these hegemonic materializations are never politically neutral. Instead, they help to reproduce specific relations of power and dominant ideologies. This is witnessed, for instance, in the current use of video games by the US military to bolster support for militarism while breeding the physical and mental skills necessary for its success within a new generation of the populace. Here 'war video games construct and imagine places like Iraq and Afghanistan as barren wastelands devoid of civilians and infrastructure in need of saving and U.S. intervention', and accordingly 'justifies intervention, control, and mastery of unused space within both virtual and real projects of colonisation' (Leonard & King, 2009, p 107). The video games example is particularly interesting in the context of our analysis in that it reveals how digital products are deployed to produce concrete mobile subjects – ones who view quite profound moral and political subjects such as war as 'games' to creatively play and win. The military is seeking not just to ideologically manufacture a new generation of willing soldiers but also to turn them into innovative martial problem-solvers who must discover inventive solutions to meet differing combat situations and personnel deployment. These virtual scenarios become, in turn, the basis for their potential future real-life survival and success.

The process of materialization can also allow people to transform from mobile resources into active (im)material creators of their own existence. Arboleda (2015) writes of the protest movement that arose as part of a collective grassroots struggle for water rights against large-scale mining companies in Bucaramanga, Colombia, in this regard. 'Communicational strategies, collaborative engagement, technoscientific debates, and legal action from activists and committed individuals can produce new experiences of collectivity and new ways of sensing and enacting urban space', she observes, and so 'Bucaramanga became at once the source of and the receptacle for an emancipatory social subject that has been able to protect its water sources from being enclosed and contaminated and ... in this way, [has] forged renewed patterns of solidarity between human and nonhuman worlds' (Arboleda, 2015, p 37). These spurred material practices associated with the aforementioned processes of contagious political reimagination and reconnection. Tellingly, she reports that 'not only were occupations, conferences, and demonstrations commonplace, but there was everyday talk in the streets about the páramo, graffiti critical of the company was sprayed all around, and there were screenings of documentaries and hiking tours through Santurbán'. For this reason, 'it was easy to see how city streets, walls, parks, and other public spaces served as the receptacle for the commons that was being produced through these myriad encounters' (Arboleda, 2015, p 44).

The distinction, hence, between social and political materials is the transition of mobile resources from an inscriptive or creative force into one that it is disruptive and emancipatory. Crucially, Arboleda concludes that 'the case of Bucaramanga evinces the reversal of a subject–object relation that characterises contemporary productive activity, because the object of production of the networks of immaterial labour engaged in the defence of the páramo was not an object but a subject, a living social subject' (Arboleda, 2015, p 48). These valuable insights point to the deeper relationship and possibilities inhering between (im)materialism, on the one hand, and guerrilla democracy, on the other.

Radical rematerializing

We believe the insights presented in this chapter, and in this book more generally raise profound questions – ones which encompass significant and urgent theoretical and political concerns. Specifically, what is the critical relationship between democracy and materialism? What constitutes a properly radical conception and praxis of democratic materialism? These important queries are, to an extent, already gestured towards in contemporary accounts of democracy, which treat it as both an 'actually existing' set of processes and institutions and an emancipatory promise that challenges and transcends these empirical realities. This dual democratic character, composed simultaneously of both the actual and the virtual, is especially relevant for this emerging age of digitalization. Already, scholars have grappled with the prospect of 'digital materialism[s]' which 'point to the often inconvenient insight that digital media research requires research into the technological infrastructures which are less easily accessible than the representative content', for the purpose of 'tracing the materiality of media in terms of components' history, socio-economic and ecological implications, or to address the materiality of allegedly immaterial research objects such as software' (Reichert & Richterich, 2015: 12).

This highlights the potential to democratize materials – or as we have referred to them, mobile resources – in order to collectively shape their articulation and use within a given social context. The materialism of democracy is, hence, as much about the mobility of matter as it is about its stability. Drawing on the work of the brilliant feminist philosopher Luce Irigaray, Stephens (2014) notes that 'fluidity is not unproblematically or unequivocally aligned with the positive and progressive; rather, its dynamic nature, its conceptualisation as a field of forces, means that one must pay attention to the specific instances of each manifestation, instead of making generalising assumptions about its effects' (p 199). Consequently, the very mobility of power lends itself to hegemony as opposed to mere completely determined domination, as 'fluidity, while important and central, while a site of possible strategic appropriation, always remains a potentiality whose outcome, by its very nature, can never be determined in advance' (p 199).

It also, however, points to the (im)material conditions that allow for the materialization of democracy, or more precisely, that determine which material forces are most amenable to particular types of viral democratic materializations. Current efforts, for example, to combine social democracy with natural resource extraction and exploitation – a strategy increasingly popularized in Latin America – ultimately confine the political generally and democracy specifically to the quite narrow ideological and empirical limits of the market. 'Relying on neo-extractivism as the main strategy for development limits the possibilities available to post-neoliberal states in terms of building more substantive democracies', notes Siegel, because 'as neo-extractivism depends on increasingly intensive and extensive resource exploitation, it is hard to reconcile with the various concerns expressed by civil society as these would require setting some limitations to resource exploitation' (Siegel, 2016, p 499).

These observations reveal, in turn, the underlying importance of dominant modes of economic production and exploitation for shaping the concrete manifestation of democracy and its perceived possibilities ideologically. In this regard, the promise of democracy is invested with actual content, and a hegemonic version of democracy is discursively linked to the material ideas and practices of freedom. This process of democratic materialization is presently witnessed in the efforts by international capitalist institutions such as the World Bank to promote types of 'entrepreneurial development' and business-led democracy globally. Critically, this contemporary instance of democratic materialization reveals who and what are given a sense of 'relative autonomy' to be an innovative force (see Cammack, 2003, p 55). In the 21st century, this 'relative autonomy' for helping democracy and freedom materialize has been progressively expanded from governing institutions and capitalists to include, under neoliberalism, entire populations. Everyone is increasingly responsible for materially adapting their lives and host contexts to better reflect these infectious market-based democratic discourses.

Fundamentally, this reflects how democracy in the current age is linked to the creative use of immaterial labour for the reproduction of capitalist exploitation and associated power relations. This perspective helps to re-uncover and refresh the vitality and relevance of historical materialism as espoused by Marxists. It is worth noting, before undertaking this critical task, that Marx's own account of historical materialism is much richer and subtler than often credited by contemporary detractors, who see in it the sins of essentialism and scientism. Indeed, for Marx, material apprehension was first and foremost depicted as a process of socialized synthesis. He declares in *Grundrisse* that

> The concrete is concrete because it is the concentration of many determinations, hence unity of the diverse. It appears in the process of thinking, therefore, as a process of concentration, as a result, not as a point of departure, even though it is the point of departure in reality and hence also the point of departure for observation [Anschauung] and conception. (Marx, 1857, p 101)

Here, physical materials can be treated as the mobile resources for materialization – the concrete but dynamic production of social and economic relations via immaterial labour. Marx again points to this phenomenon in his own theorization within *Grundrisse* (1857), where he proclaims: 'The instrument is used as an instrument, the material taken as raw material for labour. In coming into contact with labour, in being taken as its means and for its object, they are taken as objectifications of living labour, elements of the labour process' (p 299). Hence, he proclaims 'they change their form, while preserving their substance; and, from the standpoint of economics, this substance is objectified labour time. Labour is the living, forming fire, the flux and temporality of things, their shaping in the life of time' (p 361).

This paves the way for a reconsideration of both domination and democracy – one that is fully compatible with the notions of mobile power, viral hegemony and (im)materialism introduced in this book. Here domination is twofold. It is firstly the material separation of humans from their material reproduction. Returning to Marx: 'The process, therefore, which creates the capital-relation can be nothing other than the process which divorces the worker from the ownership of the conditions of his own labour' (Marx, 1867 p 874). Secondly, it encompasses the separation of people from the ability to reimagine and materially recreate their history. Thus, again, in Marx's view,

> in the history of primitive accumulation, all revolutions are epoch-making that act as levers for the capitalist class in the course of its formation; but this is true above all for those moments when great masses of men are suddenly and forcibly torn from their means of subsistence, and hurled onto the labour-market as free, unprotected and rightless proletarians. (Marx, 1867 p 876)

One of the most brilliant though often overlooked aspects of Marxist thought is its assertion that it is precisely the material practice of capitalism – its everyday inscription of people into and as exchange value – that actually socially hides the essence of, or potential for, alternative forms of value. According to Moore

> this epochal scientific discovery, while removing all appearance of contingency from the determination of value magnitudes, in no way alters the mode in which that determination takes place. Practical activity on the part of its discoverers is neither a condition for discovering this

truth nor a constitutive element of the truth discovered. (Moore, 1971, p 422)

The 'essence' of alienation is one that is (im)material and democratic – the separation from us of the possibility of contingently rematerializing existence through our immaterial labour and thus collectively resituating the very conditions of being. Illuminated, then, is how our (im)materiality concretely reproduces this democratic alienation – one that focuses our material activities and immaterial labour on reproducing the system rather than investigating its deeper materializations, building up resistances to it and producing alternatives. Indeed, 'both Marx and Engels approach the study of nature and culture from a standpoint emphasizing context, change, conflict, and emergence', notes Moore (1971, p 426).

Marxism further exposes how these dominant historic materializations innovatively reinforce not only economic domination but social inequality as well. Hartsock (1983), for instance, revisits and to an extent reinvents historical materialism in her landmark text *Money, Sex, and Power: Toward a Feminist Historical Materialism* as a source for reproducing gender and racial inequalities – highlighting how concrete practices linked to materialized social relations of money and sex provided the basis for the continual strengthening and evolution of White male power and racialized patriarchal power structures. This also points to the critical reconsideration of the 'material dialectic'. Poststructuralist thinkers, such as Derrida and Deleuze, offer a compelling foundation for what Cheah (2008) refers to as a 'non-dialectical materialism' in that it is impossible to 'know' the totality of material forces constituting the social, which themselves are impersonal and averse to easy human comprehension, let alone control, and as such, 'because Derrida understands material force as the reference to the impossible other and Deleuze views materiality in terms of impersonal and pre-individual forces, materiality, even if it is not unfigurable as such, is not easily instantiated by concrete figures that are recognizable by political discourse' (Cheah, 2008, p 143). While these critiques are certainly valuable, the focus on materialization in this analysis reintroduces the critical significance of the dialectic, though now linked inexorably to mobility and virality. More precisely, material dialectic is in the mobile synthesis of a viral discourse and a material host context, whose production rests on (im)material labour.

This highlights, in turn, the political and democratic aspects of what we term 'historical materialization'. At stake is whether this dialectic is innovative or disruptive (social or political) and in this sense offers the opportunity for contagious democratic interventions and creations or merely non-democratic forms of dynamic reproduction. Central to this immaterial dialectic is the aforementioned relation of material capabilities and disciplining discursive capacities. An important contribution of new materialism is the fresh agency given to the body (not just language) for concretely producing and allowing us to perform phenomena otherwise considered 'non-material', such as 'emotions' (see Barclay, 2017). This speaks fundamentally to the ways that bodily capabilities become translated into socialized performances and immaterial experiences. In this respect, the movement from capabilities to capacities – from the raw social material to the processed socialized materialization – is one of human becoming. It at once reveals what this 'potential' should be while also allowing the possibility for this material to be alternatively produced as something different. This harkens back to Deleuze's earlier use of new materialism or 'new vitalism', which was focused on the diverse productions of the human based on its varied dimensions and aspects. According to Ansell-Pearson (2016, p 88), 'in Deleuze's case the focus is very much on the normative and existential implications of human becomings, even when this involves the human becoming ... animal, molecular, and imperceptible'.

This reposes the question of dialectical materialism in much more political and democratic terms. At stake is not the objective movement of history but whether, politically speaking, this is innovatively reproducing and allowing for the spread of a given dominant materialization, and, democratically, what differing aspects of human potential this (im)materially reveals. This also puts into clearer critical view the materialist and democratic role of exploitation. Notably, it calls for not only a 'demystifying' of exploitation and oppression but their dematerialization and rematerialization. Guardiola-Rivera argues, hence, that the 'deflationary conception of materiality common nowadays, one that sees "signs" in the place of powerful objects (exemplars, charms, fetishes), adjudicates against the latter as mere relics of the past and can only conceive of material relations and causality in representational terms, as co-relative to our self-positing powers' (Guardiola-Rivera, 2007, p 275). Significantly, this involves looking beneath the 'representation' of power for the multitude of ways it is materialized and rematerialized. Crucial for this purpose is understanding the evolving capabilities that permit these mobile power regimes, and the infectious hegemonic capacities that permit their viral spread.

However, this approach also materially distinguishes exploitation from domination. In particular, exploitation is the immaterial way in which we use social raw materials and are used as social raw material for the maintenance and expansion of dominant socialized materializations. Domination, by contrast, is the range of concrete power relations and ideological legitimations that permit and help to legitimize these systems of (im)material exploitation. A dominant mode of (im)material production, then, is the dynamics of a system that combines exploitation and domination as a viral process of materialization and innovative re-materialization. It is one that is geographically and structurally mobile (in that, as Frank, 1967, and others pointed out in the 1970s, it can involve an uneven integration of differing forms of economic exploitation and power in the service of a dominant one), and viral in that it is centred on the diverse universalization of this mode of (im)material production. This reflects the deeper immaterial dialectic – in which a discourse adapts to materialized host contexts for its synthetic rematerialization. Absolutely crucial to remember is that manual and immaterial labour is the driver of this process (it is for this reason that we refer to it as (im)material to capture both of these aspects). What is critical then is whether we are involved in exploitive immaterial labour for reproducing dominant social materializations or political labour for their creative disruption and contagious democratic recreation.

This returns us, then, to the political dynamics at work for such material productions, or again, as we term them, rematerializations. Specifically, it sheds new light on the existence of antagonistic materials – those raw social materials that disrupt dominant materializations rather than innovatively reproducing them. Hook and Wolfe, drawing on Barad's notion of intra-action, tellingly discuss processes of 'counter-action', which can subvert hegemonic relations such as those associated with gender norms and heteronormative regimes of power. They maintain that 'although becoming is an open process, the entanglement of bodies in relation enacts a two fold [sic] mattering. This boundary making process … is ongoing. Our recounting has illustrated how binaries can and are traversed and in doing so alternative modes of living come into view' (Hook & Wolfe, 2018, pp 878–9). These material antagonisms reveal the limits of current materializations and of the concrete reimaginings of new rematerializations. The promise of democracy is then redirected and resiuated from abstract notions of emancipation to alternative and not-yet-imagined possibilities of liberatory rematerializations. In this respect, 'the concept of the body [is] depicted as always gesturing toward what is beyond and more than a body and as intrinsically oriented toward its own "elsewhere"' (Rogowaska-Stangret, 2017, p 59).

These insights, moreover, permit the denaturalizing of the social, one which, through exposing the limits of its materialization catalyzes new possibilities for virtually reimagining and actually rematerializing the social. They point to what Tuana describes as 'the urgency of embracing an ontology that rematerializes the social and takes seriously the agency where the natural is rendered apparent' (Tuana, 2008, p 188). As such, Tuana calls on us to give attention not just to intra-action as instructed by Barad but to the in-between-ness, the heterogeneity of these intra-actions, contending that 'we must attend to this porosity and to the in-between of the complex interrelations from which phenomena emerge' (Tuana, 2008, p 189). It is ironically a political rearticulation of the social as material that can be concretely redirected and remade, the rendering of the naturalized materialization of the present into a discursive configuration for its reimagination and rematerialization. Thus, 'attention to the viscous porosity of phenomena provides a Copernican revolution. ... Interactionism not only allows but compels us to speak of the biological aspects of phenomena without importing the mistaken notion that this biological component exists somehow independent of, or prior to, cultures and environments'. In this respect, 'it serves as witness to the materiality of the social and the agency of the natural' (Tuana, 2008, pp 209–210).

Critical, then, is the political articulation of the social as a globally infectious discourse that can be disrupted and alternatively materialized. This is part of a dialectic between capabilities and new capacities linked to a democratic immaterial labour of dematerializing and rematerializing. As Flatschart has recently argued, 'We need dialectics in order to make sense of this peculiar relationality of difference', one which 'acknowledge[s] that a move away from metatheory towards historicity is necessary in order to represent its materiality' (Flatschart, 2017, p 289). Indeed, such material emancipations and liberations are often found in unlikely material sources, such as dust, creating new means of materially experiencing them away from socialized *a priory* categories. Quoting Parikka, 'Dust already counts, as does a litany ... of other non-human things/processes: technologies, chemicals, rabbits, chairs, airplanes, LCD displays, ionisation, geological formations, insects, shoes, valves, density of surfaces, and skin.' However, 'instead of a list, which we only could fake to be exhaustive, let's just state that matter has its intensities, its affordances and tendencies that are not just passive, waiting for the activity of form(ing) by the human' (Parikka, 2013, p 84). Such radical political materialization, and the true revolutionary promise of democracy, is rooted in the continual processes of dematerializing and rematerializing. To this end, 'new materialism has a specific relation to a future, which also means a certain openness: materialism has to be invented continuously anew: a speculative pragmatism.' At stake is a new sort of praxis of political reimagination and rematerialization based on the ongoing (im)material dialectic of virtualization and actualization. Hence, the possibility of novel modes of existence 'cannot just be discovered dormant, formulated in a philosophy book, or a theoretical doctrine; instead, speculative mapping turns to the world of non-humans in concrete ways and often aided by artistic practices'. For this reason, both materiality and the political 'leaks in many directions. ... It is transformational, ecological, and multiscalar' (Parikka, 2013, p 86).

These insights gesture toward the need to cultivate a political ethos of radical rematerializing that brings together the insights of historical materialism and new materialism. It means discovering concrete ways of materially reproducing ourselves as active 'individuals' capable of concretely reimagining, reordering, reconnecting and when possible resituating our existence. When speaking of the 'individual', we draw inspiration from DeLanda's (2013) notion of 'flat ontology' whereby there is no hierarchy of materials but rather interconnected and socially as well as physically situated 'individuals' in continual mutual relation and transformation. The emerging and wide-ranging efforts to exploit digital fabrication and distributed manufacturing methods (such as 3D printing) for producing a 'commons-based economy' represent tangible attempts to politically rematerialize the social. The use of peer production techniques, whereby people can share ideas via open-source platforms, allows for a culture of 'designing globally and manufacturing locally' (Kostakis & Papachristou, 2014, p 434). These are already being co-opted ironically within contemporary capitalism – as evidenced in the 2012 announcement by then US president Obama of a 'a National Network for Manufacturing Innovation' meant to encourage such open-source collaboration between private and public sector organizations as well as 'insourcing' (the incentivizing of companies using these new production techniques to remain in the US as opposed to 'outsourcing' production to exploit lower labour costs). It is telling that they are explicitly referred to as 'innovative' in that they reflect the dynamic incorporation of commons values and practices for the remobilization of capitalism. By contrast, there are a growing number of studies and initiatives for exploring how such techniques can be used for politically transforming economic and social relations. These include ideas ranging from the incorporating of locally produced material into 3D production processes for producing a sustainable, digitally fabricated circular economy (Garmulewicz, 2015), to the use of local digital networks such as near-field communication for encouraging collaborative, place-based commons (see Wood, 2016), to public workshops for using these techniques to teach commons-based values and skills in schools (Stickel et al, 2017). Significantly, they can be described, using our terminology, as political rematerializations in so much as they are an attempt to employ concrete production processes and methods for radically disrupting our contemporary social world.

These 'glocal' emancipations, though, hold the possibility of leading to global revolutions. They could become a contagious means for using a wide range of social material resources to (im)materially reconnect to others across differing host contexts. This was evident, for instance, in the recent rise of the Twitter-driven Black Lives Matter movement, wherein viral hashtags and memes were used to 'forge a shared political temporality, and [gave insight into] how social media platforms can provide strategic outlets for contesting and reimagining the materiality of racialised bodies' (Bonilla & Rossa, 2015, p 4). They stand, thus, as a disruptive form of diverse universalism – in which a particular demand against injustice is adapted to specific material contexts and, through immaterial labour, in contextually radical ways. Once again, absolutely crucial is the transformation of mobile resources into political materials. This involves combining older traditions of cultural materialism – as epitomized, for instance, in the work of Raymond Williams – with new materialism. Hands writes that 'cultural materialism recognises social stratification, the centrality of contestation and the tensions between dominant, emergent, and residual class positions and the role of intention in negotiating between these positions' (Hands, 2015, p 143). This entails the distinguishing of alienating social materializations from empowering political-material potentialities.

Vital, in this regard, is the radical immaterial labour aimed at the virtual reimagination of the social linked to new material forms of reconnection. This offers the opportunity for a total reconception of social relations and possibilities for reshaping one's material context. This is witnessed, for example, in emerging notions of a 'cyborg' society, one that is populated as much by artificial intelligence and non-human consciousness as it is by human 'life'. Significantly, 'they generate, and are, in turn, generated, within new environments, or maybe a "cyborganized" order' (Luke, 1996, p 1367). This represents, again, an (im)material dialectic premised on new forms of materializations. It is one of continual 'cyborging', combining and recombining existing processes in new ways to explore what is possible as well as to expose the technological and social limits of our existing realities.

This, furthermore, is not exclusively a feature of the contemporary age. Rather, each society is composed of and reproduced by these (im)material dialectics. Indeed, as Bruster presciently reminds us, 'premodern objects were endowed with an autonomy and agency that was largely misrecognized in the wake of Enlightenment empiricism ... where and how the line between human and nonhuman, subject and object, society and nature gets drawn is always an ideological process' (Bruster, 2003, p 191). Nevertheless, in the present era, immaterial dialectics are rooted in the ability to forge novel connections, using a range of physical and digital materials. Significantly, 'these mediums instead permit individuals to democratically voice their personal dissatisfaction, to construct their own ethno-epistemic assemblages of truth-making and to mobilize a networked response that incorporates diverse viewpoints, a collective line of flight that aims to bring the disputed diagram of control into a state of crisis' (Bruster, 2003, p 191).

Additionally, this emphasis on reconnection helps to reinvigorate historical materialism by refusing to allow it to be a caricatured foil for new materialism or post-Marxist perspectives. Here, it is part and parcel of a guerrilla democratic commitment to radically and contagiously rematerialize new ways of being in the world. According to Choat, 'Rather than borrowing scientific insights into matter, historical materialism examines the historically specific power relations and divisions of labour within which modern science arose and is embedded', and as such, 'rather than extending agency to everything, historical materialism insists that we need both to understand how different agents have acquired their powers to act and to acknowledge the asymmetric power relations within which their agency is developed and enacted.' Ultimately, 'rather than opposing the ontological division of nature and society simply by pointing to their actual imbrication, historical materialism explores the historical origins and persistence of the division and the differential experience of and access to nature that is characteristic of contemporary society' (Choat, 2018, p 1040).

Represented, as well, is a materialist account of democracy. It is one fundamentally premised not just on a conflict or engagement of ideas but of diverse materializations. Just as importantly, this expands democracy to the entirety of the material and virtual world. This can include rivers and water, for instance, which serve not just as fundamental aspects of our biological and ecological survival but can become crucial parts of our political rematerialization. Thus 'natural' things such as rivers can transform into 'democratic entities' by forcing communities to interrogate, transform and rematerialize their deeper social assumptions and relationships with their environment as well as to take into account the various 'needs' and affordances of this streaming water. This speaks to a democracy grounded in an ethos of dissensus based on the continual 'redistribution of the sensible'. Such a redistribution is one that flows from the discursive to the material and vice-versa. Trumpeter (2015), for instance, notes how literature can alert people to the language of the non-human and inorganic, like stones. While this may appear only to be representational, it is in fact a political raw material, a physical book or digital text that allows for the virtual reimagination of our materialized realities. Yet such reimaginings are only made into rematerializations via the concrete potential for radical reconnections. At stake is the perpetuation of what McGregor (2014, p 212) calls 'sociomaterial movement learning', which involves establishing political networks that not only struggle for specific social demands but also gain ever-newer knowledge of how to collectively rematerialize the world.

In doing this, power and agency are displaced and distributed, so that the entire notion of 'collective learning' is redefined to include non-human matter.

This process of (im)material reconnection is rooted in the solidarity and shared capabilities of human and non-human matter. In this sense, we become united as political, material animations in a collective process of learning and engaging in creatively disruptive immaterial labour for the radical rematerialization of society. A guerrilla ethos is required for transforming the world from a collection of governable things into revolutionary mobile resources and political materials. Revealed are the revolutionary possibilities of democratic (im)materialism.

Conclusion

This chapter explored the (im)material dimensions of mobile power, viral hegemony and guerrilla democracy. To do so it drew upon theories of 'new materialism' but ultimately expanded upon them so as to better account for the immaterial and political aspects of social ordering. It introduced, for this reason, a novel concept of '(im)materialism' which highlights the immaterial necessity of continually and dynamically materializing and rematerializing the social. Significantly, this is not to assume in the slightest that humans are 'in control' or are the complete 'shapers' of their material realities – whether in the virtual or physical realms. Rather, it stresses how these material encounters are manifestations of mobile power and viral hegemony, whereby they must constantly adapt existing materials and their various concrete affordances to meet the demands of infectious discourses. Likewise, this dynamic process of (im)material socialization can also lend itself to political interventions, whereby an existent order is not just rematerialized but resituated. A core theme of this book is that this radical (im)materialism can be best expressed through a democratic guerrilla politics.

The introduction of (im)materialism obviously touches on a range of important and ongoing theoretical and political debates. Notably, it raises questions concerning concepts of historical materialism, which, in the scope of this chapter and focus of this book, we have only briefly touched upon. Yet it is worth mentioning that the original intent of new materialism was not necessarily to supplant historical materialism but to enhance it. In this spirit, the concept of (im)materialism adds to this tradition, firstly by shifting the emphasis from materialism to 'materializations. Crucial, in this regard, are how differing historical modes of economic and social production are diversely materialized across a range of host contexts in such a way that they reproduce their dominant ideological and power relations. It also points to the quite material reasons why there must be, ultimately, a 'primacy' granted to the political as opposed to the economic. Or more precisely, it recognizes that while there may be an underlying economic structure that is 'overdetermining' of social relations generally, this is only concretely manifested via contingent processes of mobile and viral materialization. Accordingly, there is always the literal and figurative space in which to locally and globally transform these relations.

The (im)material dimension forms a crucial component of the broader ways in which we are seeking to conceptually and practically reconsider power, hegemony and politics. Specifically, this book has linked social change to processes of reimagination and reconnection. This is the ongoing and dialectical relation of the virtual and actual. The political – at its most pure – is a phenomenon of 'resituation', whereby an existent 'truth' is changed, giving rise to radically new parameters for diversely organizing the social. Consequently, it is doing more than merely remobilizing a prevailing situation – it is disrupting it and threatening to completely reconfigure its possible iterations. As this chapter highlights, fundamental to both innovative remobilizing and disruptive resituating is the (im)material labour involved in continually rematerializing a social context. Politically, this can involve a range of guerrilla strategies, whereby social things are creative repurposed into political resources and in which new radical spaces can be constructed that have the prospect of fomenting a revolutionary contagion.

This analysis additionally aims to offer some prescient and timely historical insights. To a certain extent, the analysis of (im)materialism that we are proposing is trans-historical, in that there is always an element of immaterial labour that is involved in materializing any and all dominant social relations. Likewise, power and domination necessarily rely upon – though to varying degrees of intensity – the governance of 'things' and the production of active mobile resources for this purpose. This echoes, thus, the relative 'timelessness' of mobile power and viral hegemony. However, we are also making a further claim. Namely, that the growing prevalence of mobile technologies has made the reliance on mobile resources ever more critical to the resilience and spread of neoliberalism. Therefore, what is needed is a reorientation of how we view effective leadership for enacting such radical rematerializations – ones that are focused less on sovereign rule and more on flexibly taking advantage of an increasingly 'liquid' world.

7

Organic Leadership
for Liquid Times

Uber drivers in the UK have used WhatsApp extensively in their organizing of drivers – like for Deliveroo, TGI Fridays, Wetherspoons and McDonald's workers, this built upon pre-existing networks and online groups. In the UK, this mobile organizing has developed further, as witnessed in their recent strikes on 9 October 2018. They called a 24-hour strike from 1 pm, demanding increased fares of £2 per mile, for Uber's commission to be reduced to 15 percent, an end to unfair deactivations (or sacking of drivers) and bullying, and worker rights protections. 'After years of watching take-home pay plummet and with management bullying of workers on the rise, workers have been left with no choice but to take strike action', the branch chair of United Private Hire Drivers (UPHD) (the branch of the Independent Workers Union of Great Britain (IWGB) that organizes Uber drivers), James Farrar (quoted in IWGB, 2018), argued, continuing: 'We ask the public to please support drivers by not crossing the digital picket line by not using the app during strike time.'

As Farrar notes, the drivers redrew the notion of the picket line for their dispersed and digitally mediated workplace. Rather than maintaining a picket outside meeting points, taxi ranks or offices, they argued that the app should be the picket line. This was supplemented with protests outside Uber offices to provide a physical point to focus on as well. On a global level, Uber drivers have coordinated through WhatsApp, Facebook and Twitter to take joint action in the run up to Uber's IPO (initial public offering). These platforms have been key for providing the opportunities for workers to contact each other across borders, greatly lowering the administrative and logistical costs that would have been involved in doing so previously.

This growth of 'digital picket lines' reveals the importance of understanding (im)material power and politics. Here, discourses and ideologies not only operate but are framed within the public consciousness in these epidemic terms. This epidemic discursive framing can be traced back, at least, to the beginnings of the Cold War. The ability to see viruses in the decade after the Second World War fascinated scientists and the general public as, according to Wald (2017, p 158), 'unlike their bacterial counterparts, viral microbes existed on – and seemed to define – the border between the living and non-living. Viruses showed how the circulation of "information" allowed an organism to function.' It represented, in this regard,

> a gradual change through which the media portrayed the viral contagion and the changing Cold War that suggests a conceptual exchange between virology and Cold War politics. As viruses became increasingly sinister and wiley, sneaking into cells and assuming control of their mechanisms, external agents such as Communists, became viral threatening to corrupt the dissemination of information as they infiltrated the nerve centre of the state. (Wald, 2017, p 159)

It is, therefore, crucial to better critically comprehend what is required to radically manage and shape this viral culture. It requires using (im)material labour to (re)materialize the social in order to reveal its contingency and alterability.

From liquid times to revolutionary resolidifying

These concerns are, as we will now explore in this chapter, especially important during our current 'liquid times'. In a sense, it is easy to simply dismiss the question of leadership as outdated – based on sovereign and patriarchal notions of coercive, personalized and rather stagnant forms of power. Furthermore, it is understandable that many on the left, among the democratically inclined New Left in particular, remain sceptical of any notion of leadership, equating it with either a mystification of the colonial and neoliberal system it serves or with vanguard authoritarianism antithetical to its values. However, the growing importance of mobile power and viral hegemony, particularly in these increasingly liquified times, requires a critical reconsideration of what constitutes leadership and its radical possibilities. This penultimate chapter introduces the idea of 'organic leadership'– one that is based paradoxically on creatively resolidifying the social in ways that reimagine its relations and reconnect its subjects.

We approach leadership as a practice rather than a person (Raelin, 2016) – a verb rather than noun (Grint, 2005a). By this we mean that leadership is an action, linguistic and material, that does real work; it shapes, influences, inspires, repulses and so on. Contrary to the dominant accounts of leadership as a practice, even the ones that seek a democratic approach, our view of practice is one riven and shaped by conflict and antagonism. In common with most accounts of more democratic forms of leadership-as-practice (for example, Raelin, 2016), we do accept that such leadership can manifest through democratic forms of dialogue, but we go a step further and state that practices of organic leadership, a term to be developed as we continue, are constituted through intra-democratic dialogue and connection but also antagonistic opposition to hegemony. This is an opposition that takes place extra-dialogically, through acts of assertion and direct action aimed at disrupting and destructing rather than consensus building, or via intra-acts within counter-hegemonic groups aimed at strengthening connection against a status quo. Such a view accepts that leadership is a contested and collective terrain, where acts of leadership can emerge – and be opposed – anywhere in a system. Yet it does not dismiss the notion of an influential, powerful sovereign leader, or for that matter that of the singular power of an individual 'from below' articulating leadership in a way that moves others. We draw the line, however, at accounts of leadership that seek to universalize and psychologize such moments as examples of an innate and universal essence or personality owned by a discrete and bounded leader. Rather, 'leaders' are sedimentations of discursive articulations whose ability to lead with authority and power depends on a consensus among others that such a person and such articulations are to be taken seriously. Hence why leaders from corporate multinationals – not to mention White men – are taken more seriously by a configuration of the social shaped by colonial and neoliberal norms (Liu, 2020), even if movements emerge to challenge such privilege. Leaders are therefore contested symbols whose presence and interpretation can move others, and whose very meaning and identity is often hotly contested (Sinha et al, 2019).

This thus raises the important question of what precisely guerrilla democratic leadership is? We are not interested in innate leadership qualities or sovereign modes of personalized power. Instead, what is crucial is the capacity to individually and collectively 'resolidify' the 'liquid social' reflective of alternative and liberating values. Here, in politically rematerializing one's social contexts, there emerge spaces of inoculation against hegemonic infections conducive to processes of reimagining, reordering, reconnecting and resituating. 'Liquid leadership', then, denotes the shared capacities to help actualize this resolidification and then, when successful, help ensure it is contagious. It is 'organic' in so much as it emerges from a specific context and through the diverse people and things within it. It is 'guerrilla' in that it involves the disruptive repurposing of existing social structures, objects and norms to this end. And it is democratic in that it opens up, even if only locally, an opportunity for collectively shaping our existence. Fundamentally, it is the transformation of our liquid times into revolutionary resolidifications.

Liquid times

The contemporary era is becoming not just more mobile but more 'fluid'. Traditional identifications linked to geography and ethnicity are becoming dissolved and reconfigured into novel social bonding across wide distances and previously disparate demographics boundaries. This has been aided by the rise of ICTs, as indeed by the end of the 20th century the study of geography was becoming more fluid due to the interventions of both new ICTs and fresh critical perspectives such as those associated with feminism and cultural studies (Tuathail et al, 1996). We are now approaching a point at which both knowledge and connections are progressively viral – where the bond is virtual as much as it exists 'in real life'. Such a reality immediately calls into question the dominant mode of interpreting leadership as the personality and behaviour of a senior leader – such people rarely meet or engage with followers (and antagonists) face to face or in any depth. Instead, they are conglomerations of discourses, images and signs that people engage with through devices – and this stands as much for the executives of large corporations in relation to their workers as it does for citizens and political leaders. To a certain extent, this has always been true, in that even the most essentialist identities were grounded ultimately in 'imagined communities' of nationalism, race and ethnicity. Indeed, the rise of ethno-nationalist political movements in the 20th century relied upon the emergence of an effective mass media (from radios to television) for reinforcing these supposedly natural connections.

In the present period, this has been reconfigured to include a range of shifting social networks, whose ideas and potential identities can infect and thus shape those within a given host context. Significantly, such viral identities occur within overlapping host contexts, and just as importantly, individuals often belong to several, whose boundaries and relation are both customizable to their own subjecting histories and in continual flux. Perhaps the theorist who comes closest to describing this contemporary condition of fluidity is Zygmunt Bauman. He proposed, at the dawn of the new millennium, that we were entering into an age of 'liquid modernity'. He notes: 'These days patterns and configurations are no longer "given" let alone "self-evident"; there are just too many of them clashing with one another and contradicting one another's commandments, so that each one has been stripped of a good deal of compelling, coercively constraining power' (Bauman, 2000, p 6). Critically, this liquifying process has resulted not merely in the rise of individuation but of customization – whereby the social and the political are increasingly personalized rather than standardized or part of any general identification. 'The liquefying powers have moved from the "system" to "society", from "politics" to "life-policies"– or have descended from the "macro" to the "micro" level of cohabitation', maintains Bauman (2000, p 6): 'Ours is as a result, an individualised, privatized version of modernity, with the burden of pattern-weaving and the responsibility for failure falling primarily on the individual's shoulders.'

Reflected is the relation between liquid society and mobile power. Here domination is found not so much in solidifying or, as Foucault refers to it, 'paralyzing' a given social order. Instead, it is rooted, ironically, in its flexible shaping and continual adaptation. Crucially, this represents a sea change in the conventional efforts of modernity to impose a universal notion of market-based societal development. Development, and fundamentally notions of capitalist progress, is now not generalizable but customizable – ongoing and context-specific, without a final destination but rather permanently under construction and in need of innovation. Consequently, 'globalisation appears to have turned development into an otiose concept. The idea of a solid end-point has fizzled out as the liquefying power of global capital is dissolving all the boundaries that once distinguished between different countries on the road to a solid modernity' (Lee, 2005, p 70).

However, this liquifaction is also highly infectious. More precisely, it connects host contexts together in new and surprising ways. This can be achieved as a moment of 'disruptive solidity' due to a fleeting sense of collective recognition of shared truth or oppression. Returning to the insights of Bauman, he argues that 'moral moments act as catalysts that may lead to the acquisition of some solidity by a liquid society, when confronted and forced to reckon with its own past of human rights abuse, its own involvement in horrors' (Bauman, 2006, p 29). Yet this also plays into fears of being liquified – left without any certainty, sense of individual identity or common grounding. This sense of fear has catalyzed what Las Casas and Scorza (2017, p 524) refer to as a need for a 'renewed rational approach from liquid society towards rational planning' that uses participatory processes as a means for implementing 'anti-fragile strategies'.

What is clear, though, is that fear is now increasingly an endemic part of being a subject in a liquified world. These desires for solidity have given rise to novel forms of disciplinary control, in turn. The rise of big data as a tracking tool preys on these anxieties, offering an opportunity to 'know oneself' via such top-down datafication. To this end, 'what seems to be emerging now is an updated dialectic of capitalist control in which the more it disrupts societies and the people's lives within them, the greater the perceived need for rationalisation and monitoring' (Bloom, 2019, p 45). It is one that not only provides managers and those in authority with a greater ability to control subjects but also grants individuals and communities, ironically, a stronger sense of ontological security in an increasingly liquifying world.

This reinforcement of a stable self via processes of greater quantification will arguably only be exacerbated as new technologies challenge the very notion of traditional humanity. Posthumanism, in this respect, threatens to liquify contemporary human-based knowledge, providing new means to apprehend and make sense of the world. It produces '(1) cosmic nihilism, (2) molecular bio-plasticity, (3) technical accelerationism, and (4) animality', all of which challenge 'humankind's stubborn pretensions to mastery over the domain of the intelligible and the knowable' (Murphet, 2016, p 653). Here, modern existence becomes a 'style' to adopt and discard as needed. To be liquid, then, is to be stabilized as a constantly shifting subject, adapting constantly to infectious discourses, making one a personalized host to new dominating viral knowledges.

Revealed, though, are the possibilities of liquid contagions. In a sense, the present, increasingly liquid society represents the ultimate conflation of selfhood with capitalism. It is one of consuming identities, clinging and evolving to ever new 'fashionable' selves. This 'fashionable' liquid self, however, contains a multitude of radical possibilities. It points to a willingness for continual reimagination – one that, with the proper critical efforts, can be evolved from personal consumption into social reimagination and transformation. New 'utopias' must be developed, and must themselves be multiple and mobile. Hence, 'if we want to avoid a future that finds humanity groping in the dark trough of economic depression and natural catastrophe, we need to discuss and ultimately find degrees of unity around the positive features of post-capitalist alternative economic orders' (Westra et al, 2017, pp 3–4). Such desires gesture towards the importance of creating radical contagions through processes of ongoing rematerializations and ultimately democratic resituations. At stake is the ability to draw on these alternatives to engage in an inspiring counter-hegemonic project of reimagination and reconnection. Hence, 'emphasizing positive alternative economic systems fires up the imagination and brings people together in order to get closer to or even reach these alternatives.' These will further depend on the use of this liquified foundation to politically rematerialize these 'post-capitalist utopias'– translating them into concrete, everyday practices of solidarity, collaboration and mutual empowerment.

Reimagining and rematerializing governance

The growing prevalence of mobile technologies has helped to transform struggles for economic rights and worker power. Yet they also draw upon rather traditional forms of labour organizing and cultures of solidarity. This has given rise to novel digital-based struggles that rely upon a politics of reimagination and reconnection. Hence, although most Uber driver organizing, as with other kinds of platforms, has been led by worker WhatsApp groups and social media networking, in the US they have also developed new kinds of struggles. They have 'partnered with Rideshare Drivers United–Los Angeles, a democratic and independent association of US rideshare drivers seeking fair pay, transparency, a voice on the job, and community standards in the rideshare industry', according to Dolber (2019, p 4), who continues, 'with limited resources and volunteer labor, RDU was able to leverage the low cost of social media advertising, and, through app-based technologies and SMS, develop a hybrid online-offline model of organizing.' In particular, 'the success of RDU's campaign demonstrates that such a model can help overcome the obstacles endemic to building a democratic organisation of a massive, unidentified, disaggregated, and fluid workforce that can exercise real power.'

At the heart of these efforts was a radical guerrilla ethos. In particular, this involved reusing aspects of digital media advertizing developed by Facebook. RDU was able to target Uber and Lyft drivers through the granularity of the data Facebook held – albeit data that was captured to find new and innovative ways to convince people to buy things. This provided the first point of contact with drivers, using the advert as a way to direct them to the RDU website, onto a purpose-built RDU app, then into organizing conversations with volunteer organizers.

Following on from this, they developed a method for polling members about issues, ensuring that the organizing committee could understand and effectively represent the concerns of a growing organization of drivers. By 2019, RDU had grown its membership base to 2,500 and organized strikes on 25 March and 8 May in LA (Dolber, 2019, p 4). The use of social media advertizing means that efforts can be measured with the metrics and datafication that companies usually use to understand the effectiveness of their advertizing. However, in this case, the cost of recruiting drivers (taking into account the drop-off at each point of contact) was lowered to the point that they 'were able to bring the cost per member down to $0.73 by January 31st 2019' (Dolber, 2019, p 11).

The previous example reveals how the rise of a liquid society and its basis in viral knowledges and ordering requires a reconsideration of what constitutes a radical ethics. In particular, the liquifiying of established social bonds, the dissolution of traditional communities (both historically real and imagined), brings to light a seemingly simple but rather profound question: Who and what should we care about and for? The embrace of multiple selves, the subject as protagonist in a range of overlapping host contexts adapting to and trying to keep up with, often in almost real time, a range of colonizing infectious discourses, points to what may appear to be the superficiality of contemporary relationships. However, it also gestures towards the investment in possibility, a renewed attention to the various virtual trajectories that any one person can ultimately potentially actualize. There is, thus, an implicit sense of virtual care, a caretaking of prospective futures, and of the present, ensuring that one always has and knows their evolving options.

Just as significantly, it reveals the foundations for a different, more radical type of politics of plurality. In their most popular liberal form, pluralism and difference become ends in themselves, empty though normatively crucial gestures towards prioritizing values of tolerance, diversity and recognition. Processes of liquifaction, and at a deeper level their rootedness in mobile power and viral orderings, politicize this ethos in new and quite radical ways. They use it as a basis for continual disruption and resolidification. Here, the revolutionary point is not in simply introducing new marginalized voices into the civic sphere or the political realm. Nor does it follow the conventional radical democratic dictates of subverting a solid and apparently unalterable status quo. By contrast, its revolutionary ethos is discovered and made manifest precisely in allowing for the giving of fleeting stability to an otherwise liquid environment by forging seemingly incongruent but lasting reconnections. Doing so means recognizing that traditional radical democratic values are fundamental to meeting the political challenges of this emergent liquid society. 'Openness to the others, plurality, sharing and solidarity beyond differences, variation, creativity, singularity and equality, infinite justice, resistance to homogenisation, totality and atomisation, opposition to closed identities of soil, blood, community or self', says Kioupkiolis (2018, p 293), 'all these are cardinal values of a politics which aspires to equal freedom and justice in a globalised, diverse, fragmented and dramatically unequal world'. Moreover, such democratizing values of plurality and difference must be more than mere philosophical interventions and instead 'should trigger, rather, efforts to politicize the ontologies of being singular plural.'

Crucial to these efforts is encouraging local instances of rematerialization to promote global democratic resituatings of the social and its power relations. Emerging radical social movements, such as Occupy and the anti-austerity Indignados insurgency in Spain, thrive on transforming liquified host contexts into solidified political spaces open to experimentation and the contagious possibilities of disruptive creations. Here, 'they crafted open communities of political participation' as 'the movements were organized in public squares where they set up popular assemblies, creating thus spaces of free and plural action in concert' (Kioupkiolis, 2018, p 245). The use of these physical locations was itself emblematic of this attempt to politically expand democracy, as 'the very choice of public squares and streets to establish assemblies, in its contrast to decision-making behind closed doors, makes evident the will to open up political activity to any and all' (p 295). Importantly, it was not merely symbolic. Instead it was an act of guerrilla repurposing – turning these 'social spaces' into political ones for concretely actualizing a more democratic society. As such, 'their processes of collective decision-making opened political power to common citizens, striking down informal and institutional barriers to participation' and, furthermore, 'openness went hand in hand with plurality and diversity' (p 295). These movements, thus, combined a profound resistance to neoliberalism with efforts to actualize an alternative way of being. Indeed, 'the Indignados and Occupy rose up against material inequalities, debt, foreclosures and the economic system that engenders them in complicity with states', and towards these ends, 'they actively promoted diversity by foreswearing ideological closures and strict programmatic definitions and by articulating, through their assemblies, a spacious discourse hospitable to many different people' (p 295).

In these rematerialized spaces, they also redirected political conceptions of difference away from demographics, with their bio-political roots in the sovereign categorization and management of populations, into an effort to promote diverse social rationalities aimed at discovering resituated forms of egalitarian-based good governance that could spread and inform other political communities. Crucially, these political interventions imbue new meaning into notions of 'self-governance'. Here, it is precisely in these radical processes of resolidification that a novel collective self emerges. Critically, this emergent self is not inscriptive but (im)material, an identity grounded in its possibilities rather than its presumed essentialities. The philosopher Jean-Luc Nancy captures this phenomenon in his influential work *The Inoperative Community*, where he proclaims that 'a community presupposed as having to be one of human beings presupposes that it effect, or that it must effect, as such and integrally, its own essence, which is itself the accomplishment of the essence of humanness' (Nancy, 1991, p 3) Significantly, past and present economic, social and political ties (including those of support for a leader) reveal this shared 'essence'.

Singularity, in turn, becomes a radical gesture of viral reimagination and reconnection – a speculative materialization as to what a different existence may look and feel like 'in real life'. 'What is a body, a face, a voice, a death, a writing–not indivisible, but singular?', Nancy asks: 'What is their singular necessity in the sharing that divides and that puts in communication bodies, voices, and writings in general and in totality? In sum, this question would be exactly the reverse of the question of the absolute' (Nancy, 1991, pp 7–8). Solidarity, then, evolves from a sense of shared oppression – the need to build up common and convergent resistances to colonizing infections – into a revolutionary 'resemblance', in which these political communities and their members find commonality in their commitment to exploring novel social arrangements rooted in the historical realities of their given hegemonic contexts and the speculative potentialities that they contain. Returning to the insights of Nancy, he contends that 'there is no original or origin of identity. What holds the place of an "origin" is the sharing of singularities ... the origin of community or the originary community – is nothing other than the limit: the origin is the tracing of the borders upon which or along which singular beings are exposed' (Nancy, 1991, pp 33–4).

These political communities of virtual possibilities, whose foundations rest in the promotion of radical material equality and difference, provide the basis for a powerful sense of contagious agency, where through their local immanent examples of revolutionary solidification and disruptive creation, the potential for transcendence is preserved and made contagious. Nancy concludes his own reflections comparing this to a religiosity without gods, a materializing faith that the world is ours to shape and create together. 'Divine places, without gods, with no god, are spread out everywhere around us, open and offered to our coming, to our going or to our presence', he declares. 'These places spread out everywhere, yield up and orient new spaces: they are no longer temples, but rather the opening up and the spacing out of the temples themselves, a dislocation with no reserve henceforth, with no more sacred enclosures – other tracks, other ways, other places for all who are there' (Nancy, 1991, p 150).

At stake, thus, is a novel foundation for considering political ethics. Nancy offers an 'ethics of sociality without a social subject' (Korchagina & Pullen, 2016, p 12616). This, in turn, opens up novel possibilities for conceiving and investing in a democratic politics – one that can radically reimagine the possibilities of conventional bio-politics and its emphasis on managing populations. To this effect, while traditionally democracy seeks to bind people amidst their demographic and ideological differences into a common, imagined 'body politic', a radical democratic gesture would be one that reveals the profound plurality at the heart of our existence and our potential to materialize 'singular communities of contagious possibility based on equality, to make every universe a multiverse' (Prozorov, 2018, p 1101).

Rather than imagined communities of biology or nationalism, we conceive a political ethos and identity that thus celebrates, commemorates and cherishes continual processes of what we term radical resolidification. Its community, that which unites people and things, is the act of disruptive creation, the resolidification of liquid society in new emancipatory ways. Leadership, for us, therefore, signals a 'coming into being' through forms of democratic direction-setting that draw together novel connections and alliances between previously disconnected and disparate groups, who are now connected through digital articulations.

The political, within leadership and outside it, in a sense, then becomes the dual processes of building up resistances to hegemonic infections and the disruptive collective creation of unfinished realities (the 'building up' being where the leadership resides). This revolutionary act of resolidification, rematerialization and community building is, to an extent, already implied in Laclau and Mouffe's original theories of discursive hegemony. The social, by its very existence, is incomplete and available to continual alteration. It reflects 'the incomplete character of every totality necessarily lead[ing] us to abandon, as a terrain of analysis, the premise of "society" as a sutured and self defined totality.' They continue, in this respect, proclaiming that ' "society" is not a valid object of discourse. There is no single underlying principle fixing – and hence constituting – the whole field of differences. The irresoluble interiority/exteriority tension is the condition of any social practice: necessity only exists as a partial limitation of the field of contingency' (Laclau & Mouffe, 1986, p 111).

Laclau and Mouffe's initial conception of hegemony, though, is itself theoretically narrow and empirically available to reconsideration. They conceive it as the 'covering over' of this incompleteness rather than its strategic highlighting as a point of ongoing innovation. Domination is found not in 'paralyzing social relations but in making its subjects eternally responsible for its completion and improvement. 'Power exists only when it is put into action, even if, of course', according to Foucault, 'it is integrated into a disparate field of possibilities brought to bear upon permanent structures' (Foucault, 1982, p 788). Counter-hegemony, then, is adding (a practice for leadership in our schema) a sense of temporary permanency to emergent structural possibilities. Such potentials come to light, for instance, in the 'active informationalism' and 'generative time regime' marking our contemporary liquid age. In this age of rapid, almost instantaneous communication and online connections, every system is 'unfolding a self-referential world by its specific selection and synthesis of environmental data', and thus, 'to influence the becoming of a system means to generate worlds' (Löffler, 2018, p 38).

This entails, though, a process of constant (im)material enactments through which material objects help to better materialize the concrete realities of a given environment while also gesturing towards its radical virtual possibilities. These radical forms of (im)material enactments can take on a greater permanency, extending into and rematerializing conventional spaces such as classroom learning environments. For instance, emerging 'internet-based learning environment' pedagogies shift from being a unidirectional information exchange to becom[ing] a complex series of entangled movements, affects and sensations' as 'the interstices of classroom territories are rich with collaborative potential'. Far from being a 'disembodied' experience, 'the physicality of individual territory ownership is reframed through the assemblage of resources, bodies and spatial demands. Among the principals, there appears to be engagement with the agency of objects' (Charteris et al, 2017, p 818).

Here, technologies become not merely gadgets to use but extensions of one's possible selves. They are an (im)material resource for continual radical rematerialization and democratic resituation, appendages of one's emergent non-essential 'self' that allow for revolutionary ferment. One recent five-year study of students at the University of Arizona found, for instandce, that 'smartphones are not merely separate pieces of equipment, but rather appendages to the body and conduits for intensity and even transformation. Embodied and networked, mobile devices are about becomings within competing relations' (Mapes & Kimme-Hea, 2018, p 73). These findings offer, furthermore, an institutional and social basis for making an ethos of 'fragility' and liquification not something to fear but to embrace, as the foundations for one's own personal and collective development. The possibilities associated with posthumanism then present 'new constitutions of being in the world [that] are based on a creative reconceptualisation of what is already believed about the human condition, an unsettling of old ways in order to open up a mindfulness to the already hybrid place of nature in everyday life' (Sonu & Snaza, 2015, p 274).

Uncovered, thus, is a novel understanding of governance and community. Traditionally, governance is based on making subjects governable by articulating a given space as available to administrative ordering. This is premised on the fostering of an 'imagined community' as part of an essentialized or 'sovereign' people. Indeed, the political is in many ways the de-essentializing (again a verb we take to be an important practice of leadership) of this imagined community away from the tribal or hereditary and its renaturalization as a population to be governed. As such, questions of race, ethnicity, gender and class become aspects to be properly governed, linked to diverse collections of established and seemingly durable sovereign communities. The radical rematerialization of governance, by contrast, is found in the reversal of this (im)material sovereign dynamic – whereby that which is imagined allows for its concrete administration and innovation. Here, conversely, it is in the process of materializing leadership that new disruptive possibilities emerge and are actualized.

Hence, just as mobile power forces a reconsideration of what constitutes domination, so too does liquification reframe the question and possibilities of governance. Specifically, the establishment and administration of a social order is one increasingly grounded in the capacity to flexibly forge (with forging, bonding and suturing being leadership practices) a range of new connections across dynamic virtual and IRL networks. Consequently, governance revolves around managing these shifting networks, customizing information and rules so as to directly influence them based on their inessential connections – ones often based on a set of chosen preferences rather than perceived inborn similarities. We previously discussed, in this respect, the contemporary evolution from the 'governance of things' to the continual activation of 'mobile resources' and 'political materials' for this purpose. Similarly, the growth of a liquid society for whom imagined communities exist as much in virtual as in physical spaces opens the way for continually experimenting with the creation of new 'social worlds'. It is an opportunity to ceaselessly reimagine and rematerialize our governance.

Resolidifying a commons politics

Among workers organizing in the UK today, social media is increasingly playing an important role in starting campaigns. Instead of taking the paid-advertizing route like the RDU, many workers have found that social media has made it possible to connect with workers beyond their own immediate or personal networks. For example, in the UK, the TGI Fridays strike organizers have spoken about using Facebook and a form of network analysis to find workers in branches other than their own, searching for 'TGI Fridays' to see whether they could find workers who listed it as their employment on the platform, while also mapping out which geographical networks its initial team of organizers covered, to maximize the possibilities for outreach. While this may not work for finding all workers, it can then be used to start building a relationship of solidarity, and has the potential to help initiate more sustained forms of coordinating – as networks hold the potential for exponential growth. In the TGI Fridays example, initial connections snowballed, which then led to the coordination of strike action and a mass and social media campaign. Digital technologies lend themselves well to the organizing of precarious workers in hospitality, who experience different shift patterns and whose population of women workers are more likely to have extra-work family commitments that prevent them from participating in more traditional modes of organizing, such as meetings.

In other examples, social media was heavily used by the 'Mixed Fleet' British Airways cabin crew, who went on extended periods of strike in 2016–17. Given the challenges of meeting and staying in touch with other cabin crew, who often spend extended periods of time in the air and in cities across the world, social media became key to building and maintaining the morale and confidence of the strikers. Indeed, as organizers have explained, social media played a key role in the workplace, building bonds between workers – particularly allowing for asynchronous communication – which could then be leveraged to discourage scabbing and to maintain momentum throughout the strike. In 2018, workers at Ryanair organized their first strike. Like the BA Mixed Fleet strikers, they used social media extensively as part of their organizing campaign, to connect Ryanair's bases for staff, which are spread across Europe.

These wide-ranging examples gesture towards the importance of cultivating a radical (im)material politics. This involves, however, more than simply the continuous attempt to replace one hegemony with another. Instead, it must be an effort in creative disruption leading to disruptive creation. Woods (2019) captures this spirit (or at least the first part of it) in his notion of 'punk urbanism'. He notes that 'cultural geographic understandings of urban insurgency are often framed in terms of *hegemonic replacement* – the substitution of a territory's dominant urban meaning with a new dominant urban meaning – and thus frame the absence of any coherent hegemonic social and cultural geography as crisis.' However, in his view, 'these theorisations of urban insurgency thereby fail to account for contested heterogeneity within a given urban territory and functionally silence dissenting forces.' What he found compelling in the nascent punk scene was that it sought not to embrace order but rather social liminality, as a moment of permanent 'interruption' reflective of 'hegemonic displacement rather than hegemonic replacement' (Woods, 2019, p 3).

At stake, then, is the need to inject an ethos of multiple resolidifications into projects and politics of counter-hegemony. In part, this touches on emerging perspectives of distributed leadership. These theories focus commonly – as their name suggests – on spreading out leadership responsibilities and fostering a more horizontal culture of direction setting. Yet, for such values to be properly translated from theory into praxis, they must engage in processes of rematerialization. According to Harris and DeFlaminis, 'Going forward, there is a real possibility that the on-going discussion and debate about distributed leadership will reside at the interface between practice, research and theory', hence, 'entrusting the idea of distributed leadership to those who enact and practice it ... would seem not only timely but also an important step forward in the next phase of its development' (Harris & DeFlaminis, 2016, p 144). However, these would also benefit from a more thorough materialist account of such possibilities for distributing leadership. More precisely, it is a question of whether such distributed leadership serves to innovatively rematerialize the capitalist mode of production from which it emerged or whether it disrupts it and as such rematerializes possibilities for a differing type of society and economic order. Quoting Marx from the third volume of *Capital*: 'It is always the direct relationship of the owners of the conditions of production to the direct producers ... which reveals the innermost secret, the hidden basis of the entire social structure, and with it the political form of the relations of sovereignty and dependence, the corresponding specific form of the state' (Marx, 1867, p 791).

In the present era, such attempts to fundamentally subvert the relationship between owners and producers is complicated by the fact we are all increasingly tasked to produce our own productive and profitable 'realities'. We are thus materially charged and disciplined to be efficient and creative immaterial labourers. In this regard, we are part of a range of 'glocal' host contexts, all of which must innovatively adapt to infectious market discourses and make themselves more conducive to their epidemic spread. Consequently, the danger is that distributive leadership simply serves to reinforce this progressive distribution of neoliberal management in these increasingly liquid times. Such a distribution is also sustained by the fostering of 'local fears' and 'global anxieties', which simultaneously demand individuals continually 'improve' the various environments they inhabit while affectively discouraging a reimagining of alternative orderings and forms of social existence.

To make sense of the leadership required of guerrilla democracy in more depth, we return to Antonio Gramsci to provide us with the coordinates. The reason for this is that Gramsci provides us with the necessary understanding of leadership from within diverse working-class communities, but also with a means of scaling up to help us envisage a form of leadership that can connect outwards to bring together previously disparate struggles, a connecting work that is of course constituted and facilitated through the digital as well as, if not more so, through the more traditional modes of organizing. In doing so, we begin to address some of the deficiencies with collective and more critical leadership theory, which tends, on the one hand, to view leadership as accomplished through relatively harmonious forms of dialogue internal to an organization and, on the other, does not consider class struggle and notions of leadership that are shaped outside the boundaries of more conventional organizations. We refer to such leadership as 'organic leadership', a concept established by placing Gramsci's notion of the organic intellectual in conversation with his account of leadership. We recognize that the term 'organic' may be interpreted as somewhat in conflict with our emphasis on cutting-edge technology and the digital, but maintain that, as Marx interpreted technological innovation as proceeding within a 'metabolism' of nature, we can posit the organic as that which flourishes within relational communities of practice. Collective modes of production are central to Marx's notion of species-being (Marx, 2000) – we are what we practice and make together. Furthermore, technology is but one means of describing the work done on nature's materials, within which is situated the human.

For Gramsci, each social group will generate organic intellectuals, people who grow from within these groups (hence the reference to the 'organic') and who serve the purpose of shaping and making sense of that group's knowledge creation and political positioning. Trade unions will have the function of political education and training; global corporations their research and development functions; local communities their council officers who can explain housing and planning policy; friendship groups rooted in political solidarity will have members versed in Marxism; and so on, from the micro and quotidian through to the high-stakes world of national party politics. The vital thing to remember is that Gramsci's category of 'intellectual' is egalitarian – everybody has the capacity to be an intellectual but not all people exercise that capacity on behalf of their community. What differentiates an organic intellectual, for Gramsci, is therefore deep immersion in a community of struggle and practice, 'active participation in practical life, as constructor, organiser, "permanent persuader"' (Gramsci, 2007, p 10). One cannot be an authoritative intellectual for and within a community if one does not have an embodied and rich history within that community.

This puts paid to the time-honoured and tiresome debate on the role of academic intellectuals within class struggle by stating that intellectualism is not owned by any demographic and can, and should, be cultivated within all communities. It also helps us counter the issue of vanguardism, one rife not only within left movements but across the political spectrum. If localized, embodied and rich intellectual knowledge is what is most valued, then the prototype leader within such a configuration would be someone who learns representative, advocacy, research and campaigning skills through real material struggle, and who uses such learning to develop others and grow outwards to tackle ever-larger issues and causes. A classic example would be the worker who experiences exploitation at work, joins a trade union, learns through struggle, progresses through union positions and eventually becomes a parliamentarian.

Such organic intellectuals are always rooted to their communities in a symbiotic relationship, and are therefore not to be read as isolated individuals but as always a subject in relation. The organic begins to reveal a leadership subject in the sense that this is a subject well positioned both to understand struggle in embodied and experiential ways but also to help communities of struggle adapt and learn. In Gramsci's terminology, this enables 'a continual adaptation of the organisation to the real movement, a matching of thrusts from below with orders from above, a continuous insertion of elements thrown up from the depths of the rank and file into the solid framework of the leadership apparatus which ensures continuity and the regular accumulation of experience' (Gramsci, 2007, pp 188–9). This account is close to Hardt and Negri's (2017) inverting of strategy and tactics, whereby a grassroots community continuously provides overall direction and the formal leadership a know-how for short-term tactical decisions. Leadership here can be envisaged as not residing solely within the body of the organic intellectual but within the movement between intellectuals and community, a practice that, in itself, has as its aim the building of a democratic and accountable counter-hegemony (and is thus rooted in continuous struggle).

Of course, Gramsci goes beyond the confines of the localized community of practice to consider the 'outer ditches' of the social, and we are therefore left with questions of how an organic form of leadership may connect individual communities in a common form of struggle, growing the leadership across a chain of groups rather than situating it within isolated and discrete groups. For Gramsci, the answer lies in a moral direction, whereby the Italian *dirigere* in Gramsci's work is commonly translated as 'leadership'. He defines leadership in relation to what he views as its antonym, domination, prefixing 'leadership' with the adjectives 'organic' and 'moral' (2007, p 57). Leadership therefore emerges from communities, but it can also provide a moral direction to a broader hegemonic constellation of peoples – the proletariat has in the past, therefore, spoken on behalf of a broader movement, leading it because it had the moral authority and organic experience of struggle necessary to fulfil this role.

It is worth further reflecting here on the role of individual leaders in this formulation, in particular their capacity for accumulating ever-greater responsibilities and knowledge as the needs associated with functioning competently within high-stakes and time-sensitive campaigns take hold. Such is the 'sovereign' trap of leadership, whereby organizations revert to the comforting if authoritarian leadership of an individual or small vanguard, to help them through a pressured situation, a crisis (Smolović Jones et al, 2020). The problem here, of course, is that crises can be manufactured by ambitious but immoral leaders to suit their purposes (Grint, 2005b), necessitating a near-permanent reliance on said leaders, who successfully bypass or corrupt the normal checks and balances of democracy and routinized bureaucracy. Hence why some organizations, particularly those from an anarchist tradition, seek to mainstream modes of organizing that limit the scope and duration of a leader's tenure (Sutherland et al, 2014).

We finally need to consider the connective function of leaders. We live in societies where leaders and notions of leadership are either culturally salient or becoming increasingly so (Kelly, 2014), and therefore the figure of the leader is a common function through which collectives are able to form a sense of identity. Here we refuse the temptation to search for some secret essence of personality within such leaders, but instead note that the symbolism and rhetoric of leaders should be read hermeneutically and semiologically. Leaders are texts and signs that are consumed, reinterpreted and proffered by groups. Who such people really 'are' matters less than the work their images and words accomplish in the hands of others, their consumers. As such, we can refer to 'leadering' rather than 'leaders' (Sinha et al, 2019) – textual and semiological clusters and tentacles that accomplish real influencing work upon and with subjects. Leadering can help suture together diverse groups into a hegemony or counter-hegemony. For example, the resurgence of the socialist left within the Labour Party in the UK was in significant part attributable to the curious figure of Jeremy Corbyn, whose symbolism was able to unify a group of grizzled left-wing trade unionists, young New Left urban activists, experienced socialists well versed in party machinery and even elements of the 'soft' left who felt that the party had drifted too far towards neoliberal norms. What mattered here was not the essence of Corbyn or the commands he decreed (really not his style anyway) but rather the loose and flexible symbolism his 'anti-charisma' offered his followers (Sinha et al, 2019), who were able to identify in his symbolism their diverse and affectively charged reasons for supporting the political goals of socialism within a mainstream political party. Of course, even such a benign and forbearing mode of leadering can be said to hold its own dangers, not least the problem of what may happen after such a leader leaves or loses their initial appeal. After all, for all the anti-leader rhetoric of the socialists in the Labour Party, and for all the protestations that Corbyn himself was relatively insignificant compared to the movement, when it came to electing his successor, the socialists and their preferred, perfectly appealing and competent candidate, Rebecca Long-Bailey, were crushed.

While individual leaders of great symbolic appeal and/or ability are of course welcome within organic forms of leadership, we also – acknowledging the dangers of sovereign traps of leadership – need to search for alternative ways of suturing together the various organic communities necessary for a revolutionary guerrilla democracy, and the possibility of a digital commons in a liquid society provides us with this possibility. Liquid society and the technologies underpinning it open the space for a more mobile hegemony and more radically solidified counter-hegemony. Even in their early theorizations of discursive hegemony, Laclau and Mouffe seemed to realize the importance of this historical moment, noting that

> the field of historical contingency has penetrated social relations more thoroughly than in any of the previous discourses: the social segments have lost those essential connections which turned them into moments of the stagist paradigm; and their own meaning depended upon hegemonic articulations whose success was not guaranteed by any law of history. (Laclau & Mouffe, 1986, p 68)

The point, though, is not simply to reimagine but to discursively rematerialize and materially reconfigure. Hence, 'what is denied is not that such objects exist externally to thought, but the rather different assertion that they could constitute themselves as objects outside any discursive condition of emergence' (Laclau & Mouffe, 1986, p 108).

This, then, is a politics rooted in the forging of reconnections, so that new types of collective intelligence can emerge. It is not enough to have vibrant examples of counter-hegemonic communities with their own distributed leadership and thriving organic intellectuals that remain stuck within their localities – organic leadership requires a leveling upwards and outwards, to connect previously disparate struggles into a durable and dynamic movement. In theory and in practice, most leadership remains rooted within quite narrow confines – most usually the organization – and there it stays. Indeed, leadership theory still largely assumes a face-to-face presence. In the present age, we argue, an organic leadership rooted in the intellectual capacities of localized leaders must take advantage of crises in neoliberalism to open up possibilities for democratizing both the politics and the economy – as was the case in the immediate aftermath of the Egyptian revolution of 2011 (see Joya, 2011). Solidarity is grounded, therefore, in processes of radical reconnection, which can be made meaningful through democratic practice that is invigorating. Turning our attention to the Tunisian revolution, Zemni maintains that 'from a subjective sense of the injustice of urban segregation in the major coastal cities and the social disparities between these cities and the rest of the country grew a consciousness of solidarity between classes that had hitherto been socio-spatially unconnected.' This 'awareness' manifested itself in practice as 'the neighbourhood youths focused simultaneously on organizing services in their locality and on establishing solidarity networks throughout the country' (Zemni, 2017, p78). Here, leadership is constituted through fermenting 'glocal' contagions – transforming an infectious host context into a disruptive and creative political space.

This reflects the challenge of how to be a disruptive and innovative leadership subject. The former is a condition of resistant possibility while the latter is one of creative subjection. More precisely, it is a choice between the political, where context is the living material for new social possibilities, and the social, where it must merely be adapted to conform to dynamic but durable hegemonic discourses. Gray alludes to this difference in his discussion of 'post-sapiens', wherein he argues that 'the key issue is agency. Will we govern our own evolution, or is it something that will be done to us?' (Gray, 2018, p 136).

What is fundamental is the constructing of a subject who does not simply consume discourses but helps to design, test and implement them. Baker, in this regard, links 'post-work futures' and 'full automation' with a 'feminist design methodology'. She contends that 'while there is no doubt that technologies such as artificial intelligence are gradually reconfiguring work, mass media narratives and business literature have a tendency towards technological determinism, overstating the revolutionary nature of new technology and "black-boxing" the complexities of technological development'. In her view, 'in order to make an emancipatory post-work/post-capitalist future a reality, design methodologies would need an ontological reorientation that would go beyond the conceptualisation of the individualistic user-as-consumer, a project already underway in critical design and transition design' (Baker, 2018, p 540). Yet these efforts at radical redesign and rematerialization must remain vigilant, as 'disciplines can also reproduce privileged perspectives or essentialise gender' and thus require 'methods that aim to deconstruct and resist the binaries of sex and gender that manifest themselves in both design discourse and designed objects' (Baker, 2018, p 550).

This provides the foundations for collective leadership rooted not in any one person or group but in emergent contagious knowledges forged out of radical political reconnections. It is akin to what Last (2017) refers to as 'global brains' connected to a 'global commons'. Such collective forms of intelligence point to the radical potential for fostering peer-to-peer 'smart' revolutions. According to Peters and Reveley, 'As the Internet of Things evolves and connects up evermore people and digital devices, the networks in question will undoubtedly be self-organizing hybrid networks comprising both human and computer elements'. Thus, 'more work is needed to explore the interplay between the emergent properties of these networks and the coproduction not just of material or immaterial commodities, but new forms of sociality and principles of social organisation' (Peters & Reveley, 2015, pp 16–17).

This points to the potential for cultivating a renewed form of 'commons-sense' leadership. Drawing again on models of 'commons-based peer production', the goal is not to reinforce a hegemonic view of the world or to associate leadership with the creative adaptation to a mobile 'common sense'. Instead, it is rooted, perhaps above all, in showing how commons-based thinking can 'glocally' transform relations, turning social contexts into exciting political spaces for experimentation and reality building. Consequently, Barbrook-Johnson and Fornes highlight the existence of what they refer to as 'commoners' who reside and contribute to such 'open' communities. 'The core productive activity of any Commoner is to find tasks in the community, and contribute to them', they observe. 'Their ability to, and likelihood of, contributing will depend on their interests (a Commoner and task parameter), skill types (a Commoner and task parameter), and past activity' (Barbrook-Johnson & Fornes, 2017, p 2–3).

This revolutionary form of commons-sense leadership can be tested, developed and spread within the growing 'sharing economies' progressively marking the present period of liquid modernity. It involves, to a degree, constructing new types of 'sharing fictions' as a means for making popular and viral collaborative economies and social relations (Arvidsson, 2018, p 229). Specifically, those involved in the making of this new economy are often committed to the creation of 'new kinds of commons-based, virtuous markets' which are 'based on collaborative commons-based production' that 'also entails the collaborative construction of a common imaginary organized around the virtuous potential of a practice' (Arvidsson, 2018, p 289).

The next stage of revolutionary leadership, then, reaching up and beyond 'folk' communities, is the evolution from a collective common sense to commons-based collective sense. Here, the commons must be reframed from being merely ethical to being 'smart' and value creating. This gestures towards the potential for moving from competitive and collaborative advantage to the use of collective intelligence for *creating* common advantages. Bradley and Pargman describe 'the sharing economy as the commons of the 21st century', one that is 'mission driven', based on desires for 'democratising' access to 'under-utilised assets while simultaneously building a culture of trust and generosity' and to 'democratise access to information beyond the money-based economy' (Bradley & Pargman, 2017, p 243–4). These aspirations represent a 'post-capitalist ethic' whereby 'the resources in question are produced for use, rather than for exchange value, are produced by peers, rather than in hierarchical command structures, and are based on an ethic of sharing and common ownership, rather than competition and private property' (Bradley & Pargman, 2017, p 243–4). Drawing on Ostrom's famous 'commons-based resource approach', they note that in the 21st century commons, 'there is a (sometimes relatively stark) difference between ordinary "users" and contributors (volunteers, editors, hosts) who are essential for building and taking care of the human-made commons' and that 'therefore it is important to have clear contributor-interfaces and simple systems that potential contributors can plug into, yet that are also possible to adjust, making contributors want to continue to develop the collaborative work' (Bradley & Pargman, 2017, p 245). What is absolutely crucial, though, is that these become an increasing basis for how individuals organize all aspects of their existence. Bradley and Pargman maintain that 'in order for a commons regime to survive crises and recruit new users and contributors, it is important that the commoners are closely attached to the commons, that the commons is not simply a hobby but somehow becomes part of the commoners' lives, or perhaps even their livelihoods' (Bradley & Pargman, 2017, p 244–5). In our language, the commons must have an organic connection to people and specific localized communities or it risks withering.

At stake is the rethinking of the political as the creation of resolidified commons. These create the space for new collective 'selves' to emerge and become contagious. In this sense, Kirby asks arguably the fundamental political question of our liquid times: 'Can we embark on a political physics if the only constant in our rules of measurement and valuation is their provisional status? Or to put this in a way that might be more familiar to us, can we risk the suggestion that nature, in essence, is "under construction"?' (Kirby, 2017, p 20). What this requires is a radical answer for the rematerializing of power and resolidifying of social relations for producing emancipatory commons-based realities based on principles of collective, organic leadership.

Mobile strikes

A key political question of our liquid times, then, is how to create a 'mixed-media' and – perhaps more importantly, as will be shown – a 'mixed-reality' commons? The most obvious definition of mixed-media is one that integrates a range of different online, traditional and IRL knowledge sharing and consumption practices. While many commentators celebrate the organizing potential of digital technologies, Woodcock and Graham (2019, p 133) presciently warn that 'there are risks with using a platform like WhatsApp or Facebook, as they are not designed for worker organizing and lack safeguards against management surveillance or infiltration.' Nevertheless, it is often difficult to move away from such corporate networks since people are already in the habit of engaging with and checking these applications, and interrupting that cycle of behaviour seems like an additional barrier to organizing. This also reflects the need to emphasize the viral aspects of politics, of which a crucial element is the ability to distinguish between innovative and disruptive forms of leadership.

Significant for addressing these critical concerns is recognizing how mobile power involves a constant process of what can be termed 'religitimizing' hegemony. Dominant institutions and discourses are not static but must be continually rejustified. They call for 'innovative' organic leadership – one premised on the capacity of people to constantly reform a status quo in light of changing 'glocal' conditions. This can be seen, for instance, in the case of the EU and neoliberalism, witnessed specifically in the discourse around the European Union's Social Innovation Policy (EUSIP). Here it must be analyzed how these supposedly reforming measures can 'be understood as both "roll-out" and "roll-with-it" neoliberalisation, thereby relegitimizing and naturalizing neoliberalism' (Fougère et al, 2017, p 819). Significantly, through the discourse of innovation, the 'political logics of EUSIP pre-empt the critique of "roll-back" neoliberalisation and thus legitimize decreased public expenditure' (Fougère et al, 2017, p 819).

These problem spaces, moreover, point to the rise of a new challenge for leadership and radical politics: how to cope with mixed realities. Conventionally, this is linked to the fact that individuals will have diverse and often divergent perspectives on their shared reality. This problem has become perhaps particularly severe and urgent in light of the rise of the so-called post-truth society, connected to the ability of those in power to use social media to manipulate 'facts' and the networked populations who consume them. However, looking only slightly further ahead, new technologies associated with artificial intelligence, augmented reality and virtual reality will allow people to themselves manipulate their realities according to their personal preferences and desires. While admittedly we are not yet at the level of *The Matrix*, it is the case that 'digital media are providing more realistic experiences and not just for humans' (Blascovich & Bailenson,

2011, p 3). Offered is a utopian virtual existence of promised instant gratification and fulfillment. In place of shared revolution or liberation there is the prospect of a digitally aided, personalized paradise. 'Think also about a world with no putrid smells but plenty of delightful ones, where it rains only when you are inside, and where global warming is actually just a myth', proclaim Blascovich and Bailenson: 'In this world, your great-grandfather is still around and can play catch with your six-year-old daughter. There is no dental drill or swine flu in this place' (Blascovich & Bailenson, 2011, p 3).

Here, the threat of the Matrix that seemed to consume popular culture at the end of the last century has become an inviting promise of customizable reality creation in the new millennium. Yet these possibilities of producing 'infinite realities' obscure their contribution to novel forms of digital disciplining and control. It must be remembered, thus, that 'avatars also have the distinction of being completely anonymous but inherently "trackable."' Thus, the freedom of virtually and anonymously inhabiting 'any gender, age, race, species, or shape, and via the avatar', is conjoined with the fact that 'any time people enter a virtual space, they leave "digital footprints"– all the data the computer automatically collects: for example, speech, nonverbal behavior, and location' (Blascovich & Bailenson, 2011, p 5). Paradoxically, therefore, the desire to shed one's own identity and explore different selves leaves one ever more easily traced and monitarable, as 'this footprint can be used (and, in fact, is being used) by military and other government agencies to detect identity' (p 5).

At stake, then, is what would constitute a mixed-reality form of democracy that would enable ample scope for organic forms of leadership. Indeed, the very premise of traditional democracy is based on the assumption of a common *demos*. Yet in our liquid times, this demos has become progressively disaggregated, composed not merely of diverse views and experiences but fundamentally different demographics and networked relations. Imperative, thus, is to find ways to resolidify communities in ways that promote the possibilities inherent in democracy for enhancing our shared existence even amidst its existential differences and diverse virtual forms of life. This highlights the need to focus on the power of 'collective intelligence'. Landemore maintains that, 'given conditions of sufficient education and freedom among the members of a regular group of human beings, the rule of the many, defined as combination of inclusive deliberation and majority rule with universal suffrage, generally beats dictatorship as a decision-procedure regarding collective choices for that group' (Landemore, 2012, p 251). Here, the emphasis is not simply on numbers but diversity in experiences, skills and perspectives. As such, 'the general point is that it is often better to have a group of cognitively diverse people than a group of very smart people who think alike'. The reason why difference is more important to maintaining an effective and vibrant democracy than traditional 'intelligence' is that 'whereas very smart people sharing local optima will tend to get stuck quickly on their highest local common optimum, a more cognitively diverse group has the possibility of guiding each other beyond that local optimum towards the global optimum' (Landemore, 2012, p 260).

What this requires, though, is the turning of 'liberal' societies into commons ones, where those from different backgrounds and eventually living in 'different' realities can contribute to various 'glocal' commons – can move beyond the 'folk' to organic and connected forms of leadership. Landemore concludes her own analysis with a final but crucial caveat, highlighting the social and political environment necessary for ensuring that 'cognitive diversity' can evolve into 'collective intelligence'. She notes that this requires 'a specific kind of society, which might be called, broadly speaking, "liberal" … characterized, among other things, by the existence of a free "market of ideas", ensuring that the constant conflict of points of view and arguments renews perspectives, interpretations, heuristics, and predictive models – the toolbox of democratic reason'. Hence, 'the emergence of democratic reason is thus conditional on the existence of a social and cultural context that nurtures and protects, among other differences, cognitive differences' (Landemore, 2012, p 281). Yet this reliance on liberalism perhaps too easily ignores how such societies devolve into oligarchies and conformity of opinion precisely because of their basis in inequality, competition and exploitation.

Nevertheless, this central insight remains sound and instructive. The possibility of turning diversity into collective intelligence is the political transition from liberalism to the commons. In such a creative and liberated space, it becomes possible to foster a 'democratic reason' that is aimed not at profit or domination but instead at collaboration and shared gain. Here the scope of hegemony also changes from seeking to promote a new dominant discourse to the fostering of new political contagions for global transformation. Radical democracy, in turn, is reconfigured around the spread of contagious discourses of the commons within a diverse set of host contexts and the transforming of these into open political spaces. A radically democratic counter-hegemonic politics, thus, is centred on the fostering of common contagions. According to Chatterton (2016, p 404), 'What remains unarticulated in explorations of sustainability transitions is a concern about what the future actually holds if we do not somehow move against and beyond the capitalist present'. We need, therefore, to move towards a temporality of 'transition' linked to concepts of post-capitalism' that 'focus on those activities which critically intervene in and attempt to solve societal crises but in ways that foreground equality, openness and social justice'.

Necessitated, hence, is a contemporary democratic ethos that combines values of resolidification and openness. The radically democratic subject, then, is one who does more than simply participate but actively engages in (im)material processes of reimagination and reconnection for the construction of a more 'open' and commons-based political space. This requires a citizenry that is willing and able to undertake a number of valuable civic functions for this revolutionary purpose. This includes acting 'as a watchdog in monitorial processes, a partner in dialogue in deliberative processes and a partner in joined action in participatory democratic processes.' These radically democratic responsibilities rely upon 'open data' which can be used to collectively monitor 'government performance (monitorial) or a public problem (deliberative and participatory)' or act as 'the mediating tool that facilitates the interaction between the activity systems of the citizen and public administrator' (Ruijer et al, 2017, p 48). Key, in this respect, is to provide the common demos and concrete resources for citizens to not merely adapt to infectious hegemonic problemizations but rather to become disruptive problem-creators and solvers. Consequently,

> the role of citizens in participatory processes is not only to give a mandate to government, or deliberate about issues, but they also actively engage and collaborate directly in the solution of public problems, the production of services and policies and the implementation of policies in a variety of policy domains. ... They are co-creators of public goods. (Ruijer et al, 2017, p 48)

Here, 'the role of government shifts in this democratic processes from provider of services to partner' as 'open data platforms can make it easier for citizens, organisations and businesses to interact and collaborate with government organisations by offering a collaborative environment and enable participation in collective decision-making efforts about public problems' (Ruijer et al, 2017, p 51). The promotion of open data, then, is part of a larger radical democratic project of producing a commons demos that can address shared problems and cater to the needs of subjects inhabiting mixed-media realities.

Throughout this book we have analyzed how a core component of the reproduction of neoliberalism is the tasking of individuals with manufacturing and maintaining their own capitalist 'realities'. There is, hence, a deep caretaker ethics crucial to the strength of the free market, especially in these liquid times in which individuals must personally cultivate their own 'market-friendly' lives and help to innovatively adapt their host contexts to infectious market discourses and demands. The commons-based democracy advocated here, consequently, is one aimed at allowing individuals to explore ever-newer (im)material realities while also forging shared communities of creative disruption built on experimenting with new forms of egalitarianism, openness and common advantage. Peters and Heraud propose, in this spirit, the 'co-creation of social goods' using 'collective intelligence', whereby 'innovation and creativity are seen as products of social and networked environments – rich semiotic environments in which everything speaks. This collective view of creativity is seen as a product of "systems design"– platforms for collective awareness – that allows a high degree of interaction and rests on principles of distributed knowledge and collective intelligence' (Peters & Heraud, 2015, p 14). Critical, in this regard, is changing our understanding of and investment in 'learning communities' for this purpose. It demands 'co-production through networked engagement on platforms that facilitate interdisciplinary ideation [that] would require a transformation of the way power is administered' to generate a multitude of 'actors in social innovation' (Peters & Heraud, 2015, p 20).

We now return to our original question, though critically expanded: How can mixed-reality subjects help to co-produce 'glocal' commons contagions? A hint can be found in the emerging ideas around peer production linked to advances in collective intelligence. As Benkler et al note: 'Peer production systems combine novel and creative social practices and forms of organisation with the creation of truly unprecedented sources of behavioral data'. Consequently, 'this means that there are many opportunities to conduct research that cuts across traditional divisions between micro-, meso-, and macro-level social analysis' (Benkler et al, 2015, p 22). It also calls for an ongoing forensic analysis of how different 'spaces' and networks go viral – simultaneously reconfiguring existing host contexts for viral infections and producing new ones. Rose (2016) observes, hence, the need 'not to focus so much on the agency of machines and their code that we neglect the networks of humans within which digital technologies are embedded, and the thoughts, feelings, processes and practices which are then mediated by such technologies.' Doing so means, therefore, 'to think again about the different forms of human enabled and allowed now, at a moment when many of the media for articulating subjectivity have changed significantly' (Rose, 2016, p 766).

Radically democratic forms of organic leadership must be committed to the twofold task of 'viral containment' and 'contagious promotion'– both building up resistances to infections and the perpetuation of host contexts while finding disruptive ways to create more open commons spaces. Quoting Cohen (2011) about the threat of social epidemics: 'In addition to their material effects, epidemics constitute what geographers call "scalar narratives", "stories that temporally bind up different ways of construing space"'. Accordingly, 'because they compose narratives, these spatial and discursive dynamics assume temporal shapes that articulate relations of coordination and subordination among them, thereby serving as quasi-natural explanations for them.' Paradoxically, then, it is precisely through crisis that elites seek to resolidify a status quo. Yet by demanding that we go beyond the given and embrace the potential to co-produce new realities, we can expand the scope of democracy from elite management to our shared existential liberation. Imperative for such emancipatory aims is the rejection of traditional sovereignty for a distributed and mobile leadership that reflects our liquifying world. It is only in this manner that a contagious commons-based democracy can be collectively produced and promoted.

Conclusion

In this chapter we started to consider seriously how it might be possible to find durable relations of solidarity between various disparate groups to the extent that an impactful guerrilla democracy would be possible. It is here that we introduced our account of organic leadership. This type of leadership, drawing on Gramsci, acknowledged the necessity of rooting struggle in the particular, embodied and historically situated experiences of people within their communities (work, residential or otherwise) – which highlights the vital nature of cultivating and curating rich forms of knowledge and intellectual capacity. The leadership required for levelling upwards and outwards from such localized communities is moral and organic, one that never loses its symbiotic connection to community but that is capable of offering direction to a broader sphere of influence. Such leadership can of course be enabled by an appealing leader figure, but reliance on such figures is at best limited and at worst destructive. Rather, we need to be more imaginative about the digital forms through which we connect and build. Such an ethos and praxis would, in turn, foster 'revolutionary resolidifications' for concretely cultivating and experimenting with new emancipatory forms of existence in a seemingly unchangeable and amorphous liquid capitalist world.

8

Mobile Organizing in the 21st Century

This book has focused on the fundamental and increasing mobility of power and virality of order. In particular, it has sought to highlight the infectious character of hegemonic discourses and their wider epidemic threat. By contrast, it revealed the possibilities for building up 'glocal' resistances to these dominant infectious discourses and ultimately even contagious alternatives that can spread into revolutionary pandemics. Crucial, in this respect, is the challenging and evolution of social innovation for disruptive forms of political creation – ones which materialize and solidify new possibilities for a more egalitarian, free and commons-based existence locally and globally.

In many of the examples discussed throughout this book, workers have been able to use digital technologies to facilitate mobile organizing, often using them in interaction with offline methods, or combining them in new and important ways. Most workers have some kind of shared workplace – whether a physical building, some kind of space that they frequently pass through or transient points where they come into physical contact. Yet in some forms of digital work this is no longer the case. For example, with microwork, digital platforms are used to break work down into small (or micro) tasks that can then be completed very quickly by a large group of distributed workers. Perhaps the most famous of these platforms is Amazon Mechanical Turk (or AMT). The platform breaks work down into HITs – so-called Human Intelligence Tasks – often things like image labelling, transcription and so on, that can be completed in very short amounts of time. The name of the platform – as well as that of HITs – is a reference to the famed fake chess automaton that hid a person within it. The use of HITs also indicates the way that AMT presents humans as a service, completing tasks without having to be visible. Indeed, there have been cases of start-ups like Expensify, which pretended to have developed machine-learning algorithms for automated tasks, but which in fact had outsourced them to workers on AMT.

Turkopticon is a response to the challenges that AMT workers face. Two Human Computer Interaction (HCI) researchers, Lilly Irani and Six Silberman, make the case 'that human computation currently relies on worker invisibility'. They developed Turkopticon as 'an activist system that allows workers to publicize and evaluate their relationships with employers. As a common infrastructure, Turkopticon also enables workers to engage one another in mutual aid' (Irani & Silerberman, 2013). In practice this refers to a browser plug-in that overlays the interface that AMT workers use. Like on many platforms, AMT workers are reviewed by requesters (the people offering up work on the platform) – something that can greatly affect how much work they are offered. However, Amazon only provides a method for requesters to review workers, not the other way around. The Turkopticon interface provides a way for workers to rate clients offering work, and when using the plug-in they can see reviews from other workers. This reverses the panopticon-like nature of the platform – hence the name Turkopticon – and provides an important way for workers to start exerting some power over their work. In particular, they can avoid requesters that are known not to pay for work – something that is facilitated by the platform. As of 2018, Turkopticon had over 420,000 reviews of over 59,000 requesters.

From this practical use, Turkopticon integrates into the workflow of AMT workers. The idea, led by the HCI focus of Irani and Silberman, is to make it a usable tool. The system was used to identify workers who regularly left reviews, who were then invited to become moderators for a forum that AMT workers could use to discuss their work – and the problems and potential solutions they may have. Turkopticon is a particularly powerful example of a digital organizing method that starts from the problems and challenges that workers face, provides tools to combat them and opens up a space for workers' self-organizing. It has now been running for over a decade, and is in the process of being transferred to worker control and self-ownership.

This example reflects the need to reproduce not just domination but emancipation and liberation. The emphasis on mobility and virality in this book reveals how power is not just productive but dynamic and in constant reproduction. These insights chime with the groundbreaking perspectives of social reproduction theory. Quoting one of its founding and leading thinkers, Tithi Bhattacharya: 'The fundamental insight of social reproduction theory is, simply put, that human labour is at the heart of creating and reproducing society as a whole' (Bhattacharya, 2017, p 69). One of the crucial insights of this theory is that a 'tremendous amount of familial as well as communitarian work ... goes into sustaining and reproducing the worker'. At stake is uncovering the concrete labour and relations that reproduce our 'capitalist life' and how they can be redirected towards reproducing a more emancipatory form of existence. It represents attempts to materialize, as a process of critical praxis, not empirical reality but the underlying forces that give it birth and perpetuate it. The goal is to move beyond a system that exploits our (im)material labour for its own creation and maintenance. Consequently, the task must be to explore how we can evolve from social reproductions to political recreations.

Mobile power in a viral age

Significantly, a core aim of this analysis is, to an extent, both trans-historical and responding to contemporary developments. Power is always necessarily mobile, and so too is order always necessarily viral. The strength of any dominant regime of power and its associated social configuration, thus, is rooted at least in part in their capacity not just to produce subjects but to continuously and innovatively reproduce them and successfully adapt their underlying values to diverse host contexts. Yet these aspects of power and hegemony have only grown in importance due to the recent rapid rise in communication technologies. More than simply 'shrinking the world', ICTs have resituated the very composition of present-day power away from its past foundations in 'truth' and 'obedience' to its current embrace of virality and adaptability.

Emerging is a novel manifestation of capitalism, one that potently combines the traditional insatiable desires for profit and growth with a neoliberal demand for personal responsibility and creativity. Drawing on the insights of Boltanski and Chiapello, Ampuja contends that this 'new spirit of capitalism' is one marked by 'innovation fetishism' fueled by ICTs. Here, 'while neoliberalism keeps reinventing itself, it continues to draw strength from its long-standing ideological assumptions, according to which the market and the private are superior to the state and the public' (Ampuja, 2016, p 20). Importantly though, these rather inscriptive assumptions are accompanied by a sense of 'fun' and discovery. The appeal of this ideology is in large part its giving us the responsibility for innovatively ensuring its reproduction.

This points to the disciplining aspects of this technologically enhanced mobile capitalism. It is constantly reproduced and spread by the production of innovative subjects, ones who can properly shape themselves and their surrounding environments to reflect these dominant discourses and dominating practices. Its strength lies precisely in its ability to virally infect people while adapting to and transforming their culturally imagined host contexts. Modern emancipation, hence, is made possible through the building up of local resistances to these colonizing social infections and the fostering of liberatory political contagions globally.

Radical mobility

At its heart, power is always to a greater or lesser extent mobile. The original and guiding insights of Ong thus uncover something more than a timely reflection on the dynamic character of contemporary globalization and its reproduction of a diverse neoliberal world order. Rather, she brilliantly gestures towards a crucial but too often ignored aspect of power: its flexibility, adaptability and creativity. This further allows for an updating of the Foucauldian relationship between the power and the self. As Kelly (2013) presciently notes, Foucault reveals how power is formed via a set of technologies that allows for the construction of the self. However, it is perhaps more accurate to restate this notion to emphasize *the mobile* rather than merely inscriptive construction of the self. This addition of mobility opens up new vistas for understanding power and, as such, hegemony. Rosi Braidotti maintains, thus, that 'the crucial issue is that of the speeds of de/ reterritorialisation and the toxic saturation of the present by cognitive capitalism, to the detriment of the actualisation of the virtual, and the extent to which they affect knowledge practices in the contemporary university and scientific community' (Braidotti, 2017, p 87–8). Hence, a fundamental question for her (and one that we would maintain is crucial to any radical and democratic transformation of the social) is 'how to tell the difference between affirmative and reactive modes of knowledge production'. This is especially so as power is not merely inscriptive and productive but 'a multilayered and dynamic entity', and thus 'as embedded and embodied, relational, and affective subjects, we are immanent to the very conditions we are trying to change, we need to make the careful ethical distinction between different speeds of both knowledge production – with the predictable margins of institutional capitalisation – and the construction of alternative knowing subject formations' (Braidotti, 2017, 87–8).

Power and hegemony, consequently, must be treated as necessarily and eternally under construction. If there is a dominant character of hegemony, therefore, it is, of above all else, that of innovation. In the present era, such social innovation is witnessed in the ongoing development and indeed redevelopment of neoliberalism. Ordering, neoliberal or otherwise, critically revolves around the setting up of cultural parameters and institutional rules in which for such hegemonic creativity to flourish. Hence, 'what is "neo" about neoliberalism', according to Wacquant, is 'the reengineering and redeployment of the state as the core agency that sets the rules and fabricates the subjectivities, social relations and collective representations suited to realising markets' (Wacquant, 2012, p 66). Hegemony is, as such, foundationally a project composed of tricky and context-specific 'problems' to be solved. Returning to Braidotti, this speaks to the nomadic nature of contemporary existence. Stability is now a matter of semi-controlled flux in which 'a radically immanent intensive body is an assemblage of forces, or flows, intensities and passions that solidify in space, and consolidate in time, within the singular configuration commonly known as an "individual" self' (Braidotti, 2006, p 201). Just as significantly, this exchanges the notion of a 'stable' self for one that is resilient enough to be hegemonic flux. In this respect, selfhood 'does not coincide with the enumeration of inner rationalist laws, nor is it merely the unfolding of genetic data and information. It is rather a portion of forces that is stable enough to sustain and to undergo constant, though non-destructive, fluxes of transformation' (Braidotti, 2006, p 201).

Order is eternally rooted in the channeling of mobility for the establishment of contained and durable social spaces for innovative change. And with the introduction of new mobile technologies, this dimension of power and hegemony is increasing in import – witnessed in the production of the mobile subject. Here subjection is linked to the demand to be flexible, adaptive and creative. More precisely, to construct a self that is able to flexibly mutate across different imagined communities and IRL relations, in such a way that they can remain adaptable to their cultural particularities and creative enough to continually manifest dominant ideologies and values within diverse environments.

The evolution of mobility from a critical component of power to its dominant characteristic, hence, calls for novel forms of resistance and strategies for politically transforming the social. A crucial and ever more urgent question, then, is how to properly and effectively radicalize this historical condition of mobility. Critical, in this respect, is to understand the multiple and interweaving levels at which we are produced and socially activated as subjects. Braidotti declares that 'the subject is a process, made of constant shifts and negotiations between different levels of power and desire, that is to say, entrapment and empowerment' (Braidotti, 2014, p 169). Fundamental to these radicalizing efforts is to rematerialize the social by revealing how its liquification is reinforcing neoliberal power relations and inequalities so that it can be resolidified in fresh and more egalitarian ways, through mobile, democratic and organic forms of leadership. Drawing on the earlier insights of Bauman, Braidotti maintains that is crucial 'to identify lines of flight' which would foster

> a creative alternative space of becoming that would fall not between the mobile/immobile, the resident/the foreigner distinction, but within all these categories. The point is neither to dismiss nor to glorify the status of marginal, alien others, but to find a more accurate, complex location for a transformation of the very terms of their specification and of our political interaction. (2014, p 178–9)

The ultimate aim is the political channeling of mobile power into radical forms of mobile organizing and leadership. The possibilities and challenges for such radical mobility in action are evident, for instance, in contemporary cultures of digital activism in Cuba. In this respect, 'while the majority of Cubans continue to live without consistent access to the Internet, since 2007 a dedicated network of bloggers and cyberactivists has achieved international visibility and notoriety for their criticisms of the Cuban government' (Kellogg, 2016, p 23). In this study, Kellogg observes the differing, often subversive means Cubans undertook for reimagining and reconnecting their social relations. He observes the way the USB flash drive became a mobile artefact of radical knowledge sharing and resistance – reflected, for instance, in the youth he met who wore a crucifix and flash drive as a necklace. Its radical power, then, lay precisely in its portability and adaptability, making the technological limits of 'contemporary Cuban information networking' into a political strength.

This allowed, in turn, for the quite literal recirculation of power and political resolidification of the social marked by experimentations with novel democratic and commons-based governing practices. Accordingly, they served as a viral form of counter-knowledge, as 'events are recorded, and after each one Antonio and others compile and edit the videos on [their] laptop[s] and burn them onto blank compact discs. These videos, everything from round-table discussions on foreign policy to hip hop concerts, are constructed as alternative channels to the state's official news organs" (Kellogg, 2016, p 23).

This radical mobility is also characterized by a daily ethos of creative disruption, leading hopefully towards more revolutionary disruptive creations. In this sense, otherwise straightforward webpages on *Translating Cuba*, instructing people how to pay mobile phone bills also contain a revolutionary warning that 'many people want to do something to help the bloggers directly. The most important thing is to read them, talk about them, comment on their blogs, share their blogs with others, keep them IN THE PUBLIC EYE, which is a shield that helps to protect them' (Translating Cuba, 2012).

What this example shows is that the very flexibility, adaptability and creativity that have fortified and made neoliberalism so strong, are now what emboldens its resistance and counter-hegemonic transformation. Thus, Kellogg maintains that 'in Cuba, despite an apparent lack of Internet access, new technologies in conjunction with mobilised networks are profoundly changing how written narratives are produced and communicated' (Kellogg, 2016, p 46). He specifically refers, in this regard, to Voces Cubanas, which 'is a cooperative cyborg network involved in hacking the technologies it comes into contact with in order to further its political goals'. Such 'cyborg political action' is, in his view, about 'creating fluid heterogeneous networks that bend rather than break when the stakes change'. In practice this involves fostering contagious, revolutionary 'glocal' alternatives by 'hacking narratives and technologies to fit local problems and situated political ends, subverting the god-trick of author-less [sic] knowledge and binary for/against logic ... it is about establishing valuable partial understandings and using the tools at hand to build better futures' (Kellogg, 2016, p 46). Significantly, this revolutionary change is never certain and rarely immediate. Instead, it draws its resilience and excitement from revealing that another world is possible, not in our wildest dreams but in our concrete 'glocal' existence.

Viral intelligence

Conventional accounts of order and hegemony tend to focus on their ability to stabilize a political space, to reflect dominant ideas and power relations. This emphasis is apparent theoretically in Gramsci's cultural treatment of hegemony as an ongoing 'war of position' between historic blocs within a given context, or more recently Laclau and Mouffe's prioritization of dominant discourses. The spread of hegemonic knowledge and practices across contexts was thus, to an extent, underexplored. Yet the problem of discursive colonization has taken on renewed importance and urgency in light of the rise of ICTs and the more networked as well as virtual character of contemporary social relations. Even at the most banal levels of electoral politics, strategies to have candidates go viral now increasingly reign supreme. In 2019, an article in the *Washington Post* reported that presidential candidates 'hunt desperately for viral moments', and that, 'while viral moments are presented as spontaneous – and uniquely revealing about the candidates – the process can be anything but random, and the campaigns are devoting significant resources to spotting, cultivating and publicizing them' (Wang, 2019).

We have introduced the concept of viral logics as a centrepiece in the critical analysis of present-day hegemony and domination. This concentrates attention on the ability of dominant discourses to infect host contexts – highlighting the mobility of power as fundamentally malleable, mutating and colonizing. This echoes recent ideas of 'visceral identification' in that it spotlights how power and hegemony diversely materialize themselves, adapting to, disseminating across and transforming different people and places. Hayes-Conroy and Martin critically elaborate that a 'visceral approach ... centres on understanding these representations vis-à-vis an analysis of feelings that work to satisfy the always embodied process we know as identification' (Hayes-Conroy & Martin, 2010, p 272). It is therefore ever more imperative to understand not simply traditional sovereign power relations but also the more expansive growth of viral relations. Here, as has been explored throughout this book, order is akin to an infectious virus and hegemony its viral epidemic. According to Blas: 'The virus|viral relations presented reveal that a mediation, or distortion always exists between the virus and the viral, and while the viral typically has a political leaning or inclination, the virus itself is politically ambiguous. All virals are captures, identifications, speculations; and yet the virus always escapes' (Blas, 2012, p 39).

Viral politics, then, is at its heart a potent mixture of reimagination, on the one hand, and reconnection, on the other. This chimes with Nancy Fraser's 'critical reflections on the "postsocialist" condition' where she maintains that 'justice today requires both redistribution and recognition' (Fraser, 2014, p 12). These ongoing processes of critical reimagination map onto new viral terrains of political solidarity and connection. Paraphrasing Fraser (2009, p 9), it is a radical act of counter-hegemonic 'remapping' whereby, 'unlike that of impartiality, the problematic of the map can lay dormant for long historical stretches, when a hegemonic frame is naturalised and taken for granted'. Here, in her view, 'the Westphalian mapping of political space is losing its hold. Certainly its posit of exclusive, undivided state sovereignty is no longer plausible given a ramifying human-rights regime, on the one hand, and spiraling networks of global governance, on the other.' Revealed, in turn, is the emergence of what can be termed both popularly and theoretically 'smart politics'. A predominant concern is the ability to predict, direct and exploit the spread of information. The terrain of politics is not a throne or even a conventional physical space of power but an overlapping of virtual and IRL networks. 'A fundamental problem in network science is to predict how certain individuals are able to initiate new networks to spring up "new ideas"', note Hu et al: 'Frequently, these changes in trends are triggered by a few innovators who rapidly impose their ideas through "viral" influence spreading, producing cascades of followers and fragmenting an old network to create a new one' (Hu et al, 2014, p 1). More radically, these point the way to the creation of self-organizing, democratic, peer-to-peer 'trust communities'. In this regard, 'future technical systems will be increasingly characterised by openness and heterogeneity of participating elements', representing a 'novel self-organised multi-agent organization – the Trust Community' (Edenhofer et al, 2016, p 127).

Critical in this regard is not to oppose change and order, or similarly hegemony and dynamism. Indeed, the point is not merely that change is ever present but that, in fact, a hegemonic discourse and any attempt at counter-hegemony draw their strength precisely from their respective capacities to be both mobile and viral. A crucial new tool in this increasingly viral social and political environment are what Ventsel refers to as 'viral texts', which 'can function as possible discursive tools for questioning and contesting the boundaries of private and public communication' (Ventsel, 2017, p 365). Importantly, such 'virals may undermine as well as facilitate the dominant discourses and in such processes they often shift the boundaries between the public and counter-publics' (Ventsel, 2017, p 378).

Arising, hence, are exciting new viral social movements. These are marked by their ability to politically exploit technological knowledge and networks to foster creative disruptions and, over time, disruptive creations. At stake is the disruptive use of such viral technologies to undermine and overtake dominant forms of technocratic control. In such control, 'every step in society's automation process transfers power to the technocratic sphere. Technocracy works from within capitalism; it is colonizing it, eroding capitalist power from the inside out ... technocratic colonialism takes over gradually; it increases its power from within the capitalist corporation' (Morador & Vásquez, 2016, p 403). For this purpose, novel types of leaders and leadership emerge, ones founded on creating more open, transparent networks while revealing the hidden oppression, exploitation and violence of dominant ones. Thus, 'profane activists are the new heroes in history; they are organized in order to strengthen civil society. They work to defetichize [sic] technology and condemn the dehumanizing effects of automation' (Morador & Vásquez, 2016, p 404). The success of these viral movements is found precisely in their capacity to fight off hegemonic infections and foster revolutionary contagions. 'The "know-how" of these new movements and their ability to drive social transformation are expressions of a framework made up of different strategies to those proposed by traditional groups framed by political parties', Morador and Vásquez contend (2016, p 403): 'The "Do-It-Yourself" logic leads new social movements to seek alternatives that will solve their local-global issues.'

Reflected, in turn, are novel techno-political possibilities. Tellingly, the acceleration and spread of disruptive technologies are most often tinged with a profound sense of fear. This worry manifests itself within mainstream thought in the anxiety of mass unemployment due to automation. Within critical theory, it is witnessed in accelerationist ideas that the pace of capitalist technological development can quicken to such a degree that the system will burn itself out, allowing for radical alternatives to emerge and take hold in its aftermath. However, in this analysis, far from being a harbinger of death and destruction (or even apocalyptic salvation), viral technologies represent an ever-present opportunity for disruptive creation and egalitarian experimentation.

Guerrilla warfare 4.0

The last century was marked by the presence, and in places the surprising success, of revolutionary guerrilla movements. While most failed or regressed into dogmatic movements whose basis in military struggle presaged a turn toward violent authoritarianism, such a politics retains its appeal as holding out the romantic possibilities of a beleaguered and oppressed population defeating a seemingly invincible foe. Indeed for all its actual successes and failures, it is perhaps most powerful as a potent reminder that imperialism is not inevitable and no hegemonic power is unconquerable. Fast-forwarding to the new millennium, we are once again confronted with an apparently indestructible force of global capitalism. Yet now the main battlegrounds for insurgents are not mountain hideouts but subversive virtual networks.

For this reason, it is worth critically reflecting on how neoliberalism has constructed technology to reflect and reinforce its own ideologies and power relations. As Tyfield notes, 'What is systematically missing from most of this literature is any attention to the specificities of the context of neoliberalism, let alone to the detailed ways in which developments in science and innovation (and their respective institutional forms) have contributed to and been co-produced with neoliberalism' (Tyfield, 2016, p 340). It is tempting, therefore, to assume that these technologies have no radical potential – that they are merely the 'master's tools' and will inevitably lead to the reproduction of capitalism and the strengthening of existing power structures. Yet such a view, while understandable, elides just how mobile these social technologies are and consequently how ever-present their racial-political repurposing remains. The key word, in this regard, is 'co-produced', as every technological advancement requires a culture of innovation to socially sustain its mobile power and maintain its infectious hegemony. Present-day insurgency is found exactly in the concerted and ongoing evolution of these innovative capacities into disruptive capabilities.

A crucial question, then, for the contemporary democratic guerrilla is to assess how hegemonic technologies can be politically transformed into revolutionary tools for creative disruption. This is revealed, for example, in the 'analytics turn' whereby activists can assess in greater detail how their posts are being engaged with, and are thus able to constantly customize them to their target audience. The point, though, is not to inherently promote or assail any specific internet culture or platform. Instead, it is to theoretically, and as a matter of radical praxis, explore their radical possibilities for politically reimagining and reconnecting the social. At the level of hegemony, it is also necessary to continually question how to build up resistances to infectious discourses and foster the 'glocal' conditions for more revolutionary contagions.

Imperative is to cultivate a culture of guerrilla technology grounded in the ability to challenge and disrupt advancements for more radical and transformative ends. Recent theories of 'xeno-feminism' reveal this virtual and IRL bottom-up insurgency, pointing towards a post-capitalist existence. In the words of Jones: 'Xenofeminism proposes a feminist ethics for the technomaterial world, both seeking to promote feminist interventions into the shaping of science and technology as well as working to ensure that any radical technological change or alterity is considered, analysed and shaped by/through a feminist lens'. Consequently, 'xenofeminism thus asks questions of inclusion and exclusion as well as questions of fundamental structural change' (Jones, 2019, p 127).

In this techno-guerrilla spirit, our environments are reconfigured into material and immaterial resources for resistance and experimentation.

It represents a DIY ethos whereby technology is not presented as an unstoppable force that one must simply accept but as a means to take back a sense of personal and collective existential control. These techno-guerrilla insurgencies, however, are not limited to the basic overthrow of existing rulers or mere minor subversions at the edge of neoliberal power. Rather, they reflect an incipient abolitionist politics by which conventional relations can be reimagined and transcended in order to forge novel and quite revolutionary reconnections. It represents a subject unbound by liquifying traditions and embracing of experimentation and resolidified possibility. Quoting Helen Hester in this respect: 'The subject of xenofeminism is neither woman nor human, if these terms are understood as suggesting discrete entities snipped from the wider fabric of technomaterial existence. Instead, xenofeminism is interested in the assemblages within which social agents are embedded'. To this end, this perspective 'points to some of the many ways in which technological alteration might generate forms of radical alterity. ... Nature (not least as it is manifested in gendered embodiment) is viewed as a space of experimentation – not a fact to be accepted but a terrain of negotiation to be actively contested for' (Hester, 2018a, p 10).

This presages the potential for updating 20th-century guerrilla warfare. This does not consist in directly confronting sovereign power or only taking up arms against oppressive rulers, as in the past. Instead, it is bound up with the reprogramming of technology and networked systems to reflect an abolitionist spirit, experimental ethos and commons-based values. It gestures towards the disruptive creation of guerrilla technologies that can autonomously and efficiently bring a world once thought impossible into existence. This would be based on an ethos of 'collective self-reflection' rooted in the ability of human and non-human 'individuals' 'to fuse their collectively gathered data about the world and about themselves and update their distributed model base' (Ventsel, 2017). Required, in turn, is a guerrilla form of collective self-reflection based on the ongoing and context-specific rematerialization of commons intelligence.

Revolutionary (im)materialism

The growing prevalence of ICTs and digital technologies has blurred the line between the virtual and the physical, the material and the immaterial. Critically, it casts into question what constitutes labour – especially as manual forms of toil are being supplanted and progressively replaced by present-day work in the digital realm. In the contemporary age, subjects must be more than just self-disciplined. They must also be able to use these virtual and material resources to innovatively customize their realities to reflect infectious hegemonic values. 'The networked interactions of communicative capitalism do not provide symbolic identities, sites from which we see ourselves as loci of collective action', according to Dean. 'Rather, they provide opportunities for new ways for me to imagine myself, a variety of lifestyles that I can try and try on' (Dean, 2010, p 78).

This (im)material labour is both utterly inscriptive and potentially liberating. The political task of the current age, hence, is to reimagine and rematerialize new, more egalitarian worlds. Imperative to this task is the cultivation of radical forms of (im)material labour. More precisely, the ability to exploit diverse existing and emerging digital and IRL resources to 'glocally' create contagious commons-based existences. At its core it is the individual and collective effort to turn virtual possibilities into actualized realities. Foundational to this broader political project of commons creation is the dual task of resolidifying reality and revolution. It entails recognizing, perhaps first and foremost, our existence as liquified digital commodities.

Returning once more to the insights of Jodi Dean – she prophetically captured this phenomenon in her 2010 book *Blog Theory* – she says, 'Communicative capitalism designates the strange convergence of democracy and capitalism in networked communications and entertainment media.' It does so by simultaneously promoting 'democratic ideals of access, inclusion, discussion, and participation' through mobile technologies while 'the speed, simultaneity, and interconnectivity of electronic communications produce massive distortions and concentrations of wealth as communicative exchanges and their technological preconditions become commodified and capitalised' (Dean, 2010, p 10). This process of exploitative recognition – specifically concretizing through discursive processes of economic construction and oppression – reveals the commonly invisible labour producing this increasingly digital economy and society. Importantly, 'our disclosures are surveilled, archived, remembered, in ways that exceed our ability to manage or control ... the media that incite us to create and express, to offer our thoughts, feelings, and opinions freely, to participate (but in what?), deliver us up to others to use for purposes of their own' (Dean, 2010, p 56–7). Thus, what was once mere futuristic fantasy has become our daily fever dream and nightmarish reality of neoliberalism. Hence, 'what initially appears as the most separate and complete realm for living fantasies quickly opens up into the actualities of financial markets, wage labor, and exploitation' (Dean, 2010, p 119).

Yet it is precisely through this simultaneous liquifaction and resolidification that new political and existential potentialities become possible and manifest. The danger is that this creeping fluidity will harden past essentialisms. For this reason, the underlying truth of mobility must be combined with an overriding commitment to an ethics of abolitionism. Key in this respect is the adoption of a queering political spirit regarding these radical attempts at resolidification. As MacCormack insightfully observes: 'Queer theory works not to exchange binaries of masculinity/femininity, hetero/homo or even human/non-human but to theorise the spaces between and the mobilisation of categories of identity through desire' (MacCormack, 2016, p 129). Doing so as much an undertaking of disruptive creation as it is one of creative deconstruction. This radically productive and deconstructive politics is apparent, for instance, in the potentially transformative impact of new materialism on traditional humanism. 'It becomes possible to see how an idea of intelligence that is still pervasive today was forged through a highly unstable set of practices and technologies out of a dubious and now clearly indefensible amalgam of physiognomy and nineteenth-century cultural and colonial prejudice', observe Anderson and Perrin (2015, p 11): 'To approach humanism as a material configuration, and so to see "the tiny ingredients" out of which it has been made, is, therefore, to be able to expose its contingency.' Here queerness is associated not only, or in fact even primarily, with difference but with experimentation. This dynamic is captured in emerging notions of the 'experimental city', as 'the promise of learning, and by extension innovation, lends experiments considerable rhetorical power. As experimental activities reinterpret and reframe the trajectories of contemporary urban development, different frameworks are being developed to understand these processes' (Evans et al, 2016, p 2).

Just as importantly, the ontological focus of an abolitionist politics – its commitment to ushering in revolutionary new forms of social being through its elimination of the most oppressive vestiges of the old – is complemented by a queer epistemology wherein novel ways of producing, consuming and legitimizing knowledge are experimented with and ultimately embraced. Here, 'considering the political aspects of urban experimentation leads inexorably to the question of how an experiment or set of experiments drives wider transformation, including whose interests are mobilised in the process' (Evans et al, 2016, p 3). It is precisely, thus, in this ongoing dialectical dance of revolutionary abolitionist ontology and radical queer epistemology that contagious commons-based futures can be made real. Indeed, 'urban experiments intrigue because they constitute explicit attempts to stage and learn about different possible futures in the real world; their actuality matters in producing a different kind of city. They offer novel modes of engagement, governance, and politics that both challenge and complement conventional strategies in important ways' (Evans et al, 2016, p 7). At stake is nothing less than the continuous (im)material rewriting and reshaping of our still undetermined and always uncertain histories.

'Glocal' possibilities

The 21st century poses a profound conundrum for radical politics. It is clear that the new millennium has not ushered in the proverbial 'end of history'. Yet in the face of the dual forces of globalization and digitalization, new challenges have arisen. Specifically, where in the world and cyberspace will the revolution take place? As Connolly notes, 'The challenges of today solicit both an embrace of this unruly world and pursuit of new political assemblages to counter its dangers' (Connolly, 2017, p 9). For this purpose, 'militant citizen alliances across regions are needed to challenge the priorities of investment capital, state hegemony, local cronyisms, international organisations, and frontier mentalities' (Connolly, 2017, p 9). While these are most obviously – and to a certain extent most urgently – explicitly political concerns, at a deeper and arguably more fundamental level we are also here in existential territory.

What is the (im)material realm – the mix of the virtual and material sphere – where experimenting with novel forms of existence can occur and take hold? It is our argument that it in fact represents the changing geography of contemporary life generally and of social struggles specifically. To this effect, it is a space of 'geographies produced through, produced by, and of the digital' (Ash et al, 2018, p 25). These shifting (im)material geographies reflect the rise of fresh 'glocal' possibilities for reimagining, reconnecting and rematerializing the world. Imperative for realizing these revolutionary ambitions is effectively politically harnessing mobile power. While power cannot and should not be reduced to instrumentality, it nonetheless should and must be tactical.

Whereas previously the tactical could be concentrated – though never fully exhausted – by sovereign struggles for power, conceptually and concretely manifested in that 'empty space of power' so presciently theorized by Lefort (1986), we have now entered into the viral age of order, hegemony and politics. What is now primary is the viral spread and mobile adaptation of ideologies and practices, the diverse materializations of hegemonic discourses and revolutionary alternatives. The language of epidemiology is useful, in this regard, for theoretically and empirically navigating this viral age. According to Pope et al: 'Harnessing epidemiologic insights can suggest educational strategies to help address inequalities in civic engagement with added benefits of increasing overall health' (Pope et al, 2019, p 1). As such, we must search for the underlying structural causes and conditions fostering past and future hegemonic epidemics. Indeed, 'the purpose is not simply to "contain the epidemic" but to search for ways to prevent its appearance' (Pope et al, 2019, p 6). Equally significant is the critical analysis and strategic undertaking of successfully encouraging and catalyzing radical pandemics.

Integral to such a viral counter-hegemonic project is the cultivation of radical networks. Conventionally, and perhaps understandably, studies of power and hegemony focus predominantly on the ideological and cultural. Such efforts of political reimagining can by no means be made secondary. Yet just as significant are processes of political reconnection. Mobile technologies have reconfigured our relation to the material and digital environment as well as to each other. 'The question to ask is not how the young human–smartphone assemblage can be deterritorialised: it seems highly unlikely that the genie can be forced back into the bottle', argue Marchant and O'Donohoe: 'Instead, educators, policy makers and technology developers might wish to ask how capacity building within this assemblage can be developed and enhanced in positive ways' (Marchant & O'Donohoe, 2019, p 469). The inscriptive and exploitative implications of this mobile perspective are profound and increasingly clear, yet their radical potentialities are only now emerging. Traditional social geographies and boundaries, along with the identities associated with them, are rapidly liquifying. They are therefore being both clung to with renewed furious passion and deconstructed, as well as, prospectively, even abandoned.

However, these ICTs and the greater mobility (digital and physical) they permit also provide the foundation for novel networks to come to fruition – some of which expand the geographies and physical possibilities of previously territorially bounded identities and communities. Bernal's recent study of the Eritrean diaspora bears witness to such political reconnections. He writes that diasporas, much like cyberspace, are altering the meaning of territorial locations and borders, disrupting prior configurations of society and territory and making possible new spatializations of politics which are 'always both grounded and virtual' (Bernal, 2018, p 1).

This quite literally – and also figuratively – opens the space for political experimentation. As Foucault helpfully reminds us, everything is dangerous. In this sense, the danger is always double-bladed. On the one hand, it threatens the status quo in ways big and small. On the other, we must be attentive to how it particularly endangers historically marginalized groups. It thus must incorporate and embrace an ethos of expansion and inclusion. Hester again reminds us that 'any emancipatory techno-feminism must take the form of a concerted political intervention, sensitive to the fused character of the structures of oppression that make up our material world' (Hester, 2018b, p 11). This also entails taking care of these reconnections, nurturing these nascent radical resolidifications of the social and cultivating them as 'glocal' contagions for transforming, reimagining and rematerializing the social.

Mobile organizing in the 21st century

This book has sought to reconsider power and hegemony as fundamentally mobile and viral, respectively. These foundational aspects are increasingly important given the growth of mobile technologies and the viral spread of information. To this end, domination is progressively linked to the epidemic proliferation of infectious discourses. Revealed, in turn, is how neoliberalism draws strength from the (im)material labour of contemporary subjects to adapt their diverse material and digital contexts to best reflect its capitalist ideologies. Crucial is the ability of individuals and communities to inoculate themselves against these viral neoliberal discourses and exploit these built-up resistances to create disruptive revolutionary contagions. Ultimately, the emerging significance of mobile power and viral ordering can give rise to a new radical culture of disruptive creativity waged by everyday 21st-century democratic guerrillas.

It is tempting to assume that in an era of corporate globalization its struggles must be similarly global in scope. However, this is only half true. As this analysis has sought to make clear, present-day globalization is actually, and paradoxically, profoundly local. Digitalization has been complemented and reinforced by a concurrent process of 'glocalization'. It reflects how, on the one hand, neoliberal values of financialization, privatization and marketization are uniquely adapted to and seek to transform existing host contexts, and on the other, how these contexts can learn and share 'best' practices with each other. Required, hence, are similarly 'glocal' insurgencies, whereby social contexts are made into political spaces of experimentation and levelled up through organic forms of leadership. Practically, this encourages and in many ways demands a novel and more radical form of leadership and governance. Needed, though, is an alternative political spirit rooted in finding fresh means for instituting commons-based virtual and IRL networks. This disruptive and creative ethos is captured, for instance, in the GynePunk collective started near Barcelona. As Thorburn observes, 'As a queer collaboration of hackers and feminists, the GynePunk collective focuses on bodies as reconfigurable and hackable technologies, and adopts the devices of gynaecology as weapons of resistance by 3D-printing speculums and making their own centrifuges and microscopes from discarded hardware' (Thorburn, 2017, p 153).

This collective draws direct inspiration from the autonomous Marxists of the 1970s in its emphasis on using class conflict as a source for social experimentation and revolutionary creativity. This creative approach 'alters how the working class structures its resistance, again altering the capital's organisation of labour, and so on in an on-going "cycle of struggle" that sees class power decompose and recompose with differing technological capacities in different historical epochs' (Thorburn, 2017, p 155). Yet, transposed into the contemporary context, this is given a technological update and guerrilla reboot. It links to a politics of the 'cyborg' that combines an abolitionist commitment to reimagining the social with a queer epistemology of forging radical reconnections. Consequently, 'the cyborg is then a way of thinking solidarity – and composition – in transnational, intersectional terms, within and through conditions of twenty-first century techno-capitalism' (Thorburn, 2017, p 160).

This has resulted in a guerrilla democratic community marked by a willingness to concretely subvert the status quo and in doing so cultivate radically new ways of interacting and existing with each other and the world. A key and urgent political task of our time, then, is transforming mobile power into mobile organizing. Like perhaps all great historical undertakings, the roots of this struggle have sprouted up organically. In a political sense, this entails adopting refreshed democratic guerrilla strategies to creatively disrupt the status quo and disruptively recreate it from the bottom up across the physical and digital world. Importantly, 'there are multiple ways that material things are reconfigured through successive configurations of apparatus. Things are always both being and becoming, but in many different ways, and specific configurations of reality alter what those things are and what they can become' (Fowler & Harris, 2015, p 145). Similarly, as Gigi Roggero argues, the task of the militant – riffing off Churchill's metaphor of Lenin arriving like the plague in a sealed carriage to Russia – is to 'hold back the force which spreads the plague in our own body and accelerate the bacteria produced by class struggle in the body of our enemy. ... Conflict must therefore function as a plague in the enemy and as a vaccine for us, a controlled inoculation of poison to reinforce our organism' (Roggero, 2020).

It is only through paying revolutionary attention to mobile power and viral hegemony that such a radical democratic project of counter-hegemonic commons building can be both contagiously upscaled and transformatively downscaled for reimagining, reordering, reconnecting, resituating, rematerializing and resolidifying our shared existence in ways previously considered impossible.

References

Abrahamsson, S., Bertoni, F., Mol, A. and Martín, R.I. (2015) 'Living with omega-3: New materialism and enduring concerns', *Environment and Planning D: Society and Space*, 33(1): 4–19.

Abu-Lughod, J.L. (1989) *Before European Hegemony: The World System AD 1250–1350*, Oxford: Oxford University Press.

Adam, B. (2013) *Timewatch: The Social Analysis of Time*, Hoboken, NJ: John Wiley & Sons.

Agamben, G. (1998) *Homo Sacer: Sovereign Power and Bare Life*, Stanford: Stanford University Press.

Agger, B. (2011) 'iTime: Labor and life in a smartphone era', *Time & Society*, 20(1): 119–36.

Alipour Leili, M., Chang, W.T. and Chao, C. (2017) 'Driverless governance: Designing narratives toward democratic technology', *The Design Journal*, 20(1): S4343–56.

Ampuja, M. (2016) 'The new spirit of capitalism, innovation fetishism and new information and communication technologies', *Javnost-The Public*, 23(1): 19–36.

Anderson, B. (2016) 'Neoliberal affects', *Progress in Human Geography*, 40(6): 734–53.

Anderson, K. and Perrin, C. (2015) 'New materialism and the stuff of humanism', *Australian Humanities Review*, 58: 1–15.

Anon (2019) 'Digital Democracy and Data Commons (DDDC): Data control wars – Mobile social congress', Pl Manning – Mobile Social Congress, 27 February.

Ansell-Pearson, K. (2016) 'Naturalism as a joyful science: Nietzsche, Deleuze, and the art of life', *Journal of Nietzsche Studies*, 47(1): 119–40.

Arboleda, M. (2015) *Resource Extraction and the Planetary Extension of the Urban Form: Understanding Sociospatial Transformation in the Huasco Valley, Chile*, Manchester: The University of Manchester.

Arditi, B. (2012) 'Insurgencies don't have a plan – they are the plan: Political performatives and vanishing mediators in 2011', *JOMEC Journal*, (1).

Arditi, B. (2016) 'Populism as hegemony and as politics? The theory of populism by Ernesto Laclau', *Ponte*, 72(8–9): 19–42.

Arora, P. (2019) 'Benign dataveillance? Examining novel data-driven governance systems in India and China', *First Monday*, 24(4).

Arvidsson, A. (2018) 'Value and virtue in the sharing economy', *The Sociological Review*, 66(2): 289–301.

Ash, J., Kitchin, R. and Leszczynski, A. (2018) *Digital Geographies*, California: SAGE Publications.

Ayers, A.J. and Saad-Filho, A. (2015) 'Democracy against neoliberalism: Paradoxes, limitations, transcendence', *Critical Sociology*, 41(4–5): 597–618.

Ayoub, P.M. (2018) 'Protean power in movement: Navigating uncertainty in the LGBT rights revolution', in P.J. Katzenstein and L.A. Seybert (eds) *Protean Power: Exploring the Uncertain and Unexpected in World Politics*, Cambridge: Cambridge University Press, pp 79–99.

Baack, S. (2015) 'Datafication and empowerment: How the open data movement re-articulates notions of democracy, participation, and journalism', *Big Data & Society*, 2(2): 2053951715594634.

Baer, H. (2014) 'Redoing feminism within and outside the neoliberal academy', *Women in German Yearbook: Feminist Studies in German Literature and Culture*, 30: 197–208.

Baer, H. (2016) 'Redoing feminism: Digital activism, body politics, and neoliberalism', *Feminist Media Studies*, 16(1): 17–34.

Badiou, A. (2007) *Being and Event*, London: A&C Black.

Baker, P. (2016) '(Post) hegemony and the promise of populism: Reflections on the politics of our times', *Politica Comun*, 10.

Baker, S.E. (2018) 'Post-work futures and full automation: Towards a feminist design methodology', *Open Cultural Studies*, 2(1): 540–52.

Banks, D.A. (2016) *Three Theories of Praxis: Sense-Making Tools for Post-Capitalism*, New York: Rensselaer Polytechnic Institute.

Barad, K. (2007) *Meeting the Universe Halfway: Quantum Physics and the Entanglement of Matter and Meaning*, Durham, NC: Duke University Press.

Barassi, V. (2015) *Activism on the Web: Everyday Struggles against Digital Capitalism*, Abingdon: Routledge.

Barbrook-Johnson, P. and Fornes, A. (2017) *The Commoners Framework*, Github.

Barclay, J.M.G. (2017) *Paul and the Gift*, Grand Rapids, MI: Wm. B. Eerdmans Publishing.

Barisione, M. and Michailidou, A. (2017) *Social Media and European Politics: Rethinking Power and Legitimacy in the Digital Era*, New York: Springer.

Barnes, T.J. and Hannah, M. (2001) 'The place of numbers: histories, geographies, and theories of quantification', *Environment and Planning D: Society and Space*, 19(4): 379–83.

Barrett, M.A., Humblet, O., Hiatt, R.A. and Adler, N.E. (2013) 'Big data and disease prevention: from quantified self to quantified communities', *Big Data*, 1(3): 168–75.

Bassett, K. (2016) 'Event, politics, and space: Rancière or Badiou?' *Space and Polity*, 20(3): 280–93.

Bastani, A. (2019) *Fully Automated Luxury Communism*, New York: Verso.

Bates, T.R. (1975) 'Gramsci and the theory of hegemony', *Journal of the History of Ideas*, 36(2): 351–66.

Bauman, Z. (2000) *Modernity and the Holocaust*, Ithaca, NY: Cornell University Press.

Bauman, Z. (2006) *Liquid Modernity*, Hoboken, NJ: John Wiley & Sons.

Bauman, Z. (2013) *Liquid Modernity*, Hoboken, NJ: John Wiley & Sons.

Beck, U. (1992) *Risk Society: Towards a New Modernity* (vol 17), London: SAGE Publications.

Beer, D. (2015) 'Productive measures: Culture and measurement in the context of everyday neoliberalism', *Big Data & Society*, 2(1): 2053951715578951.

Bene, M. (2017) 'Go viral on the Facebook! Interactions between candidates and followers on Facebook during the Hungarian general election campaign of 2014', *Information, Communication & Society*, 20(4): 513–29.

Benedikter, R. and Siepmann, K. (2016) '"Transhumanism": A new global political trend?' *Challenge*, 59(1): 47–59.

Beniger, J. (2009) *The Control Revolution: Technological and Economic Origins of the Information Society*, Cambridge, MA: Harvard University Press.

Benkler, Y. (2006) *The Wealth of Networks: How Social Production Transforms Markets and Freedom*. London: Yale University Press.

Benkler, Y., Shaw, A. and Hill, B.M. (2015) 'Peer production: A form of collective intelligence', in M. Bernstein and T.W. Malone (eds) *Handbook of Collective Intelligence*, Cambridge, MA: Harvard University Press, pp 175–204.

Bennett, J. (2004) 'The force of things: Steps toward an ecology of matter', *Political Theory*, 32(3): 347–72.

Bennett, J. (2010) 'A vitalist stopover on the way to a new materialism', *New Materialisms: Ontology, Agency, and Politics*, 91(1): 47–69.

Bennett, W.L. (2012) 'The personalization of politics: Political identity, social media and changing patterns of participation', *The Annals of the American Academy of Political and Social Science*, 644, 20–39.

Bennett, W.L. and Segerberg, A. (2012) 'The logic of connective action: Digital media and the personalization of contentious politics', *Information, Communication & Society*, 15(5): 739–68.

Bensaïd, D. (2004) 'Alain Badiou and the miracle of the event', in P. Hallward (ed) *Think Again: Alain Badiou and the Future of Philosophy*, London: Bloomsbury, pp 94–105.

Bernal, V. (2018) 'Digital media, territory, and diaspora: The shape-shifting spaces of Eritrean politics', *Journal of African Cultural Studies*, 32(1)1–15.

Bhattacharya, T. (2017) *Social Reproduction Theory: Remapping Class, Recentering Oppression*, London: Pluto Press.

Blas, Z. (2012) 'Virus, viral', *Women's Studies Quarterly*, 40(1/2): 29–39.

Blascovich, J. and Bailenson, J. (2011) *Infinite Reality: Avatars, Eternal Life, New Worlds, and the Dawn of the Virtual Revolution*, New York: William Morrow & Co.

Bleiberg, J. and West, D. (2014) 'The explosive growth of the mobile economy will change the world', *The Brookings Institute*, 15 September, available at: www.brookings.edu/blog/techtank/2014/09/15/the-explosive-growth-of-the-mobile-economy-will-change-the-world/

Bloom, P. (2016) *Authoritarian Capitalism in the Age of Globalization*, Cheltenham: Edward Elgar Publishing.

Bloom, P. (2019) *Monitored: Business and Surveillance in a Time of Big Data*, London: Pluto Press.

Bloom, P. and Cederstrom, C. (2009) ' "The sky's the limit": fantasy in the age of market rationality', *Journal of Organizational Change Management*, 22(2): 159–80.

Bloom, P. and Dallyn, S. (2011) 'The paradox of order: reimagining ideological domination', *Journal of Political Ideologies*, 16(1): 53–78.

Bode, L. and Dalrymple, K.E. (2016) 'Politics in 140 characters or less: Campaign communication, network interaction, and political participation on Twitter', *Journal of Political Marketing*, 15(4): 311–32.

Bode, L., Vraga, E.K. and Troller-Renfree, S. (2017) 'Skipping politics: Measuring avoidance of political content in social media', *Research & Politics*, 4(2): 2053168017702990.

Bogad, L.M. (2016) *Electoral Guerrilla Theatre: Radical Ridicule and Social Movements*, Abingdon: Routledge.

Bonilla, Y. and Rosa, J. (2015) '#Ferguson: Digital protest, hashtag ethnography, and the racial politics of social media in the United States', *American Ethnologist*, 42(1): 4–17.

Brabham, D.C. and Guth, K.L. (2017) 'The deliberative politics of the consultative layer: Participation hopes and communication as design values of civic tech founders', *Journal of Communication*, 67(4): 445–75.

Bradley, K. and Pargman, D. (2017) 'The sharing economy as the commons of the 21st century', *Cambridge Journal of Regions, Economy and Society*, 10(2): 231–47.

Braidotti, R. (2000) 'Teratologies', in I. Buchanan and C. Colebrook (eds) *Deleuze and Feminist Theory*, Edinburgh: Edinburgh University Press, pp 156–72.

Braidotti, R. (2006) 'The ethics of becoming-imperceptible', in C.V. Boundas (ed) *Deleuze and Philosophy*, Edinburgh: Edinburgh University Press, pp 133–59.

Braidotti, R. (2011) *Nomadic Theory: The Portable Rosi Braidotti*, New York: Columbia University Press.

Braidotti, R. (2014) 'Writing as a nomadic subject', *Comparative Critical Studies*, 11(2–3): 163–84.

Braidotti, R. (2017) 'Critical posthuman knowledges', *South Atlantic Quarterly*, 116(1): 83–96.

Brandsen, T., Steen, T. and Verschuere, B. (2018) *Co-production and Co-creation: Engaging Citizens in Public Services*, Oxfordshire: Taylor & Francis.

Brenner, N. and Theodore, N. (2002) 'Cities and the geographies of "actually existing neoliberalism"', *Antipode*, 34(3): 349–79.

Briscoe, I. (2015) *Conflict, Security and Emerging Threats*, Netherlands: Instituut Clingendael.

Brown, P.R. and Head, B.W. (2019) 'Navigating tensions in co-production: a missing link in leadership for public value', *Public Administration*, 97(2): 250–63.

Bruster, D. (2003) 'The new materialism in early modern studies', in D. Bruster (ed) *Shakespeare and the Question of Culture*, New York: Springer, pp 191–205.

Butler, J. (2001) 'What is critique? An essay on Foucault's virtue', *Eipcp*, May: 16–22.

Cammack, P. (2003) 'The mother of all governments: The World Bank's matrix for global governance', in P. Cammack (ed) *Global Governance*, Abingdon: Routledge, pp 4–71.

Cammaerts, B. (2015) 'Social media and activism', in P. Hwa Ang and R. Mansel (eds) *The International Encyclopedia of Digital Communication and Society*, Malden: Wiley Blackwell, pp 1–8.

Campbell, A. and Gindt, D. (2018) *Viral Dramaturgies: HIV and AIDS in Performance in the Twenty-first Century*, Cham: Palgrave Macmillan.

Caplan, R. and Boyd, D. (2018) 'Isomorphism through algorithms: Institutional dependencies in the case of Facebook', *Big Data & Society*, 5(1): 2053951718757253.

Carlsson, C. and Manning, F. (2010) 'Nowtopia: strategic exodus?' *Antipode*, 42(4): 924–53.

Caramazza, G. (2019) 'Workers unite online', *Red Pepper*, available at: www.redpepper.org.uk/workers-unite-online/

Carter, D. (2017) 'Smart cities: terrain for "epic struggle" or new urban utopias?' *The Town Planning Review*, 88(1): 1.

Castells, M. (1996) *The Power of Identity: The Information Age, Economy, Society and Culture*, New Jersey: Wiley Blackwell Publishing.

Catlaw, T.J. and Sandberg, B. (2018) 'The quantified self and the evolution of neoliberal self-government: An exploratory qualitative study', *Administrative Theory & Praxis*, 40(1): 3–22.

Cavanagh, C.J. and Benjaminsen, T.A. (2015) 'Guerrilla agriculture? A biopolitical guide to illicit cultivation within an IUCN Category II protected area', *Journal of Peasant Studies*, 42(3-4): 725–45.

Chadwick, A., Dennis, J. and Smith, A. (2016) 'Politics in the age of hybrid media', in A. Bruns, G. Enli, E. Skogerbo, A. Olof Larsson and C. Christensen (eds) *The Routledge Companion to Social Media and Politics*, Abingdon: Routledge, pp 7–22.

Chandler, A.D. (1984) 'The emergence of managerial capitalism', *Business History Review*, 58(4): 473–503.

Charteris, J., Smardon, D. and Nelson, E. (2017) 'Innovative learning environments and new materialism: A conjunctural analysis of pedagogic spaces', *Educational Philosophy and Theory*, 49(8): 808–21.

Chatterton, P. (2016) 'Building transitions to post-capitalist urban commons', *Transactions of the Institute of British Geographers*, 41(4): 403–15.

Chatterton, P. (2002) ' "Squatting is still legal, necessary and free": A brief intervention in the corporate city', *Antipode*, 34(1): 1–7.

Cheah, P. (2008) 'Nondialectical materialism', *Diacritics*, 38(1/2): 143–57.

Chenou, J.-M. and Cepeda-Másmela, C. (2019) '#NiUnaMenos: Data activism from the global south', *Television & New Media*, 20(4): 396–411.

Chilvers, J. and Kearnes, M. (2020) 'Remaking participation in science and democracy', *Science, Technology & Human Values*, 45(3): 347–80.

Choat, S. (2018) 'Science, agency and ontology: A historical-materialist response to new materialism', *Political Studies*, 66(4): 1027–42.

Chow, R. (2010) 'The elusive material, what the dog doesn't understand', in S. Frost and D. Coole (eds) *New Materialisms: Ontology, Agency and Politics*, Durham, NC: Duke University Press, pp 221–33.

Cody, F. (2020) 'Millennial turbulence: The networking of tamil media politics', *Television & New Media*, 21(4): 392–406.

Cohen, E. (2011) 'The paradoxical politics of viral containment; or, how scale undoes us one and all', *Social Text*, 29(1 (106)): 15–35.

Collier, S.J. (2006) 'Global assemblages', *Theory, Culture & Society*, 23(2–3): 399–401.

Comaroff, J. and Comaroff, J.L. (2000) Millennial capitalism: First thoughts on a second coming', *Public Culture*, 12(2): 291–343.

Comor, E. (2011) 'Contextualizing and critiquing the fantastic prosumer: Power, alienation and hegemony, *Critical Sociology* 37(3): 309–27.

Conaghan, C.M. and Malloy, J. (1995) *Unsettling Statecraft: Democracy and Neoliberalism in the Central Andes*, Pittsburgh, PA: University of Pittsburgh Press.

Connolly, W.E. (2013) 'The "new materialism" and the fragility of things', *Millennium: Journal of International Studies*, 41(3): 399–412.

Connolly, W.E. (2017) *Facing the Planetary: Entangled Humanism and the Politics of Swarming*, Durham, NC: Duke University Press.

Coole, D. (2013) 'Agentic capacities and capacious historical materialism: Thinking with new materialisms in the political sciences', *Millennium: Journal of International Studies*, 41(3): 451–69.

Coole, D. and Frost, S. (2010) 'Introducing the new materialisms', in D. Coole and S. Frost (eds) *New Materialisms: Ontology, Agency, and Politics*, Durham, NC: Duke University Press, pp 1–43.

Cousins, M. and Hussain, A. (1984) *Michel Foucault*, New York: St. Martin's Press.

Crary, J. (2013) *24/7: Late Capitalism and the Ends of Sleep*, New York: Verso.

Cremin, C. (2010) 'Never employable enough: The (im)possibility of satisfying the boss's desire', *Organization*, 17(2): 131–49.

Culpepper, P.D. and Thelen, K. (2019) 'Are we all Amazon primed? Consumers and the politics of platform power', *Comparative Political Studies*, 53(2): 288–318.

Dahlberg, L. (2011) 'Re-constructing digital democracy: An outline of four "positions"', *New Media & Society*, 13(6): 855–72.

Daniel, R. and Behe, C. (2017) 'Co-production of knowledge: An Inuit Indigenous knowledge perspective', *American Geophysical Union*, Fall Meeting.

Daniels, J. (2017) 'Bodies in code', in J. Daniels and K. Gregory (eds) *Digital Sociologies*, Bristol: Policy Press, pp 335–8.

Davies, W. (2014) *The Limits of Neoliberalism: Authority, Sovereignty and the Logic of Competition*, California: SAGE publications.

Davies, W. (2015) 'How friendship became the tool of the powerful: Will Davies on social media, sharing and selling', *Verso Blogs*, 7 May, available at: www.versobooks.com/blogs/1979-how-friendship-became-the-tool-of-the-powerful-will-davies-on-social-media-sharing-and-selling

Davies, W. (2017) 'Elite power under advanced neoliberalism', *Theory, Culture & Society*, 34(5-6): 227–50.

Day, O. (2017) 'Towards a contemplative commons', *Institute for Advanced Sustainability Studies*, IASS Potsdam, 1–2.

De Angelis, D.M. (2017) *Omnia Sunt Communia: On the Commons and the Transformation to Postcapitalism*, London: Zed Books.

De Filippi, P. and Loveluck, B. (2016) 'The invisible politics of bitcoin: Governance crisis of a decentralized infrastructure', *Internet Policy Review*, 5(4): 1–28.

Dean, J. (2010) *Blog Theory: Feedback and Capture in the Circuits of Drive*, Bristol: Polity Press.

Dederer, J.M. (1983) 'Making bricks without straw: Nathanael Greene's southern campaign and Mao Tse-Tung's mobile war', *The Journal of Military History*, 47(3): 115.

DeLanda, M. (1996) 'An Interview with Manuel DeLanda', interview by Konrad Becker and Miss M, *Virtual Futures 96 Conference*, May, available at: www.t0.or.at/delanda/intdelanda.htm

DeLanda, M. (2002) 'Deleuze and the use of the genetic algorithm in architecture', *Architectural Design*, 71(7): 9–12.

DeLanda, M. (2013) *Intensive Science and Virtual Philosophy*, London: Bloomsbury.

Deleuze, G. (1968) *Difference and Repetition*, Columbia: Columbia University Press.

Deleuze, G. and Guattari, F. (1980) *A Thousand Plateaus*, London: Continuum.

Delgado, A. and Callén, B. (2017) 'Do-it-yourself biology and electronic waste hacking: A politics of demonstration in precarious times', *Public Understanding of Science*, 26(2): 179–94.

Derrida, J. (1993) *Ghostly Demarcations: A Symposium on Jacques Derrida's Spectres of Marx* (vol 33), New York: Verso.

Di Salvo, P. (2020) 'The rise of digital whistleblowing platforms – and how they work', *Global Investigative Journalism Network*, 21 September, available at: https://gijn.org/2020/09/21/the-rise-of-digital-whistleblowing-platforms-and-how-they-work/

Dolber, B. (2019) 'Building solidarity among gig workers through digital organizing', University of Pennsylvania, 8 November.

Dolber, B. (2020) 'Precarity and solidarity at neoliberalism's twilight: The potentials of transnational production autoethnography', *Cultural Studies ↔ Critical Methodologies*, 20(4): 311–21.

Dolphijn, R. and Van der Tuin, I. (2011) 'Pushing dualism to an extreme: On the philosophical impetus of a new materialism', *Continental Philosophy Review*, 44(4): 383–400.

Dolphijn, R. and Van der Tuin, I. (2012) *New Materialism: Interviews & Cartographies*, Michigan: Open Humanities Press.

Dowling, E., Nunes, R. and Trott, B. (2007) 'Immaterial and affective labour: Explored', *Ephemera: Theory and Politics in Organization*, 7(1): 1–7.

Duggan, L. (2012) *The Twilight of Equality? Neoliberalism, Cultural Politics, and the Attack on Democracy*, Boston, MA: Beacon Press.

DuPont, Q. (2017) 'Experiments in algorithmic governance: A history and ethnography of "The DAO," a failed decentralized autonomous organization', in M. Campbell-Verduyn (ed) *Bitcoin And Beyond*, Abingdon: Routledge, pp 157–77.

Dutta, T., Kim, K.H., Uchimiya, M., Kwon, E.E., Jeon, B.H., Deep, A. and Yun, S.T. (2016) 'Global demand for rare earth resources and strategies for green mining', *Environmental Research*, 150, 182–190.

Dyer-Witheford, N. (2015) *Cyber-proletariat: Global Labour in the Digital Vortex*, London: Pluto.

Eagle, N. (2010) *SMS Uprising: Mobile Activism in Africa*, Kenya: Fahamu/Pambazuka.

Eagleton-Pierce, M. (2016) *Neoliberalism: The Key Concepts*, Abingdon: Routledge.

Edenhofer, S., Tomforde, S., Kantert, J., Klejnowski, L., Bernard, Y., Hähner, J. and Müller-Schloer, C. (2016), Trust communities: an open, self-organised social infrastructure of autonomous agents', in E. André, T. Ungerer, C. Müller-Schloer, W. Reif, G. Anders, H. Seebach, J.-P. Steghöfer and J. Hähner (eds) *Trustworthy Open Self-Organising Systems*, New York: Springer, pp 127–52.

Eller, A. (2017) 'Rumors of slavery: Defending emancipation in a hostile Caribbean', *The American Historical Review*, 122(3): 653–79.

Engels, F. (1890) 'Letter to Joseph Bloch', in J. Storey (ed) *Cultural Theory and Popular Culture: A Reader*, Abingdon: Routledge, pp 71–72.

Evans, J., Karvonen, A. and Raven, R. (2016) *The Experimental City*, Abingdon: Routledge.

Faguet, J.P., Fox, A.M. and Pöschl, C. (2015) 'Decentralizing for a deeper, more supple democracy', *Journal of Democracy*, 26(4): 60–74.

Farkas, J. and Schou, J. (2018) 'Fake news as a floating signifier: Hegemony, antagonism and the politics of falsehood', *Javnost – The Public*, 25(3): 298–314.

Fattal, A.L. (2018) *Guerrilla Marketing: Counterinsurgency and Capitalism in Colombia*, Chicago: University of Chicago Press.

Fawcett, P., Flinders, M., Hay, C. and Wood, M. (2017) 'A renewed agenda for studying anti-politics, depoliticisation, and governance', in P. Fawcett, M. Flinders, C. Hay and M. Wood (eds) *Anti-Politics, Depoliticisation and Governance*, Oxford: Oxford University Press, pp 283–98.

Fenton, N. (2016) 'Left out? Digital media, radical politics and social change: Information', *Communication & Society*, 19(3): 346–61.

Fenton, N. (2018) *Digital, Political, Radical*, Hoboken, NJ: John Wiley & Sons.

Ferguson, J. (1994) *The Anti-Politics Machine: Development, Depoliticization, and Bureaucratic Power in Lesotho*, Minneapolis, MN: University of Minnesota Press.

Ferreday, D. and Harris, G. (2017) 'Investigating "fame-inism": The politics of popular culture', London: SAGE Publications.

Firchow, P., Martin-Shields, C., Omer, A. and Ginty, R.M. (2017) 'PeaceTech: The liminal spaces of digital technology in peacebuilding', *International Studies Perspectives*, 18(1): 4–42.

Fishkin, J. and Mansbridge, J. (2017) 'The prospects & limits of deliberative democracy – Introduction', *Daedalus*, 146(3): 6–13.

Flatschart, E. (2017) 'Feminist standpoints and critical realism: The contested materiality of difference in intersectionality and new materialism', *Journal of Critical Realism*, 16(3): 284–302.

Fleming, P. and Spicer, A. (2004) ' "You can checkout anytime, but you can never leave": Spatial boundaries in a high commitment organization', *Human Relations*, 57(1): 75–94.

Fleming, P. and Sturdy, A. (2009) ' "Just be yourself!": Towards neo-normative control in organisations', *Employee Relations*, 31(6): 569–83.

Foucault, M. (1973) *The Order of Things*, Abingdon: Routledge.

Foucault, M. (1975) *Discipline and Punish*, trans. A. Sheridan, Paris: Gallimard.

Foucault, M. (1982) 'The subject and power', *Critical Inquiry*, 8(4): 777–95.

Foucault, M. (1988) *Technologies of the Self: A Seminar with Michel Foucault*, Amherst, MA: University of Massachusetts Press.

Foucault, M. (1989) *Foucault Live*, New York: Semiotext.

Fougère, M., Segercrantz, B. and Seeck, H. (2017) 'A critical reading of the European Union's social innovation policy discourse: (Re)legitimizing neoliberalism', *Organization*, 24(6): 819–43.

Fourcade, M. and Healy, K. (2017) 'Seeing like a market', *Socio-Economic Review*, 15(1): 9–29.

Fowler, C. and Harris, O.J.T. (2015) 'Enduring relations: Exploring a paradox of new materialism', *Journal of Material Culture*, 20(2): 127–48.

Fox, N.J. and Alldred, P. (2016) *Sociology and the New Materialism: Theory, Research, Action*, California: SAGE publications.

Frank, A.G. (1967) *Capitalism and Underdevelopment in Latin America* (vol 16), New York University Press.

Frase, P. (2016) *Four Futures: Life after Capitalism*, New York: Verso.

Fraser, N. (2009) *Scales of Justice: Reimagining Political Space in a Globalizing World*, Chichester: Columbia University Press.

Fraser, N. (2014) *Justice Interruptus: Critical Reflections on the 'Postsocialist' Condition*, Abingdon: Routledge.

Fregonese, S. (2011) 'Beyond the domino: Transnational (in)security and the 2011 protests', *Environment and Planning D: Society and Space*, 20 October.

Fuchs, C. (2018) *Digital Demagogue: Authoritarian Capitalism in the Age of Trump and Twitter*, London: Pluto Press.

Fuchs, C. (2019) 'Karl Marx in the age of big data capitalism', in D. Chandler and C. Fuchs (eds) *Digital Objects, Digital Subjects: Interdisciplinary Perspectives on Capitalism, Labour and Politics in the Age of Big Data*, London: University of Westminster Press, pp 53–72.

Fujimoto, T. (2018) 'Ideology of AoD: Analog on digital-operating digitized objects and experiences with analog-like approach', in *2018 7th International Congress on Advanced Applied Informatics* (IIAI-AAI), IEEE, pp 901–6.

Fusaro, L. (2019) *Crises and Hegemonic Transitions: From Gramsci's Quaderni to the Contemporary World Economy*, Leiden; Boston: Brill.

Gardner, P. and Wray, B. (2013) 'From lab to living room: Transhumanist imaginaries of consumer brain wave monitors', *Ada: A Journal of Gender, New Media, and Technology*, 3: 1–39.

Garmulewicz, A. (2015) '3D printing in the commons: knowledge and the nature of digital and physical resources', Doctoral dissertation, University of Oxford.

Garrod, J.Z. (2016) 'The real world of the decentralized autonomous society', *TripleC: Communication, Capitalism & Critique, Open Access Journal for a Global Sustainable Information Society*, 14(1): 62–77.

George, J.J. and Leidner, D.E. (2019) 'From clicktivism to hacktivism: Understanding digital activism', *Information and Organization*, 29(3): 100249.

Gerbaudo, P. (2017) 'From cyber-autonomism to cyber-populism: An ideological analysis of the evolution of digital activism', *TripleC: Communication, Capitalism & Critique, Open Access Journal for a Global Sustainable Information Society*, 15(2): 477–89.

Gerhardt, H. (2020) 'Engaging the non-flat world: Anarchism and the promise of a post-capitalist collaborative commons', *Antipode*, 52(3): 681–701.

Gill, R. (2010) 'Life is a pitch: Managing the self in new media work', in M. Deuze (ed) *Managing Media Work*, London: SAGE Publications, pp 249–62.

Gill, R. (2017) 'Beyond individualism: the psychosocial life of the neoliberal university', in M. Spooner (ed) *A Critical Guide to Higher Education & the Politics of Evidence: Resisting Colonialism, Neoliberalism, & Audit Culture*. Regina, Canada: University of Regina Press, pp 193–216.

Glennie, P. and Thrift, N. (1996) 'Reworking EP Thompson's Time, work-discipline and industrial capitalism', *Time & Society*, 5(3): 275–99.

Glynos, J. and Howarth, D. (2007) *Logics of Critical Explanation in Social and Political Theory*, Abingdon: Routledge.

Glynos, J. and Howarth, D. (2019) 'The retroductive cycle: The research process in poststructuralist discourse analysis', in T. Marttila (ed) *Discourse, Culture and Organization*, New York: Springer.

Golsteijn, C., Gallacher, S., Capra, L. and Rogers, Y. (2016) 'Sensus: Designing innovative civic technology for the public good', in M. Foth, W. Ju, R. Schroeter and S. Viller (eds) *Proceedings of the 2016 ACM Conference on Designing Interactive Systems*, New York: ACM, pp 39–49.

Golumbia, D. (2013) 'Cyberlibertarianism: The extremist foundations of 'digital freedom'', Clemson University Department of English (September), available at: www.academia.edu/4429212/Cyberlibertarianism_The_Extremist_Foundations_of_Digital_Freedom

Goode, L. (2015) 'Anonymous and the political ethos of hacktivism', *Popular Communication*, 13(1): 74–86.

Gramsci, A. (1971) *Selections from Prison Notebooks*, ed and trans. Q. Hoare and G. Nowell-Smith, London: Lawrence and Wishart.

Gramsci, A. (2000) *The Gramsci Reader: Selected Writings, 1916–1935*, New York University Press.

Gramsci, A. (2007) *Prison Notebooks: Selections*, London: Lawrence & Wishart.

Gray, C.H. (2018) 'Post-sapiens: Notes on the politics of future human terminology', *Journal of Posthuman Studies*, 1(2), 136–50.

Greenberg, A. (2012) *This Machine Kills Secrets: How WikiLeakers, Hacktivists, and Cypherpunks Are Freeing the World's Information*, New York: Random House.

Greenwood, R., Díaz, A.M., Li, S.X. and Lorente, J.C. (2010) 'The multiplicity of institutional logics and the heterogeneity of organizational responses', *Organization Science*, 21(2): 521–39.

Grint, K. (2005a) *Leadership: Limits and Possibilities*, Basingstoke: Palgrave Macmillan.

Grint, K. (2005b) 'Problems, problems, problems: The social construction of "leadership"', *Human Relations*, 58(11): 1467–94.

Grosz, E. (2005) *Time Travels: Feminism, Nature, Power*, Durham, NC: Duke University Press.

Guardiola-Rivera, O. (2007) 'Return of the fetish: A plea for a new materialism', *Law and Critique*, 18(3): 275–307.

Guevara, C. (2012) *Guerrilla Warfare*, Lanham, MD: Rowman & Littlefield Publishers.

Gunder, M. (2016) 'Planning's "failure" to ensure efficient market delivery: A Lacanian deconstruction of this neoliberal scapegoating fantasy', *European Planning Studies*, 24(1): 21–38.

Gunes, C. (2013) 'Explaining the PKK's mobilization of the Kurds in Turkey: Hegemony, myth and violence', *Ethnopolitics*, 12(3): 247–67.

Gustafsson, N. (2010) 'This time it's personal: Social networks, viral politics and identity management', in D. Riha and A. Maj (eds) *Emerging Practices in Cyberculture and Social Networking*, Lieden: Brill, pp 1–23.

Habermas, J. (1984) 'Habermas: Questions and counterquestions', *Praxis International*, 4(3): 229–49.

Habermas, J. (1996) *Between Facts and Norms: Contribution to a Discourse Theory of Law and Democracy*, Cambridge, MA: MIT Press.

Hale, E. (2019) ' "Be water": Hong Kong protesters adopt Bruce Lee tactic to evade police crackdown', *The Independent*, 6 January, available at: www.independent.co.uk/news/world/asia/hong-kong-protest-latest-bruce-lee-riot-police-water-a9045311.html

Hall, S. (1992) 'The West and the rest: Discourse and power', in T. Das Gupta, C.E. James, C. Andersen, G.-E. Galabuzi and R.C.A. Maaka (eds) *Race and Racialization, 2E: Essential Readings*, Toronto: Canadian Scholars' Press, pp 85–95.

Hands, J. (2015) 'From cultural to new materialism and back: The enduring legacy of Raymond Williams', *Culture, Theory and Critique*, 56(2): 133–48.

Hannerz, U. (2006) 'Studying down, up, sideways, through, backwards, forwards, away and at home: Reflections on the field worries of an expansive discipline', in S. Coleman and P. Collins (eds) *Locating the Field: Space, Place and Context in Anthropology, 42*, London: Bloomsbury, pp 23–42.

Hardt, M. and Negri, A. (2004) *Multitude: War and Democracy in the Age of Empire*, London: Penguin.

Hardt, M. and Negri, A. (2017) *Assembly*, Oxford: Oxford University Press.

Hareven, T.K. (1991) 'The history of the family and the complexity of social change', *The American Historical Review*, 96(1): 95–124.

Harrigan, N., Achananuparp, P. and Lim, E.-P. (2012) 'Influentials, novelty, and social contagion: The viral power of average friends, close communities, and old news', *Social Networks*, 34(4): 470–80.

Harris, A. and DeFlaminis, J. (2016) 'Distributed leadership in practice: Evidence, misconceptions and possibilities', *Management in Education*, 30(4): 141–46.

Hartsock, N.C.M. (1983) *Money, Sex, and Power: Toward a Feminist Historical Materialism*, New York: Longman's.

Harvey, D. (2003) 'The right to the city', *International Journal of Urban and Regional Research*, 27(4): 939–41.

Hassan, R. (2007) *24/7: Time and Temporality in the Network Society*, Palo Alto, CA: Stanford University Press.

Hayes-Conroy, A. and Martin, D.G. (2010) 'Mobilising bodies: Visceral identification in the slow food movement', *Transactions of the Institute of British Geographers*, 35(2): 269–81.

Hearn, J., Biricik, A., Sadowski, H. and Harrison, K. (2014) 'Hegemony, transpatriarchies, ICTs and virtualization', in J. Hearn, M. Blagojević and K. Harrison (eds) *Rethinking Transnational Men: Beyond, Between and Within Nations*, New York: Routledge, pp 91–108.

Heeg, S. (2019) 'Neoliberalism and neoliberalization: Helpful devices for the analysis of urban development in the Middle East and North Africa', *Middle East-Topics & Arguments*, 12: 18–26.

Heilmann, S. and Perry, E.J. (2011) 'Embracing uncertainty: Guerrilla policy style and adaptive governance in China', in *Mao's Invisible Hand*, Lieden: Brill, pp 1–29.

Hemsley, J. (2016) 'View of studying the viral growth of a connective action network using information event signatures', *First Monday*, 21(8), available at: http://dx.doi.org/10.5210/fm.v21i8.6650

Hennessy, R. (2017) *Profit and Pleasure: Sexual Identities in Late Capitalism*, Abingdon: Routledge.

Hester, H. (2018a) *Xenofeminism*, Hoboken, NJ: John Wiley & Sons.

Hester, H. (2018b) 'Xenofeminist ecologies: (Re)producing futures without reproductive futurity by Helen Hester (Laboria Cuboniks) philosopher', *Map Magazine*, available at: https://mapmagazine.co.uk/xenofeminist-ecologies

Heynen, N. (2010) 'Cooking up non-violent civil-disobedient direct action for the hungry: "Food Not Bombs" and the resurgence of radical democracy in the US', *Urban Studies*, 47(6): 1225–40.

Hobson, K. and Lynch, N. (2016) 'Diversifying and de-growing the circular economy: Radical social transformation in a resource-scarce world', *Futures*, 82, 15–25.

Holloway, T. (2018) 'Neoliberalism and the future of democracy', *Philosophy Today*, 62(2): 1–31.

Hom, A.R. (2010) 'Hegemonic metronome: The ascendancy of Western standard time', *Review of International Studies*, 36(4): 1145–70.

Hook, G.A. and Wolfe, M.J. (2018) 'Affective violence: Re/negotiating gendered-feminism within new materialism', *Journal of Gender Studies*, 27(8): 871–80.

Horpedahl, J. (2015) 'Ideology Über Alles? Economics bloggers on Uber, Lyft, and other transportation network companies', *Econ Journal Watch*, 12(3): 360–74.

Howarth, D., Glynos, J. and Griggs, S. (2016) 'Discourse, explanation and critique', *Critical Policy Studies*, 10(1): 99–104.

Hu, Y., Havlin, S. and Makse, H.A. (2014) 'Conditions for viral influence spreading through multiplex correlated social networks', *Physical Review X*, 4(2): 021031.

Huault, I., Perret, V. and Spicer, A. (2014) 'Beyond macro-and micro-emancipation: Rethinking emancipation in organization studies', *Organization*, 21(1): 22–49.

Hughes, C. (2017) 'How Momentum delivered Labour's stunning election result – and how the Tories are trying to copy it', *The Independent*, 19 July, available at: www.independent.co.uk/news/long_reads/momentum-labour-jeremy-corbyn-election-result-how-they-did-it-grassroots-movement-a7847421.html

Irani, L.C. and Silberman, M.S. (2013) 'Turkopticon: Interrupting worker invisibility in amazon mechanical turk', *Proceedings of SIGCHI*, April, Paris.

Ishkanian, A. and Glasius, M. (2018) 'Resisting neoliberalism? Movements against austerity and for democracy in Cairo, Athens and London', *Critical Social Policy*, 38(3): 527–46.

Israel, J. (2009) *A Revolution of the Mind: Radical Enlightenment and the Intellectual Origins of Modern Democracy*, Princeton, NJ: Princeton University Press.

Ives, P. (2004) *Language and Hegemony in Gramsci*, London: Pluto Press.

IWGB (2018) 'Uber drivers to strike for 24 hours in London, Birmingham and Nottingham', IWGB, available at: https://iwgb.org.uk/post/5bbb3ff1bf94a/uber-drivers-to-strike-for

Jaeger, H.-M. (2007) '"Global civil society" and the political depoliticization of global governance', *International Political Sociology*, 1(3): 257–77.

Jay, M. (1995) 'The limits of limit-experience: Bataille and Foucault', *Constellations*, 2(2): 155–74.

Jones, B. and O'Donnell, M. (2017) 'A Brexit from neoliberalism?' in M. O'Donnell and B. Jones (eds) *Alternatives to Neoliberalism: Towards Equality and Democracy*, Bristol: Policy Press, pp 245–65.

Jones, E. (2019) 'Feminist technologies and post-capitalism: Defining and reflecting upon xenofeminism', *Feminist Review*, 123(1): 126–34.

Joya, A. (2011) 'The Egyptian revolution: Crisis of neoliberalism and the potential for democratic politics', *Review of African Political Economy*, 38(129): 367–86.

Kanna, A. (2010) 'Flexible citizenship in Dubai: Neoliberal subjectivity in the emerging "city-corporation"', *Cultural Anthropology*, 25(1): 100–29.

Karatzogianni, A. (2015) *Firebrand Waves of Digital Activism 1994–2014: The Rise and Spread of Hacktivism and Cyberconflict*, New York: Springer.

Katzenstein, P.J. and Seybert, L.A. (2018) *Protean Power: Exploring the Uncertain and Unexpected in World Politics* (vol 146), Cambridge: Cambridge University Press.

Kellogg, S. (2016) 'Digitizing dissent: Cyborg politics and fluid networks in contemporary Cuban activism', *Teknokultura*, 13(1): 19–53.

Kelly, M.G.E. (2013) 'Foucault, subjectivity, and technologies of the self', in C. Falzon, J. Zawicki and T. O'Leary (eds) *A Companion to Foucault*, Hoboken, NJ: John Wiley & Sons, pp 510–25.

Kelly, P. (2016) *The Self as Enterprise: Foucault and the Spirit of 21st Century Capitalism*, London: CRC Press.

Kelly, S. (2014) 'Towards a negative ontology of leadership', *Human Relations*, 67(8): 905–22.

Kelly, P., Campbell, P. and Howie, L. (2019) *Rethinking Young People's Marginalisation: Beyond Neo-Liberal Futures?* Abingdon: Routledge.

Kelty, C.M. (2017) 'Too much democracy in all the wrong places: Toward a grammar of participation', *Current Anthropology*, 58(15): S77–90.

Ketter, E. and Avraham, E. (2012) 'The social revolution of place marketing: The growing power of users in social media campaigns', *Place Branding and Public Diplomacy*, 8(4): 285–94.

Kinder, K. (2016) *DIY Detroit: Making Do in a City Without Services*, Minneapolis, MN: University of Minnesota Press.

Kioupkiolis, A. (2018) 'Commoning the political, politicizing the common: Community and the political in Jean-Luc Nancy, Roberto Esposito and Giorgio Agamben', *Contemporary Political Theory*, 17(3): 283–305.

Kioupkiolis, A. and Katsambekis, G. (2016) *Radical Democracy and Collective Movements Today: The Biopolitics of the Multitude Versus the Hegemony of the People*, Abingdon: Routledge.

Kirby, V. (2017) 'Matter out of place: New materialism in review', in V. Kirby (ed) *What if Culture Was Nature all Along*, Edinburgh: Edinburgh University Press, pp 1–25.

Klinger, U. and Svensson, J. (2015) 'The emergence of network media logic in political communication: A theoretical approach', *New Media & Society*, 17(8): 1241–57.

Korchagina, N. and Pullen, A. (2016) 'Jean-Luc Nancy and the promise of corporeal ethics in organizations', presentation at the 74th Academy of Management, Anaheim, CA, 4–9 August.

Kostakis, V. and Papachristou, M. (2014) 'Commons-based peer production and digital fabrication: The case of a RepRap-based, Lego-built 3D printing-milling machine', *Telematics and Informatics*, 31(3): 434–43.

Klooster, W. (2014) 'Slave revolts, royal justice, and a ubiquitous rumor in the age of revolutions', *William & Mary Quarterly*, 71(3): 401–24.

Kremers, R. and Brassett, J. (2017) 'Mobile payments, social money: Everyday politics of the consumer subject', *New Political Economy*, 22(6): 645–60.

Kushner, D. (2014) 'The masked avengers', *The New Yorker*, 8 Sep, available at: www.newyorker.com/magazine/2014/09/08/masked-avengers

Lacan, J. (1977) 'The function and field of speech and language in psychoanalysis', in *Écrits: A Selection*, Abingdon: Routledge, pp 30–113.

Laclau, E. (2018) *On Populist Reason*, London: Verso.

Laclau, E. and Mouffe, C. (1986) *Hegemony and Socialist Strategy: Towards a Radical Democratic Politics*, New York: Verso.

Laclau, E. and Mouffe, C. (1987) 'Post-Marxism without apologies', *New Left Review*, 166(11–12): 79–106.

Lamonica, M. (2014) 'The spiralling energy consumption behind your smart phone', *The Guardian*, 10 September, available at: www.theguardian.com/sustainable-business/2014/sep/10/energy-consumption-behind-smart-phone

Landemore, H. (2012) 'The mechanisms of collective intelligence in politics', in J. Elster and H. Landemore (eds) *Collective Wisdom: Principles and Mechanisms*, Cambridge: Cambridge University Press, pp 251–89.

Lange, B. and Bürkner, H.-J. (2018) 'Flexible value creation: Conceptual prerequisites and empirical explorations in open workshops', *Geoforum*, 88: 96–104.

Laqueur, W. (2019) *Guerrilla: A Historical and Critical Study*, Abingdon: Routledge.

Larsson, C.W. and Stark, L. (2019) *Gendered Power and Mobile Technology: Intersections in the Global South*, Abingdon: Routledge.

Larsson, G. (2017) 'Apostasy and counter-narratives – two sides of the same coin: The example of the Islamic State', *The Review of Faith & International Affairs*, 15(2): 45–54.

Las Casas, G. and Scorza, F. (2017) 'A renewed rational approach from liquid society towards anti-fragile planning', in *International Conference on Computational Science and its Applications*, Cham: Springer, pp 517–26.

Last, C. (2017) 'Global commons in the global brain', *Technological Forecasting and Social Change*, 114: 48–64.

Laurell, C. and Sandström, C. (2016) 'Analysing Uber in social media – disruptive technology or institutional disruption?', *International Journal of Innovation Management*, 20(5): 1640013.

Lazzarato, M. (1996) 'Immaterial labour', in A. Pendakis, J. Diamanti, N. Brown, J. Robinson and I. Szeman (eds) *Contemporary Marxist Theory*, London: Bloomsbury, pp 77–92.

Lee, P.S., So, C.Y. and Leung, L. (2015) 'Social media and umbrella movement: Insurgent public sphere in formation, *Chinese Journal of Communication*, 8(4), 356–75.

Lee, R.L.M. (2005) 'Bauman, liquid modernity and dilemmas of development', *Thesis Eleven*, 83(1): 61–77.

Leerssen, J. (2011) 'Viral nationalism: Romantic intellectuals on the move in nineteenth-century Europe', *Nations and Nationalism*, 17(2): 257–71.

Lefort, C. (1986) *The Political Forms of Modern Society: Bureaucracy, Democracy, Totalitarianism*, Cambridge, MA: MIT Press.

Leipold, S. and Winkel, G. (2017) 'Discursive agency: (Re-) conceptualizing actors and practices in the analysis of discursive policymaking', *Policy Studies Journal*, 45(3): 510–34.

Leitner, H., Sheppard, E.S., Sziarto, K. and Maringanti, A. (2006) 'Contesting urban futures: Decentering neoliberalism', in H. Leitner, J. Peck and E.S. Sheppard (eds) *Contesting Neoliberalism: Urban Frontiers*, New York: Guilford Press.

Lemke, T. (2014) 'New materialisms: Foucault and the "government of things"', *Theory, Culture & Society*, 32(4): 3–25.

Leonard, D.J. and King, C.R. (2009) 'Replaying empire: Racialized violence, insecure frontiers, and displaced terror in contemporary video games', *Ethnicity and Race in a Changing World*, 1(2): 2–14.

Leung, D.K. and Lee, F.L. (2014) 'Cultivating an active online counterpublic: Examining usage and political impact of Internet alternative media', *The International Journal of Press/Politics*, 19(3): 340–59.

Levinson, J. (1985) *Guerrilla Marketing*, Boston, MA: Houghton Mifflin Harcourt.

Leyshon, A. and Thrift, N. (2007), 'The capitalization of almost everything: The future of finance and capitalism', *Theory, Culture & Society*, 24(7–8): 97–115.

Lezaun, J., Marres, N. and Tironi, M. (2016) 'Experiments in participation', in U. Felt, C.A. Miller, L. Smither-Doerr and R. Fouché (eds) *The Handbook of Science and Technology Studies*, Cambridge, MA: MIT Press, pp 195–221.

Lima, V. (2020) 'Sustainable citizenship and the prospect of participation and governance in the digital era', in V. Lima (ed) *Participatory Citizenship and Crisis in Contemporary Brazil*, New York: Springer.

Liu, H. (2020) *Redeeming Leadership: An Anti-racist Feminist Intervention*, Bristol: Bristol University Press.

Loader, B.D. and Mercea, D. (2011) 'Networking democracy? Social media innovations and participatory politics', *Information, Communication & Society*, 14(6): 757–69.

Luke, T.W. (1996) 'Liberal society and cyborg subjectivity: The politics of environments, bodies, and nature', *Alternatives*, 21(1): 1–30.

Lukes, S. (2004) *Power: A Radical View*, London: Macmillan International Higher Education.

Lupton, D. (2016) *The Quantified Self*, Hoboken, NJ: John Wiley & Sons.

Lysaker, O. (2017) 'Institutional agonism: Axel Honneth's radical democracy', *Critical Horizons*, 18(1): 33–51.

Löffler, D. (2018) 'Distributing potentiality: Post-capitalist economies and the generative time regime', *Identities: Journal for Politics, Gender and Culture*, 15(1–2): 8–44.

MacCormack, P. (2016) 'Queer posthumanism: Cyborgs, animals, monsters, perverts', in N. Giffney and M. O'Rourke (eds) *The Ashgate Research Companion to Queer Theory*, Abingdon: Routledge, pp 129–44.

Makovicky, N. (2014) 'Me, Inc.? Untangling neoliberalism, personhood, and postsocialism', in Makovicky (ed) *Neoliberalism, Personhood, and Postsocialism: Enterprising Selves in Changing Economies*, Abingdon: Routledge, pp 1–16.

Maly, I. (2020) 'What WhatsApp conversations reveal about the far right's ideology', *Fair Observer*, 29 October, available at: www.fairobserver.com/region/europe/ico-maly-dutch-far-right-forum-democracy-thierry-baudet-far-right-ideology-news-154241/

Manacorda, M. and Tesei, A. (2020) 'Liberation technology: Mobile phones and political mobilization in Africa', *Econometrica*, 88(2): 533–67.

Mao Tse-tung (1965) 'A single spark can start a prairie fire', in *Selected Works* (vol 1, English edition), Peking: FLP, p 124.

Mao Tse-tung and Griffith, S.B. (1964) *On Guerrilla Warfare*, North Chelmsford, MA: Courier Corporation.

Mapes, A.C. and Kimme-Hea, A.C. (2018) 'Devices and desires: A complicated narrative of mobile writing and device-driven ecologies', in J. Alexander and J. Rhodes (eds) *The Routledge Handbook of Digital Writing and Rhetoric*, Oxfordshire: Taylor and Francis, pp 73–83.

Marchant, C. and O'Donohoe, S. (2019) 'Homo prostheticus? Intercorporeality and the emerging adult-smartphone assemblage', *Information Technology & People*, 32(1).

Martin, J. (2013) *Chantal Mouffe: Hegemony, Radical Democracy, and the Political*, Abingdon: Routledge.

Marx, K. (1857[1993]) *Grundrisse: Foundations of the Critique of Political Economy*, London: Penguin.

Marx, K. (1867[1976]) *Capital: A Critique of Political Economy*, London: Penguin.

Marx, K. (1955) *The Poverty of Philosophy*, çev.

Marx, K. (2000) *Early Writings*, London: Penguin.

Marx, K. and Engels, F. (1848[1967]) *The Communist Manifesto*, trans. S. Moore, London: Penguin.

Massey, A. and Johnston-Miller, K. (2016) 'Governance: public governance to social innovation?' *Policy & Politics*, 44(4): 663–75.

Massey, D. (1995) 'Thinking radical democracy spatially', *Environment and Planning D: Society and Space*, 13(3): 283–8.

Mbembe, A. (2003) 'Politics, the work of death, and the "becoming subject"', *Public Culture*, 15, 11–40.

McGregor, C. (2014) 'From social movement learning to sociomaterial movement learning? Addressing the possibilities and limits of new materialism', *Studies in the Education of Adults*, 46(2): 211–27.

Mercille, J. (2008) 'The radical geopolitics of US foreign policy: Geopolitical and geoeconomic logics of power', *Political Geography*, 27(5): 570–86.

Mitra, A. (1998) 'Virtual commonality: Looking for India on the internet', in S.G. Jones (ed) *Virtual Culture: Identity and Communication in Cybersociety*, California: SAGE Publications, 55–79.

Moore, P.V. (2017) *The Quantified Self in Precarity: Work, Technology and What Counts*, Abingdon: Routledge.

Moore, P.V. and Robinson, A. (2016) 'The quantified self: What counts in the neoliberal workplace', *New Media & Society*, 18(11): 2774–92.

Moore, S. (1971) 'Marx and the origin of dialectical materialism', *Inquiry*, 14(1–4): 420–9.

Morador, F.F. and Vásquez, J.C. (2016) 'New social movements, the use of ICTs, and their social impact', *Revista Latina de Comunicación Social*, 71: 398.

Mossey, S., Bromberg, D. and Manoharan, A.P. (2019) 'Harnessing the power of mobile technology to bridge the digital divide: A look at US cities' mobile government capability', *Journal of Information Technology & Politics*, 16(1): 52–65.

Mouffe, C. (1989) 'Toward a radical democratic citizenship', *Democratic Left*, 17(2): 6–7.

Mouffe, C. (1992) 'Citizenship and political identity', *October*, 61: 28–32.

Mouffe, C. (1995) 'Feminism, citizenship, and radical democratic politics', in S. Seidman and L. Nicholson (eds) *Social Postmodernism: Beyond Identity Politics*, Cambridge: Cambridge University Press, pp 315–31.

Mouffe, C. (2013) *Agonistics: Thinking the World Politically*, London: Verso.

Mouffe, C. (2019) *For a Left Populism*, London: Verso..

Moulaert, F., Jessop, B. and Mehmood, A. (2016) 'Agency, structure, institutions, discourse (ASID) in urban and regional development', *International Journal of Urban Sciences*, 20(2): 167–87.

Murphet, J. (2016) 'A modest oroposal for the inhuman', *Modernism/Modernity*, 23(3): 651–70.

Müller, M. (2017) '"Brand-centred control": A study of internal branding and normative control', *Organization Studies*, 38(7): 895–915.

Nancy, J.-L. (1991) *The Inoperative Community* (vol 76), Minneapolis, MN: University of Minnesota Press.

Nash, G. (2005) *The Unknown American Revolution: The Unruly Birth of Democracy and the Struggle to Create America*, New York: Viking Books.

Nikolaeva, A., Adey, P., Cresswell, T., Lee, J.Y., Nóvoa, A. and Temenos, C. (2019) 'Commoning mobility: Towards a new politics of mobility transitions', *Transactions of the Institute of British Geographers*, 44(2): 346–60.

Norris, A. (2002) 'Against antagonism: On Ernesto Laclau's political thought', *Constellations*, 9(4): 554–73.

Norval, A.J. (2004) 'Hegemony after deconstruction: The consequences of undecidability', *Journal of Political Ideologies*, 9(2): 139–57.

Norval, A.J. (2007) *Aversive Democracy: Inheritance and Originality in the Democratic Tradition*, Cambridge: Cambridge University Press.

Norval, A.J. (2009) 'Democracy, pluralization, and voice', *Ethics & Global Politics*, 2(4): 297–320.

Nyabola, N. (2018) *Digital Democracy, Analogue Politics: How the Internet Era is Transforming Politics in Kenya*, London: Zed Books.

O'Leary, R. (2019) *The Ethics of Dissent: Managing Guerrilla Government*, Washington, DC: CQ Press.

Ong, A. (1999) *Flexible Citizenship: The Cultural Logics of Transnationality*, Durham, NC: Duke University Press.

Ong, A. (2006) *Neoliberalism as Exception: Mutations in Citizenship and Sovereignty*, Durham, NC: Duke University Press.

Ong, A. (2007) 'Neoliberalism as a mobile technology', *Transactions of the Institute of British Geographers*, 32(1): 3–8.

Ong, A. and Collier, S. (2005) *Global Assemblages: Technology, Politics, and Ethics as Anthropological Problems*, London: Blackwell.

Ortner, S.B. (1995) 'Resistance and the problem of ethnographic refusal', *Comparative Studies in Society and History*, 37(1): 173–93.

Ossewaarde, M. and Reijers, W. (2017) 'The illusion of the digital commons: "False consciousness" in online alternative economies', *Organization*, 24(5): 609–28.

O'Sullivan, P. (1996) 'Dominoes or dice: Geography and the diffusion of political violence', *Journal of Conflict Studies*, 16(2): 97–108.

Palczewski, C.H. (2001) 'Cyber-movements, new social movements, and counterpublics', in R. Asen and D.C. Brouwer (eds) *Counterpublics and the State*, New York: State University of New York Press, pp 161–86.

Panitch, L. (2019) *Renewing Socialism: Democracy, Strategy, and Imagination*, Abingdon: Routledge.

Panizza, F. (2005) 'Introduction', in F. Panizza (ed) *Populism and the Mirror of Democracy*, New York: Verso.

Papadopoulos, D. (2010) 'Insurgent posthumanism', *Ephemera: Theory & Politics in Organization*, 10(2): 134–51.

Papadopoulos, D. (2018) *Experimental Practice: Technoscience, Alterontologies, and More-than-Social Movements*, Durham, NC: Duke University Press.

Parikka, J. (2012) 'New materialism of dust', *Artnodes*, 12, available at: www.raco.cat/index.php/Artnodes/article/view/263139

Parikka, J. (2013) *What Is Media Archaeology?* Hoboken, NJ: John Wiley & Sons.

Peck, J. (2010) *Constructions of Neoliberal Reason*, Oxford: Oxford University Press.

Penney, J. (2016) 'Motivations for participating in "viral politics": A qualitative case study of Twitter users and the 2012 US presidential election', *Convergence*, 22(1): 71–87.

Peters, M.A. and Heraud, R. (2015) 'Toward a political theory of social innovation: collective intelligence and the co-creation of social goods', *Journal of Self-Governance & Management Economics*, 3(3): 7–23.

Peters, M.A. and Reveley, J. (2015) 'Noosphere rising: Internet-based collective intelligence, creative labour, and social production', *Thesis Eleven*, 130(1): 3–21.

Pope, A., Cohen, A.K. and Duarte, C. (2019). 'Making civic engagement go viral: Applying social epidemiology principles to civic education', *Journal of Public Affairs*, 19(1): e1857.

Porchon, T. (2019) 'Cyber picketing in workplace disputes', *Freeths*, available at: www.freeths.co.uk/2019/06/25/cyber-picketing-in-workplace-disputes

Porter, T. (1995) 'Innovation in global finance: the impact on hegemony and growth since 1000 AD', *Review*, 18(3): 387–429.

Porter, T.M. (1996) *Trust in Numbers: The Pursuit of Objectivity in Science and Public Life*, Princeton, NJ: Princeton University Press.

Postill, J. (2014) 'Democracy in an age of viral reality: A media epidemiography of Spain's indignados movement', *Ethnography*, 15(1): 51–69.

Prozorov, S. (2018) 'A thousand healths: Jean-Luc Nancy and the possibility of democratic biopolitics', *Philosophy & Social Criticism*, 44(10): 1090–109.

Punathambekar, A. (2015) 'Satire, elections, and democratic politics in digital India', *Television & New Media*, 16(4): 394–400.

Rachman, G., Mander, B., Dombey, D., Wong, S. and Saleh, H. (2019) 'Leaderless rebellion: How social media enables global protests', *The Financial Times*, 25 October, available at: www.ft.com/content/19dc5dfe-f67b-11e9-a79c-bc9acae3b654

Raelin, J.A. (2016) 'It's not about the leaders: It's about the practice of leadership', *Organizational Dynamics*, 45(2): 124–31.

Rajan, K.S. (2017), *Pharmocracy: Value, Politics, and Knowledge in Global Biomedicine*, Durham, NC: Duke University Press.

Rancière, J. (2013) *The Politics of Aesthetics*, London: Bloomsbury.

Redfield, P. and Robins, S. (2016) 'An index of waste: Humanitarian design, "dignified living" and the politics of infrastructure in Cape Town', *Anthropology Southern Africa*, 39(2): 145–62.

Reichert, R. and Richterich, A. (2015) 'Introduction: Digital materialism', *Digital Culture & Society*, 1(1): 5–17.

Reischauer, G. (2018) 'Industry 4.0 as policy-driven discourse to institutionalize innovation systems in manufacturing', *Technological Forecasting and Social Change*, 132: 26–33.

Rekret, P. (2014) 'Generalized antagonism and political ontology in the debate between Laclau and Negri', in A. Kioupkiolis and G. Katsembekis (eds) *Radical Democracy and Collective Movements Today: The Biopolitics of the Multitude Versus the Hegemony of the People*, Farnham: Ashgate Publishing, pp 133–48.

Ridout, T.N., Fowler, E.F., Branstetter, J. and Borah, P. (2015) 'Politics as usual? When and why traditional actors often dominate YouTube campaigning', *Journal of Information Technology & Politics*, 12(3): 237–51.

Roggero, G. (2020) '"A science of destruction": An interview with Gigi Roggero on the actuality of operaismo', *Viewpoint Magazine*, available at: https://viewpointmag.com/2020/04/30/a-science-of-destruction-an-interview-with-gigi-roggero-on-the-actuality-of-operaismo/

Rogowska-Stangret, M. (2017) 'Corpor (e) al cartographies of new materialism: Meeting the elsewhere halfway', *Minnesota Review*, 88(1): 59–68.

Rojecki, A. and Meraz, S. (2016) 'Rumors and factitious informational blends: The role of the web in speculative politics', *New Media & Society*, 18(1): 25–43.

Rose, G. (2016) 'Cultural geography going viral', *Social & Cultural Geography*, 17(6): 763–7.

Rose, J. and Spencer, C. (2016) 'Immaterial labour in spaces of leisure: Producing biopolitical subjectivities through Facebook', *Leisure Studies*, 35(6): 809–26.

Roskamm, N. (2015) 'On the other side of "agonism": "The enemy," the "outside," and the role of antagonism', *Planning Theory*, 14(4): 384–403.

Rowe, E., Lubienski, C., Skourdoumbis, A., Gerrard, J. and Hursh, D. (2019) 'Templates, typologies and typifications: neoliberalism as keyword', *Discourse: Studies in the Cultural Politics of Education*, 40(2): 150–61.

Ruijer, E., Grimmelikhuijsen, S. and Meijer, A. (2017) 'Open data for democracy: Developing a theoretical framework for open data use', *Government Information Quarterly*, 34(1): 45–52.

Rushton, S. (2013) 'Direct democracy in Reykjavík: The wisdom of the Icelandic crowd-sourcers', *Truthout*, 3 October.

Sarkar, S. (2014) 'The unique identity (UID) project, biometrics and re-imagining governance in India', *Oxford Development Studies*, 42(4): 516–33.

Saroshisar (2016) 'Role of cell phones in Arab Spring', *Revoevoref*, 29 February, available at: https://revoevoref.wordpress.com/2016/02/29/role-of-cell-phones-in-arab-spring/

Schmidt, J. (2013) 'The empirical falsity of the human subject: New materialism, climate change and the shared critique of artifice', *International Policies, Practices and Discourses*, 1(3): 174–92.

Scott, K., Martin, D.M. and Schouten, J.W. (2014) 'Marketing and the new materialism', *Journal of Macromarketing*, 34(3): 282–90.

Schnoll, H.J. (2015) *E-Government: Information, Technology, and Transformation*, Abingdon: Routledge.

Schradie, J. (2019) *The Revolution that Wasn't: How Digital Activism Favors Conservatives*, Cambridge, MA: Harvard University Press.

Schrock, A.R. (2016) 'Civic hacking as data activism and advocacy: A history from publicity to open government data', *New Media & Society*, 18(4): 581–99.

Schüll, N.D. (2016) 'Data for life: Wearable technology and the design of self-care', *BioSocieties*, 11(3): 317–33.

Seear, K. and Fraser, S. (2016) 'Addiction veridiction: Gendering agency in legal mobilisations of addiction discourse', *Griffith Law Review*, 25(1): 13–29.

Selke, S. (2016) *Lifelogging: Digital Self-Tracking and Lifelogging: Between Disruptive Technology and Cultural Transformation*, New York: Springer.

Senellart, M. (1995) 'A crítica da razão governamental em Michel Foucault', *Tempo Social*, 7(1/2): 1–14.

Seymour, R. (2019) *The Twittering Machine*, New York: Verso.

Shamir, R. (2008) 'The age of responsibilization: On market-embedded morality', *Economy and Society*, 37(1): 1–19.

Siegel, K.M. (2016) 'Fulfilling promises of more substantive democracy? Post-neoliberalism and natural resource governance in South America', *Development and Change*, 47(3): 495–516.

Simon, H.A. (2019) *The Sciences of the Artificial*, Cambridge, MA: MIT Press.

Simon, J., Bass, T., Boelman, V. and Mulgan, G. (2017) 'Digital Democracy: The Tools Transforming Political Engagement', *NESTA*.

Sinha, P., Smolović Jones, O. and Carroll, B. (2019) 'Theorizing dramaturgical resistance leadership from the leadership campaigns of Jeremy Corbyn', *Human Relations*, 74(2): 0018726719887310.

Sites, W. (2007) 'Contesting the neoliberal city? Theories of neoliberalism and urban strategies of contention', in H. Leitner, J. Peck and E.S. Sheppard (eds) *Contesting Neoliberalism: Urban Frontiers*, New York: Guilford Press, pp 116–38.

Smith, A. M. (2012) *Laclau and Mouffe: The Radical Democratic Imaginary*, Oxfordshire: Taylor & Francis.

Smolović Jones, O., Smolović Jones, S. and Grint, K. (2020) 'Understanding sovereign leadership as a response to terrorism: A post-foundational analysis', *Organization*, 27(4): 537–56.

Söderberg, J. (2018) 'A response to Steve Fuller: The differences between social democracy and neoliberalism', *LSE Blog*, 21 August, available at: https://blogs.lse.ac.uk/europpblog/2018/08/21/a-response-to-steve-fuller-the-differences-between-social-democracy-and-neoliberalism/

Sonu, D. and Snaza, N. (2015) 'The fragility of ecological pedagogy: Elementary social studies standards and possibilities of new materialism', *Journal of Curriculum and Pedagogy*, 12(3): 258–77.

Srnicek, N. and Williams, A. (2015) *Inventing the Future: Postcapitalism and a World Without Work*, New York: Verso.

Staab, P. and Nachtwey, O. (2016) 'Market and labour control in digital capitalism', *TripleC: Communication, Capitalism & Critique, Open Access Journal for a Global Sustainable Information Society*, 14(2): 457–74.

Steen, T., Brandsen, T. and Verschuere, B. (2019) 'Public administration into the wild: Grappling with co-production and social innovation', in A. Massey (ed) *Elgar Research Agendas*, 63–78, Edward Elgar Publishing.

Stephens, E. (2014) 'Feminism and new materialism: The matter of fluidity', *InterAlia: Pismo Poświęcone Studiom Queer*, 9: 186–202.

Stickel, O., Aal, K., Fuchsberger, V., Rüller, S., Wenzelmann, V., Pipek, V., Wulf, V. and Tscheligi, M. (2017) '3D printing/digital fabrication for education and the common good', in *Proceedings of the 8th International Conference on Communities and Technologies*, pp 315–18.

Sullivan, N. (2012) 'The somatechnics of perception and the matter of the non/human: A critical response to the new materialism', *European Journal of Women's Studies*, 19(3): 299–313.

Sun, T. (1963) *Sun Tzu: The Art of War*, Oxford: Oxford University Press.

Sutherland, N., Land, C. and Böhm, S. (2014) 'Anti-leaders(hip) in social movement organizations: The case of autonomous grassroots groups', *Organization*, 21(6): 759–81.

Swan, M. (2013) 'The quantified self: Fundamental disruption in big data science and biological discovery', *Big data*, 1(2): 85–99.

Taber, R. (2017) 'Rumor and report in Affiches Américaines: Saint-Dominigue's American revolution', *Age of Revolution*, available at: https://ageofrevolutions.com/2017/09/13/rumor-and-report-in-affiches-americaines-saint-domingues-american-revolution/

Tan, C. (2019) 'Parental responses to education reform in Singapore, Shanghai and Hong Kong', *Asia Pacific Education Review*, 20(1): 91–9.

Terrier, J. and Wagner, P. (2006) 'The critique of organized modernity', in P. Wagner (ed) *The Languages of Civil Society*, Oxford: Berghahn Books, pp 206–22.

Thomassen, L. (2005) 'Antagonism, hegemony and ideology after heterogeneity', *Journal of Political Ideologies*, 10(3): 289–309.

Thompson, E.P. (1967) 'Time, work-discipline, and industrial capitalism', *Past & Present*, 38: 56–97.

Thorburn, E.D. (2017) 'Cyborg witches: Class composition and social reproduction in the GynePunk collective', *Feminist Media Studies*, 17(2): 153–67.

Tobias, S. (2005) 'Foucault on freedom and capabilities', *Theory, Culture & Society*, 22(4): 65–85.

Törnberg, P. (2018) 'Echo chambers and viral misinformation: Modeling fake news as complex contagion', *PLoS one*, 13(9): e0203958.

Translating Cuba (2012) *Translating Cuba*, available at: https://translatingcuba.com/direct-help-to-bloggers/

Trumpeter, K. (2015) 'The language of the stones: The agency of the inanimate in literary naturalism and the new materialism', *American Literature*, 87(2): 225–52.

Tuana, N. (2008) 'Viscous porosity: Witnessing Katrina', in S. Alaimo and S. Hekman (eds) *Material Feminisms*, Bloomington, IN: Indiana University Press, pp 188–213.

Tuathail, G.Ó. and Toal, G. (1996) *Critical Geopolitics: The Politics of Writing Global Space* (vol 6), Minneapolis, MN: University of Minnesota Press.

Tucker, E. (2017) '"There's an app for that": Ghost hunting with smartphones', *Children's Folklore Review*, 38: 27–38.

Tufekci, Z. (2019) 'The Hong Kong protesters aren't driven by hope', *The Atlantic*, 12 November, available at: www.theatlantic.com/international/archive/2019/11/escalating-violence-hong-kong-protests/601804/

Tyfield, D.P. (2016) 'Science, innovation and neoliberalism', in S. Springer, K. Birch and J. MacLeavy (eds) *Handbook of Neoliberalism*, Abingdon: Routledge, pp 340–50.

Udayagiri, M. and Walton, J. (2003) 'Global transformation and local counter movements: The prospects for democracy under neoliberalism', *International Journal of Comparative Sociology*, 44(4), 309–43.

Uy, M.A., Chan, K.Y., Sam, Y.L., Ho, M.H.R. and Chernyshenko, O.S. (2015) 'Proactivity, adaptability and boundaryless career attitudes: The mediating role of entrepreneurial alertness', *Journal of Vocational Behavior*, 86, 115–23.

Vachhani, S.J. and Pullen, A. (2019) 'Ethics, politics and feminist organizing: Writing feminist infrapolitics and affective solidarity into everyday sexism', *Human Relations*, 72(1): 23–47.

Van der Tuin, I. and Dolphijn, R. (2010) 'The transversality of new materialism', *Women: A Cultural Review*, 21(2): 153–71.

Vázquez-Arroyo, A.Y. (2008) 'Liberal democracy and neoliberalism: A critical juxtaposition', *New Political Science*, 30(2): 127–59.

Ventsel, A. (2017) 'Viral communication and the formation of counter-publics', *Lexia, Rivista di Semiotica*, 25–26: 365–80.

Vlachokyriakos, V., Crivellaro, C., Le Dantec, C.A., Gordon, E., Wright, P. and Olivier, P. (2016) 'Digital civics: Citizen empowerment with and through technology', in *Proceedings of the 2016 CHI Conference Extended Abstracts on Human Factors in Computing Systems*, pp 1096–99.

Wacquant, L. (2012) 'Three steps to a historical anthropology of actually existing neoliberalism', *Social Anthropology*, 20(1): 66–79.

Walberg, S. (2007) 'Cyber-proletariat and cyber-bourgeoisie: A Foucauldian investigation of the cyber-workplace', *The International Journal of the Humanities: Annual Review*, 5(2): 29–36.

Wald, P. (2017) *Contagious: Cultures, Carriers, and the Outbreak Narrative*, Durham, NC: Duke University Press.

Wang, A.B. (2019) 'Candidates hunt desperately for viral moments', *The Washington Post*, 24 June, available at: www.washingtonpost.com/politics/candidates-hunt-desperately-for-viral-moments/2019/06/24/bd995a88-9126-11e9-aadb-74e6b2b46f6a_story.html

Warner, M. (2002) 'Publics and counterpublics', *Public Culture*, 14(1): 49–90.

Wasserman, H. (2011) 'Mobile phones, popular media, and everyday African democracy: Transmissions and transgressions', *Popular Communication*, 9(2): 146–58.

Weisgerber, C. and Butler, S.H. (2016) 'Curating the soul: Foucault's concept of hupomnemata and the digital technology of self-care', *Information, Communication & Society*, 19(10): 1340–55.

Westra, R., Albritton, R. and Jeong, S. (2017) *Varieties of Alternative Economic Systems: Practical Utopias for an Age of Global Crisis and Austerity* (vol 229), Abingdon: Taylor & Francis.

Whitson, J.R. (2013) 'Gaming the quantified self', *Surveillance & Society*, 11(1/2): 163–76.

Wiig, A. and Wyly, E. (2016) 'Introduction: Thinking through the politics of the smart city', *Urban Geography*, 37: 485–93.

Willmott, H. (1993) 'Strength is ignorance; slavery is freedom: Managing culture in modern organizations', *Journal of Management Studies*, 30(4): 515–52.

Wolfe, C. (2007) 'Bring the noise: The parasite and the multiple genealogies of posthumanism', in M. Serres (ed) *The Parasite*, London: University of Minnesota Press, pp xi–xxvvii.

Wood, E.M. (2006) 'Logics of power: A conversation with David Harvey', *Historical Materialism*, 14(4): 9–34.

Wood, J. (2016) *Digital Ways of Making, Commons-based Making and Digital Fabrication: A Practice Based Study of Design Making for the Coming Age of Networked Digital Artefacts*, Doctoral dissertation, Goldsmiths, University of London.

Woodcock, J. (2017) 'Automate this! Delivering resistance in the gig economy', *Metamute*, available at: www.metamute.org/editorial/articles/automate-delivering-resistance-gig-economy

Woodcock, J. and Graham, M. (2019) *The Gig Economy: A Critical Introduction*, Bristol: Polity Press.

Woodford, C. (2016) *Disorienting Democracy: Politics of Emancipation*, Oxfordshire: Taylor & Francis.

Woods, M. (2019) 'Punk urbanism: Insurgency, crisis, and cultural geography', *Social & Cultural Geography*, 1–20.

Wyatt, T. (2019) 'Foodbank app run by newly elected Tory MP charges charities to use it', *The Independent*, 14 December, available at: www.independent.co.uk/news/uk/politics/foodbank-app-miriam-cates-mp-conservative-general-election-universal-credit-a9245901.html

Yamamoto, M., Kushin, M.J. and Dalisay, F. (2015) 'Social media and mobiles as political mobilization forces for young adults: Examining the moderating role of online political expression in political participation', *New Media & Society*, 17(6): 880–98.

Ylönen, M. (2016) *Neoliberalism and Technoscience: Critical Assessments*, Abingdon: Routledge.

Yun, J.J. (2015) 'How do we conquer the growth limits of capitalism? Schumpeterian Dynamics of Open Innovation', *Journal of Open Innovation: Technology, Market, and Complexity*, 1(2): 17.

Zemni, S. (2017) 'The Tunisian revolution: Neoliberalism, urban contentious politics and the right to the city', *International Journal of Urban and Regional Research*, 41(1), 70–83.

Žižek, S. (1993) *Tarrying with the Negative: Kant, Hegel, and the Critique of Ideology*, Durham, NC: Duke University Press.

Index